Making History

John Colet

To John and Aelda Callinicos

Making History

Agency, Structure and Change in Social Theory

Alex Callinicos

Polity Press

First published 1987 by Polity Press in association with Basil Blackwell.
First published in paperback 1989

Editorial Office:
Polity Press, Dales Brewery, Gwydir Street,
Cambridge CB1 2LJ, UK

Basil Blackwell Ltd
108 Cowley Road, Oxford OX4 1JF, UK

British Library Cataloguing in Publication Data

Callinicos, Alex
    Making history: agency, structure and
    change in social theory.
    1. Social structure
    I. Title
    305'.01   HM73
    ISBN 0–7456–0179–0
    ISBN 0–7456–0180–4 Pbk

Typeset in Sabon on 10½/12pt
by Cambrian Typesetters, Frimley, Camberley, Surrey
Printed in Great Britain by
T. J. Press Ltd, Padstow.

CONTENTS

PREFACE

Individuals are dealt with here only in so far as they are the personifications of economic categories, the bearers of particular class-relations and interests.

Karl Marx, *Capital*

Everyone has their own good reasons.

Jean Renoir, *La Règle du jeu*

The two sentences quoted above define the scope of this book. The first is Marx at his most austerely structural, concerned with analysing the objective relationships in which human beings find themselves, rigorously abstracting from individuals' perspectives and purposes. The second comes from a film one of whose triumphs lies in the sympathetic reconstruction of the motives and interests of a diverse and conflicting group of people. Although it sums up the approach of one of the century's supreme artists, Renoir's remark could also be taken to epitomize the tradition in social theory most strongly opposed to Marx's (Max Weber was its greatest exponent) which set itself the task, not of uncovering structures, but of understanding persons. The book seeks to establish the extent to which the two perspectives, of structural explanation and intentional understanding, are compatible with one another. My aim has not been to blur real differences, setting in their place a shallow syncretism, but it seems to me that no worthwhile social theory can do without variants of both perspectives. This is so especially for Marxism, which stakes its claim on human beings' capacity to sweep away millenia of exploitation and oppression. I leave it to the reader to decide how successful my attempted reconciliation has been.

It remains only to acknowledge some debts. The past decade has been a rich one for social theory in the English-speaking world. I am grateful to those, such as Jerry Cohen and Anthony Giddens, who have been willing to stick their necks out and offer grand theories, providing others, such as myself, with the less creative and easier work of criticizing what they have come up with. The stimulus they have provided will be obvious in what follows.

There are other, more personal debts. David Held has been a model editor – patient, sympathetic and tough. Mike Rosen made very helpful comments on a version of the first three chapters. Chris Harman read the whole manuscript, his detailed and stimulating notes on which I have repaid with the grossest ingratitude by inserting criticisms of his own views in the final text. Parts of draft chapters were presented as papers to the Political Theory Workshop at the University of York. I would like to thank those present for their comments. I am also grateful to the members of the Philosophy Department at York, during a very happy year in which I wrote this book.

There are two final debts. It was thanks to Joanna Seddon that I observed the historian's almost alchemical gift of transmuting old records in archives into the struggles and passions of the once-living human beings of whom these documents are the traces. But it was from my father and mother that I learned to value history and to see its connection with liberty. I am therefore dedicating *Making History* to them.

INTRODUCTION

I shall be concerned in this book with the respective roles played by
social structures and human agency in history. This issue has come to
assume an increasing importance because of the growing convergence
of history and social theory.

Some of the most important and widely read sociological treatises
of recent years have shared a preoccupation with explaining processes
of historical change – Barrington Moore's *The Social Origins of
Dictatorship and Democracy* (1966); Immanuel Wallerstein's *The
Modern World System* (1974, 1980); Theda Skocpol's *States and
Social Revolution* (1979) and Michael Mann's *The Sources of Social
Power* (volume I, 1986). So considerable has been the impact of this
body of writing that it has given rise to the notion of a distinctive
discourse called 'historical sociology'. Indeed, the late Philip Abrams
went so far as to argue that 'in terms of their fundamental
preoccupations, history and sociology are and have always been the
same thing.' Their 'common project', Abrams contended, has been 'a
sustained, diverse attempt to deal with what I shall call the
problematic of structuring', by which he meant 'the real relationship
of structure and action, the structural conditioning of action and the
effects of action on structure'.[1]

Other sociologists, for example Anthony Giddens, made similarly
emphatic assertions of the essential unity of their discipline and
history: '*There simply are no logical or even methodological
distinctions between social sciences and history – appropriately
conceived.*'[2] There have been some signs of these efforts to break
down the barriers between different disciplines being reciprocated by
historians. Certainly many of the most innovative historical studies of
recent years have been methodologically self-conscious works drawing
often on social sciences such as anthropology, economics and
sociology, as well as on the skills of the novelist and the psycho-

analyst in order to reconstruct past events and situations. Among the most outstanding examples of this trend are Theodore Zeldin's *France 1848–1945*; Peter Brown's *The World of Late Antiquity*; Emmanuel Le Roy Ladurie's *Montaillou*; Carlo Ginzburg's *The Cheese and the Worms* and Keith Thomas's *Religion and the Decline of Magic*.[3]

A third current has helped to bring together history and social theory, namely the rise of what is sometimes called 'Anglo–Marxism', the remarkable penetration of English-speaking intellectual culture by Marxism over the past twenty years. Perry Anderson, one of the chief architects of Anglo–Marxism, has noted that its emergence has involved 'the rise of Marxist historiography to its long overdue salience within the landscape of socialist thought as a whole'.[4] The privileged relation between Marxism and history is indicated by the very name the former has often adopted – 'historical materialism'. But this conceptual connection has not prevented politico-economic analysis and philosophical reflection forming the central focus of classical and Western Marxism respectively.

The higher profile of historical writing in the resurgent Marxism of the English-speaking world is best considered under three headings. First, there is the work of a group of older historians, all active in the Communist Party (CP) Historians Groups after the Second World War (although most subsequently left the CP, for example, as a result of the crisis precipitated by the Hungarian Revolution of 1956).[5] To show the contribution of these historians to the intellectual standing of Marxism one has merely to mention their names: Christopher Hill, Eric Hobsbawm, E. P. Thompson, George Rudé, Rodney Hilton, Victor Kiernan, G. E. M. de Ste Croix. Secondly, a number of younger historians, for example, Perry Anderson, Robert Brenner and Chris Wickham, have made outstanding recent contributions. A common characteristic of their work is the influence of philosophical analyses of the basic concepts of historical materialism, which form the third feature of contemporary Marxist historiography.[6]

As Anderson notes, the essays by Louis Althusser and Étienne Balibar in *Reading Capital* (1965) 'pioneered closer theoretical scrutiny of the canons of historical materialism'.[7] The reception of Althusser's writings into the English-speaking world has been marked by great controversy, which reached its climax at the end of the 1970s with Edward Thompson's magnificent, if vastly overstated polemical broadside, *The Poverty of Theory*, and Anderson's measured and conciliatory response, *Arguments within English Marxism*. The outcome, the latter suggested, was that 'theory is now history, with a seriousness and severity it never was in the past; as history is equally theory, in all its exigency, in a way that it typically evaded before.'[8]

This statement can be taken to summarize the broader trends among non-Marxist sociologists and historians to which I have already referred. The debate over Althusser was, however, exemplary in another respect. At its heart was the question of the relation between structure and subject. Anderson indeed argued that this 'has always constituted one of the central problems of historical materialism'. He pointed to

> the permanent oscillation, the potential disjuncture in Marx's own writings between his ascription of the primary motor of historical change to the contradiction between the forces of production and the relations of production, on the one hand ... and to the class struggle, on the other hand ... The first refers essentially to a structural, or more properly interstructural, reality: the order of what contemporary sociology would call system integration (or for Marx latent disintegration). The second refers to the subjective forces contending and colliding for mastery over social forms and historical processes: the realm of what contemporary sociology would call social integration (which is equally disintegration or reintegration). How are these two distinct types of causality, or principles of explanation, to be articulated in the theory of historical materialism?[9]

The present book sets out to answer this question. Althusser's failure to do so correctly is one of the main reasons for the collapse of his philosophical enterprise. Conceiving history as 'a process without a subject', he treated human agents as the 'bearers' or 'supports' of objective structures and subjectivity itself as a construct of ideology. While Althusserian Marxism undoubtedly helped to stimulate concrete historical studies by providing certain tools of analysis, its reduction of agency to structure denied it the means to conceptualize struggle and change. One of the main attractions of the poststructuralism of Michel Foucault, Jacques Derrida *et al.*, which arose amid the ruins of Althusserianism, was surely its openness to the contingencies, the uncertainties, the instabilities of history.[10]

The question of structure and subject has been placed firmly at the top of the agenda for social theory by the recent emergence in the English-speaking world of a version of Marxism which treats individual action as primary, reducing social structures to the consequences of such action. I have in mind here most of the practitioners of what has come to be known as 'analytical Marxism'.[11]

The founding text of this philosophical current is Jerry Cohen's

Karl Marx's Theory of History – a Defence (1978), a work governed,
he says, by 'two constraints: on the one hand, what Marx wrote, and,
on the other, those standards of clarity and rigour which distinguish
twentieth-century analytical philosophy'. Cohen's is 'an old-fashioned
historical materialism . . . in which history is, fundamentally, the
growth of human productive power, and forms of society rise and fall
accordingly as they enable or impede that growth'.[12] He therefore
accords primacy to the productive forces and insists accordingly that
'Marxism is *fundamentally* concerned not with behaviour, but with
the forces and relations constraining and directing it.'[13] For Cohen,
that is, structure takes priority over agency in the explanation of
historical change. However, many other analytical Marxists, most
notably Jon Elster and John Roemer, have opted instead for the
doctrine of methodological individualism, according to which social
structures are the unintended consequences of individual human
action. This move has been accompanied by the attempt to
reconstruct Marxism using tools provided by rational-choice theory,
a cluster of disciplines such as game theory formed largely as
generalizations of the basic postulates of neo-classical economics. In
the process many of Marx's principal tenets – for example, the labour
theory of value and the law of the tendency of the rate of profit to fall
– have been abandoned. It is therefore hardly surprising that Elster
should conclude his lengthy and detailed study of Marx by declaring:
'It is not possible, today, morally or intellectually, to be a Marxist in
the traditional sense.'[14]

One reason for my writing this book is that I dissent most strongly
from this judgement. My aim is to examine the questions of agency,
structure and historical change from the standpoint of classical
Marxism, the central corpus of historical materialist theory and
revolutionary socialist politics developed by Marx and Engels, Lenin
and Trotsky, Luxemburg and Gramsci. In making this theoretical and
political commitment clear, I should also emphasize that I do not
claim in what follows to be stating 'what Marx really said'. As I have
argued elsewhere, most notably in a book called *Is There a Future for
Marxism?*, Marxism is a complex and contradictory body of theories
whose meaning is contested by a diversity of political currents. To
carve out a Marxist tradition from this mass of conflicting elements is
to take sides; Walter Benjamin's dictum that the past itself is at stake
in political struggles is nowhere more true than in the case of
Marxism.[15] This does not mean, of course, that one can, or should
read into texts what one likes, but my concern with Marxism here is
not primarily exegetical. In what follows I shall, to the best of my
abilities, be guided by three constraints – not merely by 'what Marx

[and his successors] wrote', and the 'standards of clarity and rigour' developed by analytical and other philosophers, but also by what appears to be the truth, even if it conflicts with Marxist 'orthodoxy'.

The shape of my argument is as follows. The first two chapters are concerned with the two main terms of the problem – agency and structure. Chapter 1 considers briefly different senses of historical agency (section 1.1), then focuses on the most subtle and plausible account of human action, the 'orthodox conception of agents' refined by the analytical tradition, according to which human beings act rationally in the light of beliefs and desires (section 1.2). After dismissing some bad arguments for this theory, I point to a good one, namely that it issues from the kind of account of human nature which the inadequacies of post-structuralism show that we need and which Marx had (section 1.3). There then follows an apparent digression, to the effect that Marx's theory of exploitation involves an implicit moral theory, (section 1.4) whose relevance will become clearer in chapters 3 and 5. Finally, I argue that the orthodox conception of agents is consistent with invoking structures to help explain human action (section 1.5).

Chapter 2 begins with some very general remarks on the purpose of the concept of social structure (section 2.1), followed by a consideration of the concrete theory of structure provided by historical materialism (section 2.2), a critical discussion of Cohen's 'orthodox' historical materialism (section 2.3) and an account of the 'rational-choice Marxism' of Elster, Roemer, *et al.* (section 2.4). The latter's methodological individualism is then examined at length, and the dilemma of structure and action rejected in favour of an account of the powers that agents derive from their position in the relations of production (section 2.5). This leaves us with as much of historical materialism as we could reasonably desire, namely classical Marxism (section 2.6).

Chapter 3 examines some of the theoretical problems arising from the interaction of structure and agency, commencing with an account of the formidable challenge to any generalizing social theory represented by the hermeneutic tradition of Heidegger and Gadamer (section 3.1). One recent attempt, by W. G. Runciman, to reconcile this tradition's preoccupation with the interpretation of human action with the identification of causal patterns, is then shown to be unsuccessful (section 3.2). I argue, however, that Donald Davidson's realist theory of interpretation, introduced here to help refute Runciman, captures what is valid in the hermeneutic tradition, is superior to Jürgen Habermas's theory of communicative action and is consistent with the general theory of structure and agency developed

in chapters 1 and 2 (section 3.3). The utilitarian theory of action
underpinning rational-choice theory is then held to be wanting, above
all because of the narrowly instrumental conception of rationality it
uses to explain human behaviour (section 3.4) but the concept of
interests, now conceived as the hinge connecting structure and action,
is retained from that theory (section 3.5).

Chapters 4 and 5 explore in more concrete terms how human
beings draw on the powers they derive from their position in the
relations of production to sustain, but also to transform societies.
Chapter 4 begins by introducing the concept of collective agents such
as classes and nations (section 4.1). The formation of such collectivities depends crucially on the beliefs agents have, which raises the
question of ideology. Various difficulties with the Marxist theory of
ideology and with the 'dominant ideology thesis', which claims that
the popular acceptance of ruling-class ideology is the cement of the
social order, are considered (section 4.2). Then I defend a more
modest, but still important role for ideologies as articulations of
interests and the means by which agents are invited to accept a certain
identity ('interpellated') (section 4.3). The traditional objection to
Marxism – that it fails to account for the strength of national
identifications and the associated military conflicts between nation-
states – is then discussed and dismissed with the help of Brenner's
historical writings (section 4.4), prior to some brief observations on
the question of base and superstructure (section 4.5).

Chapter 5 is to some degree an extended reflection on Walter
Benjamin's 'Theses on the Philosophy of History'. It is concerned
with epochal social transformations, the replacement of one mode of
production with another. The chapter begins with a discussion of
Benjamin's account of revolution as a Messianic irruption into the
everyday course of events, which bears strong similarities to Sartre's
discussions of series and fused groups (section 5.1). Marx's analysis
of the working class, whose struggle provides a continuity between
the everyday and the revolutionary, is then defended against
theoretical and empirical objections (section 5.2). Two arguments
purporting to show the irrationality of socialist revolution are then
considered and rejected: the importance of the claim, first made in
section 1.4, that workers have moral reasons for overthrowing
capitalism here becomes clear (section 5.3). Benjamin's idea that
revolutions necessarily seek to restore past states of affairs is
discussed, but I argue that this does not apply to socialist revolutions
(section 5.4), the structural reasons for whose distinctiveness are the
subject of my concluding reflections (section 5.5). Thus my fundamental theme is illustrated – structure and agency are so closely

interwoven that to separate either and give it primacy over the other is a fundamental error.

As the preceding outline ought to have made clear, this is, or aspires to be, a philosophical book. That is, it seeks to appraise the adequacy of concepts, the consistency of propositions and the validity of arguments. It is not, however, concerned with the philosophy of history, at least in the sense in which this subject is conceived in the analytical tradition, which seems to concentrate on such matters as the truth-conditions of historical sentences and the objectivity of historical knowledge. I shall assume, without argument, that historical sentences are usually meaningful and that we have good reasons for holding some at least to be true. If anything, this book is closer to traditional speculative philosophy of history, as practised by Condorcet or Hegel, since it is concerned mainly with the mechanisms through which human beings transform their societies and, for better or worse, push history onwards. Nevertheless, the sort of conceptual clarification pursued here cannot substitute for, and at best may serve as a preliminary to, empirical enquiry.

This raises the question of the discussions of historical writing which follow. Recent debates, as well as the pleasure and instruction I have gained from reading history, have convinced me that Marxist theory can develop only in the closest dialogue with historical research.[16] Working historians sometimes complain that historical sociologists do not original research but weave their interpretations from the studies of others. I do not think that this criticism is a valid one but it would not in any case be appropriate to make it of this book. Historical writings are cited here to illustrate arguments or pose problems, not in support of some factual account of concrete historical processes. The texts selected reflect the vagaries of my own reading, which is that of a dilettante and not a historian.

Finally, the book is ultimately an attempt to grapple with a political problem, albeit by tortuously indirect means. The 1980s have been a terrible decade for socialists, in the Western world at least. Stridently selfish, aggressive and complacent right-wing politics has been in the ascendancy. The means of mass destruction have been piled up till they reach into the heavens themselves. The episodes of heroic working-class struggle which have brought light into the general darkness have all, from *Solidarność* in Poland to the miners' strike in Britain, ended in crushing defeat. No wonder that men and women lose faith in their capacity to change the world. Now I do not believe that writing a book on agency will alter matters – a sort of reverse feat to Dr Johnson's refuting Berkeley by kicking a stone. But every little bit helps. If I can help to undermine the idea that the only avenue

to improvement open to people is the pursuit of individual interest
and to demonstrate that human beings possess the power collectively
to make history, then a blow will have been struck against the
ideology of the New Right. Like their writings, this book engages in
what Althusser called the 'class struggle in theory', though in the
name of a different class from the one they champion.

CHAPTER 1

SUBJECTS AND AGENTS

1.1 THREE CONCEPTS OF AGENCY

'Men make history, but they do not make it just as they please: they
do not make it under circumstances chosen by themselves, but under
circumstances directly encountered, given and transmitted from the
past.'[1] This celebrated passage from the beginning of *The Eighteenth
Brumaire of Louis Bonaparte* is Marx's most important statement of
the relationship between structure and subject. The solution it offers
to the problem appears to be that 'circumstances' operate primarily
through setting limits to individual or collective action, restricting the
range of alternatives open to agents. The formula suffers from a
fundamental flaw, namely that it conceives the role of structure as
essentially negative, as simply a constraint on action (see section 2.5).
There is, however, a further difficulty, which I wish to consider here,
namely the ambiguous way in which Marx seems to conceive of
agency.

Perry Anderson suggests that we can distinguish three ways in
which human beings can be said to 'make history', each involving a
different sort of goal for their activity. The first and most typical form
of historical action is the pursuit of 'private' goals – 'cultivation of a
plot, choice of a marriage, exercise of a skill, maintenance of a home,
bestowal of a name'. The second kind of agency, like the first,
operates within the framework of existing social relations, pertaining
to the kind of ventures involving 'public' goals, for example, 'political
struggles, military conflicts, diplomatic transactions, commercial
explorations', that are the stuff of conventional narrative history.
Finally, there is the 'unprecedented form of agency' involved in the
collective pursuit of global social transformation, which first appeared
in the American and French Revolutions but acquired full expression
only with the emergence of the workers' movement and revolutionary
Marxism: here, 'for the first time collective projects of social

transformation were married to systematic efforts to understand the processes of past and present, to produce a premeditated
future.'[2]

The point of these distinctions is to overcome the abstract polarity
between structure and agency represented by Althusser and Thompson
respectively. For Althusser history is 'a process without a subject or
goals'. Change occurs as a result of the accumulation of structural
contradictions. Human beings' role within this process is merely to
act as 'bearers' of the structures in conflict. People's conception of
themselves as agents participating in historical struggles does not
correspond to reality, but arises from their formation within ideology
as subjects, constituted by the illusion of their coherence and
autonomy. Thompson's response to this 'theoretical anti-humanism'
is essentially to affirm the opposite. History is the process through
which human beings constantly make and remake their lives.
Structures – modes of production – represent limits to human
practice, obstacles to be overcome by men and women in their
struggle to assume conscious control of the social world. The task of
the historian is uncover the eternal conflict between human agents
and the objective conditions of their actions.

The resolution of this debate lies, Anderson believes, in the
recognition that the scope for human action, especially in his third
sense of 'self-determination', depends on historically specific conditions. Althusser's structuralism and Thompson's humanism may
each, in particular circumstances, be true. Grasping this depends,
however, on making the appropriate conceptual discriminations
between different kinds of action:

> The two antagonistic formulae of a 'natural–human process without a
> subject' and 'ever-baffled, ever-resurgent agents of an unmastered
> practice' are both claims of an essentially apodictic and speculative
> character – eternal axioms that in no way help us to trace the actual,
> variable roles of different types of deliberate venture, personal or
> collective, in history. A *historical*, as opposed to an axiomatic
> approach to the problem would seek to trace the *curve* of such
> enterprises, which has risen sharply – in terms of mass participation
> and scale of the objective – in the last two centuries, from previously
> low levels.[3]

The distinctions drawn by Anderson – between routine conduct,
public initiatives and self-determination – are helpful. They provide a
corrective to other invocations of undifferentiated 'agency' against
structures than Thompson's. Thus Anthony Giddens writes:

Foucault's 'archaeology', in which human beings do not make their own history but are swept along by it, does not adequately acknowledge that those subject to the power of dominant groups themselves are knowledgeable agents, who resist, blunt or actively alter the conditions of life that others seek to thrust upon them.[4]

Giddens's failure to discriminate between kinds of agency in the way Anderson does leads him to ignore the fact that there are two very different ways in which the resistance of subordinate groups may 'actively alter' their 'conditions of life'. Change may arise as an unintended consequence of molecular acts of resistance. But the change may not be consciously initiated by or benefit the resisters: thus the modern factory may have been introduced by capital to eliminate the 'dishonesty and laziness' (i.e. resistance) of workers employed under the putting-out system.[5] Resistance, however, may also generate collective agents capable of pursuing the conscious goal of social change. Action in pursuit of such collective projects of transformation will no doubt have unanticipated consequences, but here it is possible to appraise the outcome in the light of its distance from the goal originally and consciously espoused. Discussions of the Russian Revolution and its fate are an obvious example of this kind of appraisal. Individual action is often self-defeating, but rarely outside Napoleonic fantasies does this failure take the form of the shipwreck of some attempt to achieve social change. Such attempts usually involve a degree of collective organization, from the Jacobin Clubs to *Solidarność*.

Valuable though Anderson's discussion of agency therefore is, it nevertheless has a major lacuna. He does not consider in any depth what the different forms of agency have in common, beyond defining agency as 'conscious, goal-directed activity'.[6] But it is the nature and implications of agency thus conceived that are at the centre of most of the debates about the status and character of social science in the past hundred years. Perhaps the most influential tradition in mainstream social theory, that associated with Max Weber, has argued for the primacy of agency over structures (in the sense that the latter are to be conceived simply as the unintended consequences of individual action) precisely on the grounds that human beings are distinguished from the rest of nature by their engaging in 'conscious, goal-directed activity'.[7] Similar considerations are among those which led to the emergence of 'rational-choice Marxism', i.e. that species of analytical Marxism which espouses methodological individualism (Jon Elster, John Roemer *et al.*).

In what follows, I shall first consider the model of human action

that underpins the Weberian argument and establish that such a way
of thinking about human beings, as acting in the light of beliefs and
desires, could only be formulated in definite historical conditions
(section 1.2). Nevertheless, the theory is, I believe, true, in part
because of the kind of account of human nature that we must accept
(section 1.3). This account has important consequences for our
conception of morality (section 1.4); nevertheless, viewing human
beings as acting for reasons and in that sense goal-directed,
does not require that we accept methodological individualism
(section 1.5).

1.2 THE ORTHODOX CONCEPTION OF AGENTS

The broad outlines of the argument for methodological individualism
have changed little since Weber's time, though it has been much
refined by analytical philosophers. Elster writes: 'intentional explanation is the feature that distinguishes the social sciences from the
natural sciences.'[8] To explain an action intentionally is to ascribe to
the agent beliefs and desires which caused him so to act. Thus, an
agent desires that *p*, believes that doing *x* will bring it about that *p*,
and therefore does *x*.

Intentional explanation involves distinguishing human action in
certain respects from the rest of nature: 'Intentional behaviour is
essentially related to the *future*. It is action guided by a goal that is
absent, not-yet-realized, merely imagined or represented. As noted by
François Jacob, men can choose between unactualized possibles,
whereas natural selection can choose only among the actual alternatives.'[9] Obviously this presupposes some account of the distinct
properties of human agents. Daniel Dennett specifies six necessary
conditions of 'personhood':

[i]   Persons are *rational beings*;
[ii] persons are beings to which . . . *intentional predicates* [i.e. beliefs
      and desires], are ascribed;
[iii] whether something counts as a person depends in some way on an
      attitude taken toward it, a *stance adopted* with respect to it;
[iv] the object towards which this personal stance is taken must be
      capable of *reciprocating* in some way;
[v]   persons must be capable of *verbal communication*;
[vi] [persons are] *conscious* in some special way [namely they are
      aware of having engaged in actions and therefore can be held
      responsible for them].[10]

Strictly speaking, only conditions [i], [ii] and [iii] are necessary to the existence of an 'intentional system', that is, 'a system whose behaviour can be – at least sometimes – explained by relying on ascriptions to the system of beliefs and desires (and hopes, fears, intentions, hunches . . .)'.[11] Animals and (Dennett believes) at least some computers are intentional systems in this minimal sense. But they lack the ability, dependent on the possession of language, to engage in the practice of giving reasons for one's actions and therefore the ability to form second-order desires, i.e. consciously to alter one's desires and thereby one's conduct.

The notion of an intentional system (and the broader conception of a person which Dennett develops from it) is an explanatory concept. Predictions about people's conduct can be derived from it, by means of explanations of the following form: 'If someone desires something, and believes that by A-ing he can best get it, and other things are equal, then he A's.'[12] Crucial to the explanatory character of ascriptions of belief and desire is Dennett's first condition of personhood, namely that people are rational.

Packed in here are in fact two distinct, though perhaps related conceptions of rationality. The first one could call the interpretive. Current discussion of it is dominated by the work of Donald Davidson.[13] My account of it here will be summary, but we shall return to it in chapter 3. The thought is that intentional explanation is an interpretive process, inseparable from assigning a sense to the actor's utterances. But people's observable behaviour typically admits of more than one interpretation. How do we know *which* beliefs and desires to assign to others? Only by relying on a normative principle of rationality. As Dennett puts it, 'we get round the "privacy" of beliefs and desires by recognizing that in general anyone's beliefs and desires must be those he "ought to have" given the circumstances.'[14] The assumption that agents are rational specifies what beliefs and desires they 'ought to have'.

Graham Macdonald and Philip Pettit break down this assumption as follows. First, we should treat agents as 'attitudinally rational', that is 'disposed at least to change one's beliefs so as to eliminate counter-examples and inconsistencies', in other words, 'to make moves to ensure that . . . [one's] beliefs were true'.[15] Secondly, agents must be regarded as 'behaviourally rational', acting in the light of their beliefs and desires, so that if someone desires that *p*, believes that doing *x* will bring it about that *p* and other things are equal (there are no conflicting desires etc.), then if he or she does not do *x*, the antecedent, with its ascription of belief and desire and *ceteris paribus* clause, must be false.[16]

The second conception of rationality is perhaps best regarded as a specification of the first. It is essentially Weber's notion of instrumentally rational (*zweckrational*) action, where rationality involves the selection of the most effective means to achieving a given end. Thus, to quote Elster, 'the usual way to define rational behaviour is by invoking some notion of optimization. One argues, that is, that the rational agent chooses an action which is not only *a* means to his end, but *the best* of all the means which he believes to be available.'[17]

This second conception of rationality (which we shall call the optimizing principle to distinguish it from the rationality principle proper) is an important one for methodological individualists. Since the latter explain social structures in terms of individuals they cannot invoke generalizations which make reference to the properties of social structures and the like. To do so would be to commit the crime of historicism denounced by Popper and his followers. The virtue of the optimizing principle is that it provides an explanatory generalization by means of which to animate the models of individualist social theory. These models need not confine themselves to descriptions of individuals and their circumstances; they can, given the assumption that agents optimize, and given the beliefs and desires of the individuals concerned, explain why they do what they do.[18]

Although there are important connections between the optimizing principle and the assumption that agents are behaviourally and attitudinally rational, they are logically distinct propositions.[19] Recognizing this is important partly because it allows us to explore the implications of the sort of intentional explanations we have been considering for the truth or otherwise of methodological individualism (hereafter MI). Macdonald and Pettit argue that the 'orthodox concept of agents' involved in intentional explanation implies the truth of MI. They say that 'accepting the orthodox conception of agents means rejecting the claim that institutions have explanatory autonomy', where 'explanatory autonomy' is defined as follows:

> One sort of entity X exists over and beyond another sort Y if and only if the following condition is met: that the addition of terms by means of which we refer to X-type things enables us to give explanations of events, taken under certain descriptions, that we cannot account for in a language with terms for referring to Y-type items.[20]

So the 'explanatory (or methodological) collectivist' holds that action cannot be explained solely in terms of individuals' properties, beliefs, desires etc., but that these explanations must also make irreducible reference to institutions (or more generally to structures: I shall give a more precise way of understanding 'structures' in chapter 2). There are two main premisses of Macdonald's and Pettit's attempted proof of this doctrine's falsehood:

[1] If the explanatory collectivist says that there are some events which can be explained by reference to institutions, but not by reference to individuals, then he is denying the truth of the orthodox conception of agents. At least with respect to the behaviour involved in those events he is saying that it is not the rational outcome of the agents' beliefs and desires . . .

[2]   the claim of this conception is undeniable.[21]

Both these assertions are false. Establishing that [1] is not true is the more important task, since I think both that the orthodox conception of agents is true and that it does not imply MI. However, I shall only begin to address [1] towards the end of this chapter, and its falsehood can only be definitively established once my general account of the relation between structure and agency is completed at the end of chapter 3. For the present, I wish to consider only [2], which concerns the status of the orthodox conception, as a way of beginning to establish why we should think it true (although, again, that task will only be completed with the discussion of interpretation in chapter 3).

Macdonald and Pettit make out [2], the claim that the orthodox conception of agents is 'undeniable', less by making explicit arguments than by drawing a contrast between 'action-explanation' and explanation in the natural sciences. The latter is 'nomothetic', that is, events are explained in terms of generalizations or laws (Greek *nomoi*) which may always in principle be revised in the light of empirical evidence. Action-explanations, however,

postulate only indubitable explanatory principles and in the exercise there can never be a possibility of revising the principles and recasting the explanations. We approach an individual action secure in the possession of these principles: they formulate what it is for a piece of behaviour to count as an action, issuing from an appropriate rationalizing state of mind.

Consequently,

the social scientist concerned with making sense of a piece or pattern of behaviour is not required or allowed to turn his attention to the explanatory principles which are put at his disposal by the orthodox conception of agents. His part is to take these principles on faith and to devote himself exclusively to the consideration of how the behaviour can best be subsumed under them.[22]

Now all this is decidedly odd. One's suspicions are aroused by the very use of the word 'indubitable', a term used by philosophers at least since Descartes's time to shore up some especially shaky assertion. In what sense is the orthodox conception 'indubitable'? Is it a logical truth? Surely this cannot be Macdonald's and Pettit's claim? Perhaps they are making a psychological generalization, that people cannot imagine the falsehood of the orthodox conception. But this is demonstrably false.

One aspect of the orthodox conception is the idea, implicit in the notion of an intentional *system*, of the coherence of the agent. We explain action by ascribing beliefs and desires because the agent is capable of forming beliefs and desires. To put it another way, it is the *agent*, not some aspect or part of him, that has beliefs and desires. But thus conceiving the agent as in some sense a unity is certainly not indubitable.

Consider, for example, the opening words of Gilles Deleuze's and Félix Guattari's *Mille plateaux*:

> We wrote *Anti-Oedipus* together. As each one of us was many, that was already quite a crowd. Here we've utilized everything that came to hand, from nearby as well as from far away. We've handed out clever pseudonyms, for purposes of disguise. Why have we kept our names? Through habit, merely through habit. To disguise ourselves in turn. To render imperceptible, not ourselves, but what makes us act, feel or think. Also, because it's nice to talk like everybody else, and to say the sun is rising, where everybody knows that this is just a manner of speaking. Not to arrive at the point where one no longer says I, but at the point where saying or not saying I is of no importance. We are no longer ourselves. Each will recognize his own. We have been helped, inspired, multiplied.[23]

Deleuze and Guattari, in their extraordinary *magnum opus*, *Capitalisme et schizophrénie* (the two volumes of which are *l' Anti-Oedipe* and *Mille plateaux*), present a view of reality as consisting in supra- and sub-individual multiplicities whose nature changes according to the assemblage (*agencement*) in which they find themselves:

> It is only when the multiple is effectively treated as a substantive, as multiplicity, that it loses all relationship to the One as subject or as object, as natural or spiritual reality, as image and world. There is no unity here to serve as pivot in the object, or ground of division in the subject. . . . A multiplicity has neither subject nor object, but only determinations, magnitudes, dimensions which cannot increase in number without its changing in nature. . . . An assemblage is precisely this growth of dimensions in a multiplicity which necessarily changes in nature as it augments in connections.[24]

To conceive of the subject as an enduring and coherent unity may, on this view, be faithful to the conventions of ordinary language, but it bears as much relation to the truth as does Ptolemaic astronomy.

One may naturally be tempted to dismiss this as a piece of post-structuralist *Schwärmerei*. However, cultures seem to have existed where conceiving 'each one of us' as 'many' was deeply embedded in everyday discourse. A. W. H. Adkins argues that Homeric Greece was one such culture:

> The Homeric *psuché* has no specific mental or emotional functions in life: it is simply that whose presence ensures that the individual is alive. To observe the mental and emotional activity of Homeric man, we must turn to . . . other words . . . whose conventional renderings, all of which are somewhat misleading, are *thumos*, 'spirit'; *kradie, etor, ker*, 'heart'; *phrenes*, 'mind' or (physiologically) 'diaphragm', or 'lungs'; *nōos*, 'mind'. The manner in which these words are used, if we take it seriously, reveals a psychological landscape quite different from our own. We are accustomed to emphasize the 'I' which 'takes decisions', and ideas such as 'will' or 'intention'. In Homer, there is much less emphasis on the 'I' or decisions: the Greek words just mentioned take the foreground, and enjoy a remarkable amount of democratic freedom. Men frequently 'act as their *kradie* and *thumos* bids them' [*sic*: Homer uses a singular verb]: Odysseus (*Odyssey* IX, 302) was wondering whether to attack the Cyclops when 'another *thumos* restrained him'; Athena tells Telemachus to give her on some future occasion (*Odyssey* I, 316) 'whatever gift his *etor* bids him give'; and 'grief came upon Achilles, and his *etor* debated between two alternatives in his shaggy chest' (*Iliad* I, 188). Examples could be multiplied: this is 'ordinary language' in Homer.[25]

This conception of the self has further ramifications:

> Similarly, there is little mention of the body as a whole, much of its parts; and these may be spoken of as initiating action in the same manner as *thumos* and similar psychological phenomena. (Indeed, the distinction between psychological and physiological phenomena is not relevant to the Homeric poems). . . . Again, the 'spectral balance' is frequently present as a psychological model of the passage from thought to action: the Homeric Greek says 'it seemed better to me . . .', not 'I decided . . .'. Furthermore, the gods are often portrayed as initiating a human action by 'putting into a man' a drive (or an idea), which again suggests that Homeric man was highly aware of the spontaneous element in his psychological experience; and he is very emotional, and distinguishes between his emotional responses in a manner unfamiliar to us. In fact, it might be said that Homeric man experiences himself as a plurality, rather than a unity, with an indistinct boundary.[26]

If Adkins is right, the Homeric self was more like a Deleuzian multiplicity than the unified intentional system characterized by the 'orthodox conception' of agents. He suggests that 'it is not the fragmentation of the Homeric personality, but the development in other cultures of the ego-centred personality, that requires explanation'.[27] Other considerations support the view that the 'orthodox conception' is a historically specific, perhaps unique set of beliefs, rather than, as Macdonald and Pettit call it, 'common knowledge'.[28]

The concept of intentional explanation involves a distinction between two kinds of events, namely those that under some description, can be characterized as actions, accounting for which requires the ascription of beliefs and desires to agents, and those that are mere physical movements. Weber has some such distinction in mind when he writes: 'We shall speak of "action" in so far as the acting individual attaches a subjective meaning to his behaviour.'[29] But this isolating action presupposes drawing a broader distinction between the human and the physical worlds, such that each world operates in a significantly different manner. The human world may be subject to the general laws of nature, but it also involves the existence of intentional behaviour which cannot be explained, at least so far as social science is concerned, solely in terms of these laws.

There is a good case for saying that drawing this kind of distinction between the human and the physical, action and movement is historically quite rare. Jürgen Habermas points to 'the peculiar *confusion between nature and culture*' characteristic of 'mythical thought':

> What *we* find most astonishing is the peculiar leveling of the different domains of reality: nature and culture are projected onto the same plane. From this reciprocal assimilation of nature to culture and conversely culture to nature, there results, on the one hand, a nature that is outfitted with anthropomorphic features, drawn into the communicative network of social subjects, and in this sense humanized, and on the other hand a culture that is to a certain extent naturalized and reified and absorbed into the objective nexus of operations of anonymous powers.[30]

Habermas's account of mythical thought was drawn from the work of anthropologists. But rarely has what he had in mind been better described than by Carlo Levi in his portrait of the peasants of the remote Lucanian village to which he was exiled under Mussolini in the 1930s:

They are literally *pagani*, 'pagans', or countrymen, as distinguished from city-dwellers. The deities of the state and the city can find no worshippers here on the land, where the wolf and the ancient black boar reign supreme, where there is no wall between the world of men and the world of animals and spirits, between the leaves of the trees above and the roots below. They cannot have even an awareness of themselves as individuals, here where all things are held together by acting upon one another, and each one is a power unto itself, working imperceptibly, where there is no barrier that can not be broken down by magic. They live submerged in a world that rolls on independent of their will, where man is in no way separate from his sun, his beast, his malaria, where there can be neither happiness, as literary devotees of the land conceive it, nor hope, because these two are adjuncts of personality and here there is only the grim passivity of a sorrowful Nature ... To the peasants everything has a double meaning ... People, trees, animals, even objects and words have a double life. Only reason, religion, and history have clear-cut meanings ... And in the peasants' world there is no room for reason, religion, and history. There is no room for religion, because to them everything participates in divinity, everything is actually, not merely symbolically, divine: Christ and the goat; the heavens above, and the beasts of the field below; everything is bound up in natural magic. Even the ceremonies of the church become pagan rites, celebrating the existence of inanimate things, which the peasants endow with a soul, and the innumerable earthy divinities of the village.[31]

The distance between such ways of thinking and the 'orthodox conception of agents' is evident. But there is good reason to believe that forms of 'mythical thought' have been prevalent through much of human history and that sharply distinguishing between the human and the physical is a relatively novel procedure. Such a distinction was implied by what Bernard Williams calls the 'absolute conception of reality' formulated by the founders of modern physics in the seventeenth century.[32] Galileo and Descartes identify the physical world with the realm governed by efficient causes, whose regularities are captured in mechanical laws of nature. The human is sharply separated from the physical thus conceived and identified with the Cartesian self and its private mental activities, the sphere to which final causes are henceforth banished. The effect is, as it were, to peel thoughts and purposes off from nature, restricting them to the inner world of the subject.[33] The implications of this conceptual revolution were perhaps only fully articulated in Kant's critical philosophy, with its clear demarcation between theoretical and practical reason, the former providing the only knowledge we have, of a Newtonian natural world subject to laws of mechanical causality, while the latter grounds our moral conduct in human freedom, whose exercise occurs beyond the chain of physical causes. Weber's account of intentional explanation draws on the use by neo-Kantian philosophers of this distinction to argue that our knowledge of the human world is very different from that of the physical.

Habermas, himself very much the heir of the neo-Kantian tradition, argues that the formulation of the 'absolute conception of reality' was an essential prerequisite for the development of the sort of conception of human agents involved in intentional explanation:

> Only to the extent that the formal concept for an *external world* develops . . . can the complementary concept of the *internal world* or of subjectivity arise, that is, a world to which the individual has privileged access and to which everything is attributed that cannot be incorporated in the external world.[34]

Two qualifications must be made to the claim that the 'orthodox conception of agents' is a comparatively recent innovation. First, it would be absurd to suggest that earlier conceptions are absolutely discontinuous with those embodied in the notion of intentional explanation. The influence of Greek thought on analytical philosophy of mind evident, for example, in recent discussions of Aristotle's views on weakness of will, would suffice to refute any such suggestion. However, Aristotle's writings on such topics apply a corpus of concepts significantly different from those involved in the 'absolute conception of reality'. The behaviour of all entities, not just human beings, is to be explained teleologically, in terms of the purposes they strive to achieve and all living organisms, plants and animals as well as humans, possess a soul (*psuchē*), which is not distinct from the body but the principle of its organization. The theoretical context of Aristotle's discussions of the human soul is therefore profoundly different from that surrounding the 'orthodox conception'.

The case of Greek thought is anyway a rather special one. Michel Foucault puts it very well when he writes of 'a practice doubtless constitutive of Western philosophy, of interrogating at once the difference which keeps us at a distance from a thought in which we recognize the origins of our own and the proximity that remains despite this separation, which we ceaselessly widen.'[35]

One reason for this proximity – and it is my second qualification of the claimed novelty of the 'orthodox conception' – is the contribution which Greek thought and more especially that of Plato, made to the formation of the 'absolute conception of reality'. This can be seen in at least two ways. First, Plato in particular developed a conception of thought as *theōria*, the disinterested contemplation of being. Both Plato and modern physical science agree in thinking, as Charles Taylor puts it, that 'a theoretical understanding aims at a disengaged perspective. We are not trying to understand things merely as they impinge on us, or are relevant to the purposes we are pursuing, but rather grasp them as they are outside the immediate perspective of our goals and desires and activities.'[36]

Secondly, Plato differed from Aristotle's more teleological understanding in regarding mathematics as essential to discovering the inner structure of nature, a view which helped to shape Galileo's revolutionary identification of the physical with the quantitative and therefore non-purposive.[37]

The upshot of these considerations is to suggest that the 'orthodox conception of agents' belongs to a historically specific intellectual context, one that involves the combination of an essentially Platonic notion of theoretical understanding with the more modern idea that it is legitimate to interfere in nature in order to know it. To assert, as Macdonald and Pettit do, that this conception is 'indubitable', 'undeniable', or 'common knowledge' is therefore to display one of analytical philosophy's most characteristic blindnesses, namely its lack of any historical self-consciousness, its characteristic failure to recognize the historical distance that often separates theoretical writings and the imprint left on them by the distinctive circumstances in which they emerge.[38]

There is, however, a line of defence open to Macdonald and Pettit. This is to assert that whatever view of the world agents may have, mythical or otherwise, they nevertheless apply the 'orthodox conception of agents' in their daily transactions with one another. One way of making out this claim would be to argue that understanding another person neccessarily involves ascribing beliefs and desires to the other. Such an argument might be thought to give the 'orthodox conception' apodictic status if it could be shown to be a case of a transcendental argument. Arguments of this kind, modelled on Kant's Transcendental Deduction of the Categories in the *Critique of Pure Reason*, take some indisputable feature of our experience, and then seek to show what must be the case if this feature is to exist.[39] In this case understanding would be the indisputable feature and the 'orthodox conception' what must be true for understanding to be possible. Macdonald and Pettit may have some such claim in mind when they call the 'orthodox conception' 'undeniable' but they do not present it explicitly or argue for it. We shall return to such matters when considering the question of interpretation in chapter 3.

1.3 HUMAN NATURE: THE NEED FOR A
PHILOSOPHICAL ANTHROPOLOGY

One conclusion that might be drawn from the considerations adduced in the previous section is that the 'orthodox conception of agents' is false, or, for those of a more relativist persuasion, that it happens to be what we, as participants in a culture shaped by the seventeenth-century scientific revolution, hold true without our having reasons for doing so that transcend our immediate socio-historic context. The latter view would be espoused by Richard Rorty, while the stronger claim of falsehood appears to be implicit in post-structuralist thought. The impact of the latter (and of Adkins's history of Greek conceptions of the self) can be seen in this recent remark by William Connolly, the author of a systematic attempt to use the 'orthodox conception' to elucidate political theory: 'Any argument seeking to defend modern postulates of agency and responsibility must retreat from the claim that these are universal orientations presupposed in all human societies and merely lifted to a peak of realization in modernity.'[40]

There are, nevertheless, good reasons for holding the orthodox conception to be true. I shall begin to present them here in the form of a critique of post-structuralism's treatment of the subject. This will involve negative and positive stages – first, the difficulties in which Foucault's effacement of the subject places him and then the necessity of adopting a notion of human nature which implies the orthodox conception of agents.

Foucault himself argued that it was the epistemological inadequacy of the hitherto dominant 'philosophy of subject', the failure of successive attempts to found knowledge and meaning upon the Cartesian self, or its Kantian shadow, the transcendental subject, which gave rise to post-war French 'anti-humanism'.[41] From being constitutive, the subject could be shown to be constituted, the effect, in particular, of specific social practices. Althusser's claim that individuals are formed into subjects within ideology was one attempt to make out this thesis.[42] Foucault indeed came to describe his whole project as the attempt 'to create a history of the modes by which, in our culture, human beings are made into subjects'.[43]

Discipline and Punish (1975) and the first volume of the *Histoire de la sexualité* (1976) represent one version of Foucault's history of the subject. Here his central concept is that of 'power–knowledge', the relations of domination that articulate discursive and non-discursive practices into a historically specific apparatus (*dispositif*), an assemblage of heterogeneous elements.[44] The two examples of such apparatuses which Foucault gives are first, the disciplines, the practices of surveillance and control which developed in a wide variety of institutions – prisons, schools, asylums, factories – in the nineteenth century, and secondly, sexuality, which he conceives as not a biologically given substance but rather a historically specific set of social practices constructed around the belief that the truth about human beings lies in their sex.

Now one property of these practices is that they constitute subjects. Foucault writes: 'It is already one of the prime effects of power that certain bodies, certain gestures, certain discourses, certain desires, come to be identified and constituted as individuals. The individual, that is, is not the *via-à-vis* of power; it is, I believe, one of its prime effects.'[45] Thus the disciplines form individuals as 'docile bodies' ready to work at the pace and in the manner required of them.

It is important to stress here that Foucault is not thinking of the sort of process envisaged by Parsons, where subjects internalize prevailing norms and values; it is their very existence *as subjects* possessing the capacity so to internalize that is a 'prime effect' of power. At the same time, however, Foucault conceives power as an inherently antagonistic relation: 'power is war, a war continued by other means.'[46] This leads him to claim that 'where there is power, there is resistance and that however, or rather for the same reason, the latter is never in a position of exteriority with respect to power.'[47]

As many commentators have observed, this view of power gives rise to the following problem: granted that 'power is "always already there", that one is never "outside" it, that there are no "margins" for those who break with the system to gambol in', how is resistance possible?[48] The problem does not arise in pluralist political science, where power tends to be conceived thus: 'A has power over B to the extent that he can get B to do something that B would not otherwise do.'[49] Power is here a relationship between agents with their own wants, some of which at least were formed outside this relationship. But Foucault conceives subjects as themselves among 'the prime effects of power', and therefore he cannot appeal to their recalcitrant wants to explain resistance.

In the first volume of the *Histoire de la sexualité* Foucault spoke of 'the body and its pleasures' as the basis for a 'counter-attack' against the 'apparatus of sexuality'.[50] But this seemed more an act of desperation than a solution to the problem of resistance, appearing as it did to posit a natural man repressed by social relations. The *aporia* of power and resistance may help to explain the major shift in Foucault's thought that occurred between the first volume of the

Histoire, which appeared in 1976, and the second and third volumes, which were published only days before his death in June 1984. The extent of the shift is indicated by the following remark: 'Power is exercised only over free subjects, and only in so far as they are free.'[51] The distance between 'docile bodies' and 'free subjects' appears vast.

More concretely, Foucault introduces the notion of a form of power-relation other than the 'techniques of domination' he had studied in *Discipline and Punish*, namely what he called 'technologies of the self'.[52]

> By that it is necessary to understand the reflective and voluntary practices by which men, not only fix the rules of their conduct, but seek to transform themselves, to modify themselves in their singular being, and to make of their life a work which bears certain aesthetic values and obeys certain stylistic criteria.[53]

The main example of such an 'aesthetic of existence' analysed in the second and third volumes of the *Histoire* is that of the 'government of pleasures' (*chrēsis aphrodisiōn*) practised by free male citizens in classical antiquity, the techniques through which they so regulated their behaviour as to fit them to play their part in both household and city.

Now what is striking about these descriptions of 'technologies of the self' is that they seem to accord to subjects an active role in their own making. This certainly is what is suggested by such formulations as 'reflective and voluntary practices', 'men . . . seek to transform themselves, to modify themselves.' Power, Foucault says, is 'basically . . . a question of government', where 'to govern . . . is to structure the possible field of action of others.'[54] But what are we to make of power-relations which involve structuring *our own* 'possible field of action'? Foucault says nothing about the sort of personal motives or social mechanisms which might lead to the development of 'technologies of the self'; indeed, given his earlier preoccupation with power-knowledge he says surprisingly little about the relation between the *chrēsis aphrodisiōn* and the public world of the ancient *polis*.[55]

What makes Foucault so intriguing and challenging a thinker is his belief – evident in the attempt to write histories of the truth, sexuality, the subject – that what we think of as enduring and fundamental aspects of existence are nothing but historical constructs formed by a specific regime of social practices. Behind this lies a thoroughgoing nominalism, which treats all substances as contingent unities, temporary resting-points in the endless play of difference, a position obviously akin to Deleuze's and Guattari's.[56] The difficulties in which

Foucault found himself around the question of resistance and his subsequent development of the concept of 'technologies of the self' show one respect in which this nominalism is untenable (there are others, but it is unnecessary to consider them here).

Put simply, it does not seem that Foucault can, even in his own terms, do without some account of the properties that all subjects share. Such an account seems to be required by the notion of an 'aesthetic of existence' which is a practice of *self*-government. That is, there are some aspects of human subjects which are not simply socially constructed and which may provide both motives for and means of acting. In other words, even Foucauldian genealogy requires the concept of an enduring human nature.

Those who never doubted the necessity of such a concept will not find this conclusion very striking. It is indeed a tribute to both the rhetorical skills of the proponents of Parisian anti-humanism and the genuine insights which they offered, that the following remark by Ian Hacking does not seem merely to celebrate an absurdity: 'Foucault was that rare nominalist apprised of the . . . evident fact that, if there is no intrinsic human nature, there is no salvation, period.'[57] *No* intrinsic human nature? Are there really no properties which human beings share? Or perhaps the thought is that these properties are irrelevant to any understanding of human history. But is it really plausible to say that if human beings photosynthesized (to take an admirable example of Stephen Jay Gould's) this would make no difference to their history?[58]

I speak here of the concept of an enduring human nature rather than of the orthodox conception of agents. There is a close relationship between the two notions, which will be further explored below and in section 3.3. But the orthodox conception, while its truth may require the existence of a common human nature, does not itself make reference to specifically human needs and capacities in stating what it is to be an agent. This partly reflects the circumstances of its formulation. Thus Dennett's definition of personhood given in section 1.2 above is to some degree at least a response to developments in artificial intelligence and is formulated so that a computer could, at least in principle, meet these conditions. Whatever its virtues, it abstracts from one central fact about human beings, namely that they are *embodied* agents, whose intentional activities flow from the capacities they possess and are intelligible in the light of the needs they share as members of the same natural species. Conceiving the subject as a disembodied self is, of course, also central to the philosophical tradition from Descartes to Kant.

The orthodox conception is therefore best seen as part of a broader

account of human nature, one which, as Norman Geras puts it, treats
human beings as, 'like all other species, material and natural beings,
"irredeemably" rooted in a given biological constitution, *absolutely
continuous* with the rest of the natural world.'[59] The discontinuity
implied in the use of intentional explanations, ascribing beliefs and
desires to human agents on the assumption of their rationality, is to
be seen as a consequence of this 'given biological constitution', rather
than as marking an unbridgeable chasm separating the human and
the natural. Such a perspective is also reflected in David Wiggins's
definition of a person as 'any animal the physical make-up of whose
species constitutes the species' typical members thinking intelligent
beings, with reason and reflection, and typically enables them to
consider themselves, the same thinking things, in different times and
places'.[60]

Mary Midgley, the contemporary philosopher who has perhaps
stressed most strongly the unity of human beings with the rest of
nature, suggests that we conceive of the 'nature of a species' as 'a
certain range of powers and tendencies, a repertoire, inherited and
forming a fairly firm characteristic pattern'. The account she then
gives of the nature of the human species serves admirably to illustrate
why Foucault as well as many Marxists have been deeply suspicious
of such a notion. Social relations in our own as well as other species
involve rank, Midgley claims, since they are a generalization of the
relation between parent and child. Thus: 'Our natural interest in
dominance is not a lust for oppression. It is a taste for order, one that
can get out of hand. Based on the relation of child to parent, it is
essentially protective.'[61]

To avoid such canonizations of social oppression, Geras, in his
outstanding attempt to demonstrate Marxism's dependence on a
theory of human nature, suggests that we distinguish between 'human
nature', 'a constant entity, the set of all (relatively) permanent human
characteristics', and the 'nature of man', 'the all-round character of
human beings in some given context. Whilst the first usage makes of
human nature something unchanging by definition . . . the second
leaves open the degree of mutability in the *nature of man*.'[62] Such a
distinction removes a traditional Marxist objection to the notion of
human nature, namely that forms of behaviour arising within specific
social relations (say, egoism and competitiveness under capitalism)
are treated as 'permanent human characteristics'. Geras's usage
allows us to regard these as aspects rather of the 'nature of man'
under capitalism.

What, then, can be said about the genuinely 'permanent characteristics' constituting human nature? In the first place, they include not

just the 'range of powers and tendencies' referred to by Midgley, but also certain distinctive needs. This point needs to be stressed in the light of the way in which subjectivity is often conceived as something ethereal, non-bodily, even by those committed to understanding human beings as historically situated agents. Thus Agnes Heller rightly objects to Habermas's theory of communicative action because 'the creature-like aspects of human beings are missing . . . Habermasian man . . . has no body, no feelings; the "structure of personality" is identified with cognition, language and interaction.'[63] Important though the questions of the body and of human needs are for an account of agency, I shall, however, not deal with them here.[64]

Human nature, of course, consists in capacities as well as needs. An account of these capacities is central to Marx's philosophical anthropology, developed chiefly in the *Economic and Philosophic Manuscripts of 1844* and *The German Ideology*. Elster summarizes this theory of human nature thus: 'Marx distinguishes men from other animals on the basis of (i) self-consciousness, (ii) intentionality, (iii) language, (iv) tool-using, (v) tool-making and (vi) co-operation.'[65] Marx in fact varies his stress on these different features. Thus he writes in the *Manuscripts*:

> The animal is immediately one with its life-activity. It does not distinguish itself from it. It is *its life-activity*. Man makes his life-activity itself the object of his will and consciousness. He has conscious life-activity . . . Conscious life-activity distinguishes man immediately from animal life activity.[66]

By contrast, Marx declares in *The German Ideology*: 'Men can be distinguished from animals by consciousness, by religion or anything else you like. They themselves begin to distinguish themselves as soon as they begin to *produce* their means of subsistence, a step which is conditioned by their physical organization.'[67]

The contradiction between these passages is only apparent. Central to Marx's account of human labour is its *redirective* character, namely the fact that human beings' ability consciously to reflect on their activity allows them to modify and improve on prevailing productive techniques. Rather than being tied to the fixed repertoire of behaviour characteristic of other species, human productive activity is distinguished by its flexibility, by the indefinite variety of ways in which human beings may meet their needs by virtue of their cognitive capacities.[68] Marx's conception of human labour as necessarily a social activity is closely related to his view of language as 'the immediate actuality of thought': 'Language is as old as consciousness, language *is* practical, real consciousness that exists for

other men as well, and only therefore does it exist for me.'[69] Indeed,
in a polemic against the 'Robinsonades' of Rousseau and Smith,
Marx makes the connection between the social character of language
and that of labour explicit: 'Production by an isolated individual
outside society . . . is as much of an absurdity as is the development of
language without individuals living together and talking to each
other.'[70]

It should be clear, then, that Marx's philosophical anthropology
ascribes to human beings conditions [iv], [v] and [vi] of Dennett's
definition of personhood, namely reciprocity, the capacity to engage
in verbal communication and self-consciousness. The extent to which
historical materialism is consistent with the three more basic
conditions defining an intentional system, and in particular rationality
and intentionality, will be explored in section 1.5 and in chapters 2
and 3. It is worth noting, however, how well Marx's stress on labour,
language and co-operation accords with the findings of such branches
of empirical inquiry as biology, palaeontology, archaeology and
anthropology.

Thus the neurobiologist Steven Rose writes:

> *Homo sapiens* have a number of distinct advantages over their nearest
> relatives today; a somewhat larger brain-size in proportion to body
> weight, a hand-structure which makes the operation and manipulation
> of tools vastly easier than for even a chimpanzee, vocal cords which,
> unlike those of the apes, permit the clear articulation of sounds and the
> capacity to live in social groups . . . It is undoubtedly the social
> character of human relationships which has enabled them to exploit
> their other – perhaps only marginal – evolutionary advantages. From
> this and the use of tools comes the key characteristic of humans living
> in society; the change in their relationship to the natural world, such
> that they come to attempt to manipulate and control it. From this, and
> the activity of *production* of goods to satisfy wants, which flows from
> it, comes the steady transformation of human social relationships
> which characterizes the history of the last few hundred thousand years.
> The social, productive mode of life of *Homo sapiens* demands the
> capacity not only to be able to learn individually, but to signal
> meaningfully between members of the group; that is, to communicate.
> And the ability to communicate, first face to face in speech, later at a
> distance by writing, made possible the decisive evolutionary break-
> through in human history. Learned information could now be
> transferred between human individuals and, by means of oral and later
> written communications, between generations as well. It became
> unnecessary for each generation to learn afresh everything its ancestors
> had painfully and slowly accumulated.[71]

1.4 HUMAN NATURE: MORALITY, JUSTICE AND VIRTUE

What, then, are the implications of the sort of notion of human nature sketched out above? More specifically, how does it relate to the concepts and propositions of historical materialism as a scientific research programme? Norman Geras, arguing against the view that the notion of human nature has no explanatory role, which is instead performed by Marx's theory of history, emphatically declares:

> A concept of human nature, encompassing at once the common needs and the general and distinctive capacities of humankind, plays an important, a quite fundamental role there [i.e. within historical materialism] in accounting for those specifically human relationships that are production relations and for that specifically human type of process of change that is history.

The reason is that 'there are features of the relations in question that are due precisely to the *nature of the entities they relate*, that is to say, to the general make-up of human beings, to human nature.'[72]

One can readily agree with this, and still want to know more about the precise relationship between Marx's philosophical anthropology and his theory of history. This is especially so since, as Geras concedes, concepts such as those of the forces and relations of production occupy the foreground of Marx's account of historical development from the mid-1840s onwards, whereas the *1844 Manuscripts* are organized around an essentially Hegelian schema, in which history is seen as the loss (alienation) and recovery of man's essential powers.[73] G. A. Cohen has argued recently that Marx's 'theory of history does not require or derive from the anthropology'. The reason is that

> production in the philosophical anthropology is not identical with production in the theory of history. In the anthropology men are by nature creative beings. They flourish only in the cultivation and exercise of their manifold powers, and they are especially productive – which is say, *here*, creative – in the condition of freedom conferred by material plenty. But in the theory of history people produce not freely but because they have to because nature does not otherwise supply their wants; and the development in history of the productive power of *man* (as such, as a species) occurs at the expense of the creative capacity of the *men* who are the agents and victims of that development.[74]

Cohen here points to an ambiguity in Marx's thought reflected in his apparently contradictory views on labour under communism – on the one hand, it will then become 'not only a means of life but life's prime want', on the other it is 'a realm of necessity', the 'realm of freedom' lying 'beyond the sphere of actual material production'.[75]

Cohen's solution is effectively to assign the former view to Marx's anthropology, the second to his theory of history. Part of his concern so to separate the two seems to be his belief that 'the philosophy anthropology is false, because it is one-sided.'[76] We shall take a rather oblique look at his reasons for believing this in section 4.4. In the meantime, it is worth emphasizing that Cohen's argument for the independence of historical materialism from Marx's anthropology does not actually contradict Geras's claim that the former requires *some* account of human nature. Cohen points out that in his own argument for a version of historical materialism in which the productive forces have primacy 'the premisses are scarcity, intelligence, and rationality: nothing about humanity being by nature productive enters those premisses.'[77] No, but to assume, as he does, that agents are intelligent and rational is implicitly to assert something about the 'permanent characteristics' of human beings, even if it is not to endorse Marx's own account of human nature. (We shall consider Cohen's assumptions much more closely in the next chapter.)

Cohen's discussion of Marx's anthropology raises another question – whether there is (or should be) an ethical dimension to the latter's thought. For it is difficult not to see the claim that human beings 'flourish only in the cultivation and exercise of their manifold powers, and ... are especially productive ... in the condition of material plenty' as both a sketch of the good life and a yardstick by which to appraise concrete societies. Elster accurately summarizes Marx's attitude in both the *Manuscripts* and mature works such as *Capital*: 'Marx himself condemned capitalism mainly because it frustrated human development and self-actualization. Correlatively, he saw communism as a society in which men could become fully human, that is fully realize their potential as all-round creators.'[78] But do not such apparently ethical judgements conflict with the condemnations of morality in the writings of Marx and his successors?[79]

The question is one which has been much discussed in relation to the more specific question of whether or not Marx had a theory of justice. Without entering into that controversy, I wish simply to refer to the magisterial survey and resolution of the argument provided, once again, by Norman Geras. He concludes that 'Marx did think capitalism was unjust but he did not think he thought so.'[80] Or, in Jon Elster's stronger version of the same claim: 'like M. Jourdain, he did not know how to describe correctly what he was doing; unlike him, he actually went out of his way to deny that the correct description was appropriate.'[81]

On this interpretation Marx had what Elster calls a 'hierarchical' theory of justice, spelt out in the *Critique of the Gotha Programme*. There Marx distinguishes between the distributive principles operative in the transition from capitalism to communism (the dictatorship of the proletariat) and in communism itself. The first, the contribution principle as it has come to be known ('From each according to his capacity, to each according to his work') rewards people in proportion to the labour they contribute. Though it is an improvement on capitalism, Marx nevertheless stresses the principle's limitations:

> This *equal* right is an unequal right for unequal labour. It recognizes no class differences, because everyone is only a worker like everyone else; but it tacitly recognizes unequal individual endowment and thus productive capacity as natural privileges. *It is, therefore, a right of inequality, in its content, like every right.*

These defects reflect the extent to which the new order is 'still stamped with the birthmarks of the old society from whose womb it emerges'. Only after a considerable further development of the productive forces 'can the narrow horizon of bourgeois right be *crossed* in its entirety and society inscribe on its banners: From each according to his ability, to each according to his needs!'[82] Those who ascribe to Marx a theory of justice think that this second criterion, the needs principle, forms the core of the theory. The contribution principle, Elster suggests, 'is a Janus-like notion. Looked at from one side, it serves as a criterion of justice that condemns capitalist exploitation as unjust. Looked at from the vantage point of fully developed communism, it is itself inadequate by the higher standard expressed in the needs principle'.[83]

Surely this interpretation conflicts with Marx's rejection of morality? The crucial issue here turns on what one understands by 'morality'. Those who have argued that Marxism and morality are incompatible have tended to conceive of the latter along Kantian lines, that is, as consisting in a set of universally applicable general norms.[84] This form of ethical thinking gives rise to what Steven Lukes calls the 'morality of *Recht*', in which people are regarded as having rights irrespective of the circumstances and consequences of their actions, an approach which Marx certainly did reject both because, as he argues in his discussion of the contribution principle, rights based on general standards fail to address people's specific needs, and because they reflect and do not abolish the antagonisms of capitalist society.[85] The other prevailing conception of morality is the utilitarian, where actions are judged in terms of their consequences, or more specifically their contribution to the sum of human welfare. Marx was equally hostile to this approach, for reasons which we will explore in section 3.4.

There is, however, another conception of morality available to Marx, namely that of Aristotle. The kinship between the two thinkers has been stressed by a number of commentators, starting with Lukács and Marcuse, and is brought out in a way relevant to the present discussion by Richard W. Miller:

> In the history of philosophy, Marx and Aristotle are the most striking and attractive contrasts to both alternatives [i.e. the morality of *Recht* and utilitarianism]. As against rights-based morality, both judge institutions by the kinds of lives they promote and judge proposed rights by assessing the consequences, of embodying them in institutions. At the same time, their general conceptions of the kinds of lives worth promoting are highly similar, and emphatically opposed to utilitarianism. In short, as political philosophers they are non-utilitarian consequentialists.[86]

Marx and Aristotle are opposed to utilitarianism in the sense that 'the goal of society is to promote good lives on the part of its members', where 'the good life must give priority to the exercise of the best human capacities, the ones which most remove a person farthest from an animal existence', rather than, as Bentham sees it, maximizing pleasure, where pleasures can aggregated into a sum (transcending individuals) of human welfare, to which specific pleasures simply contribute in proportion to their supposedly measurable intensity and duration. Similarly, rights are 'to be chosen by assessing their consequences for people governed by them', rather than on the basis of some more universal norm. This is not to say that Marx's and Aristotle's conceptions of the good are identical. Aristotle, Miller observes 'employs fixed hierarchical rankings of human capacities in which what is less than best should, so far as possible, contribute to the activity of the best.' Since for Aristotle the best consists in *theõria*, 'the contemplation of eternal truths', and only a few are capable of performing this activity, the result is to license the most extreme social inequality. Marx, by contrast, believed that 'the most desirable life is many-sided, expressing a diversity of intellectual, perceptual, and manual activities, and overcoming the distinction between mind-work and hand-work.'[87]

The needs principle can thus be taken as stating the basis on which distribution would have to be organized for the good life, as Marx conceives it, to be realized. He emphasizes, as we have seen, that applying this principle depends on historical circumstances and in particular on the sort of development of the productive forces following the overthrow of capitalism which would permit the abolition of the distinction between mental and manual labour, a distinction which Aristotle, unlike Marx, believes to be inherent in human nature. At the same time, the contribution principle identifies as unjust the social mechanism through which people are prevented from pursuing the good life in class society, namely the appropriation of surplus labour.

There is another respect in which Marx can be said to be an Aristotelian. Aristotle's account of morality appraises action, not in terms of rights or utility, but rather in the light of the virtues that they may embody, where virtues are dispositions to behave and feel in certain ways. Alasdair MacIntyre is the philosopher to have offered the most illuminating recent discussion of the virtues. They are, he says, 'precisely those qualities the possession of which will enable individuals to achieve *eudaimonia* [well-being] and the lack of which will frustrate progress towards that *telos*'. There is, he stresses, an internal relation between *eudamonia* and the virtues: 'What constitutes the good for man is a complete human life lived at its best, and the exercise of the virtues is a necessary and central part of such a life, not merely a preparatory exercise to secure such a life.' Possession of the virtues does not consist in a set of natural dispositions but rather depends on the development of the capacity to make judgements, which involves crucially discriminating how to behave in specific circumstances. The right cannot therefore be captured in a set of rules, as the morality of *Recht* would have us suppose. Furthermore, 'the virtues find their place not just in the life of the individual, but in the life of the city'; 'the individual is indeed intelligible only as a *zōon politikon*.'[88]

MacIntyre, attracted though he is to such a virtue-based morality, doubts whether it can be sustained today. Perhaps the most important reason for this scepticism is the following:

> Is it possible to be an Aristotelian and yet to view the city-state in a historical perspective as only one – even if a very important one – in a series of social and political forms in and through which the kind of self which can exemplify the virtues can be found and educated and in which the self can find its arena?

MacIntyre thinks that modernity is not such a form, and is therefore left 'waiting not for a Godot, but for another – doubtless very different – St Benedict' to create, amid the ruins of our civilization, the communal forms of living in which the virtues could flourish.[89]

As some commentators have observed, Marx does seem to have thought that certain virtues could be cultivated even in capitalist society. These are specifically the solidarity and heroism displayed by workers in the class struggle against capital: think, for example, of Marx's praise of the Communards in *The Civil War in France*. Frederick G. Whelan suggests that 'the proletarian virtue that Marx admires resembles, and may be derivative of, the civic virtue that was a distinctive component of earlier republican traditions in political thought', by which he means the classical republicanism of Machiavelli and Rousseau, who conceived agents as citizens, the members of a political community, rather than as the bearers of rights or the maximizers of utilities.[90] Alan Gilbert espouses a similar view of Marx, in attributing to him an Aristotelian 'moral realism' whose ethical standards do not all vary with 'the waxing and waning of modes of production':

> Marx's vision of a working-class community, transforming itself through public action, revived and transformed the ancient *polis*. Under socialism the role of co-operative political activity, a good in itself, carried at least equal weight with the ultimate end of individual self-realization under communism. Marx regarded this political activity as a component of the final good and not merely a means to it.[91]

Such an implicit moral theory (and it can only be treated as implicit in Marx's thought) is not open to the sort of objection that the classical Marxist tradition has had to attempts – usually influenced by some version of Kantian morality – to ground socialism ethically. This objection was, as Perry Anderson notes, not so much to morality, as to *moralism*,

> the vain intrusion of moral judgements in lieu of causal understanding – typically, in everyday life and in political evaluations alike, leading to an 'inflation' of ethical terms themselves into a false rhetoric, which lacks the exacting sense of material care and measure that is inseparable from true moral awareness.[92]

A virtue-based morality involves crucially the exercise of judgement concerning the circumstances and consequences of action, a process which necessarily requires the development of a 'causal understanding' of these circumstances and consequences. Morality thus conceived is perfectly consistent with what Geras calls the 'salutary impulse' behind 'Marx's disavowal of all commitment to ethical principle', whose 'positive core is the conviction that ideals alone are an insufficient tool for human liberation and the consequent dedication to trying to grasp the material preconditions of this (historically unavoidable alienations, unfreedoms and injustices included) and the social agencies capable of bringing it about'.[93]

At the same time, however, this account of the sort of morality to which Marx's arguments committed him is vulnerable to two sorts of objections. The first concerns the question of whether the sort of many-sided realization of human capacities which constitutes *eudaimonia* under communism is in fact feasible.[94] The second, raised for example by Steven Lukes, centres on the claim that Marx's rejection of the morality of *Recht* and his consequentialism contributed to the disasters of Stalinism by justifying all means by the end, communism.[95] To deal with either of these questions would, however, take us too far from the main concerns of this book.

1.5 PRACTICAL REASON AND SOCIAL STRUCTURES

The upshot of the preceding two sections is to embed the orthodox conception of agents in a broader theory of human nature. As David Wiggins puts it, 'the constitution that is seen in its causal relations with the contingencies of human history and geography is a constitution supervenient on contingencies of human *biological* constitution.'[96] The approach developed here can be seen as naturalistic, in the sense of treating both the boundaries between human beings and the physical world and those between philosophy and the sciences as relative. We have seen also that the sort of view of human nature developed here will impose constraints on our explanations of social events and can be made to issue in an ethical theory. (I should hasten to emphasize, however, that this latter theory is not 'ethical naturalism' of the sort condemned by G. E. Moore, where the referents of terms such as 'good' are thought to be ultimately physical properties. It does, however, seem to involve commitment to some form of moral realism, that is, to the claim that moral judgements are true or false, and not, as many have thought, merely expressions of desire or imperatives. This approach seems, in any case, broadly consonant with the neo-Aristotelian drift of much contemporary moral philosophy.[97])

It should be clear enough that this conception of human nature and the account of agency it implies has nothing to do with the 'philosophy of subject' which led Foucault, Althusser and others to embrace anti-humanism. To view human beings as animals of a certain kind capable of engaging in a range of intentional activities is in no sense to endorse an epistemology in which the subject is the foundation of knowledge or the source of meaning. But it is still to conceive human beings as centres capable of initiating action, rather than as bundles of drives and desires constructed within social relations. To distinguish the view of human nature here defended from the 'philosophy of subject' undoubtedly central to Western philosophy from Descartes through Kant to Husserl, I prefer to speak in this book of 'agents', with the connotation this term has of the operation of causal powers in the physical as well as the human world, rather than of 'subjects'. But this is not meant to suggest that the explanation of human behaviour does not involve the use of those distinctive principles embodied in the orthodox conception of agents.

There remains, however, the question left over from section 1.2, of whether or not the orthodox conception thus woven into an account of human nature requires methodological individualism (MI), i.e. the claim that the explanation of social events can only be in terms of individuals, their states and properties. Let us recall that Graham Macdonald and Philip Pettit argued that the orthodox conception does involve MI, since to accord 'explanatory autonomy' to social structures, that is, to refuse to reduce them to the consequences, intended or otherwise, of individual action, is to suggest that at least some social events are not 'the rational outcome of the agents' beliefs and desires', and is thus to contradict the 'indubitable' orthodox conception. While I have sought to undermine the idea that the orthodox conception is 'undeniable', I still think it to be true, and therefore I must either accept MI or undermine MacDonald's and Pettit's inference from the orthodox conception to MI.

Let us consider the form of action-explanation. It can be cast into an inference (indeed the structure of action-explanations derives from what Aristotle called the 'practical syllogism'):[98]

(1) A desires that p
(2) A believes that q, namely that doing x will bring it about that p
(3) Therefore A does x.

There are various ways in which such a piece of practical reasoning may be defeasible. For example, there is the case of what Aristotle called *akrasia*, or incontinence, where A desires that p and believes that q, but nevertheless does y rather than x out of weakness of will.[99] There is another way in which the inference from (1) and (2) to (3) may be defeated. It may be that A cannot do x because he is prevented from doing it, or because doing it is beyond his powers. In this case A embarks on x, but is prevented from accomplishing it. So here we have, instead of (3)

$$(3') \text{ A tries to do } x.^{100}$$

Let consider a particular instance of this latter case (chosen, in part, because it concerns one of a class of agents whose pursuit of *eudaimonia* played little part in Aristotle's philosophy). Spartacus is a Thracian slave owned by a *lanista*, a trainer of gladiators, in Capua in the first century before Christ. Spartacus naturally wishes to return to Thrace, and believes correctly that to realize this desire he must first leave the gladiator's school. But his attempts to do so are frustrated by the guards employed (or, more likely, themselves owned) by the *lanista*.

In this case, Spartacus's lack of power to realize his desire is not, in any very interesting sense, a physical disability. It arises from social relations. These are not simply the structure of power within the gladiators' school, but also the broader relationships involved in the enforcement of slave-owners' rights by the Roman state. This would become clear enough if Spartacus were (as of course he did) to rouse his fellow gladiators against the *lanista* and his guards, and then organize a more general slave revolt. The military power of Rome would be (and was) mobilized to crush the rebels, and thus to eliminate a serious threat to the slave relations of production essential to the appropriation of surplus labour in that society.[101]

The significance of this example is that in our explanation of what took place, why (3') (Spartacus's unsuccessful escape) happened rather than (3) (his departure from the gladiatorial school), we must make reference to social structures, since it is they which account for Spartacus's inability to realize his desire. Thus, we have here a case in which social structures (the class relations of Roman society) have what Macdonald and Pettit call 'explanatory autonomy' since our explanation invokes them as well as Spartacus's beliefs and desires. Does this not contradict the orthodox conception, since we here have a social event which is not simply the 'rational outcome of the agents' beliefs and desires'? No, since, as we have seen, for the conclusion of an action-explanation to be validly inferred, that is, for (3) to follow from (1) and (2), we require also

(4) A has the power to do x, and is not prevented from doing it.

Usually (4) is just treated as part of the general assumption that other things are equal, along with assumptions, for example, that A has no stronger or equally powerful conflicting desires. But to do so is to consign to the *ceteris paribus* clause features of A's social context that

are crucial both to whether he can perform the action he believes will
realize his desires and to what the actual outcome will be. Actions
consist in the exercise of powers, and the powers agents have depend
on and are determined in part by social structures. That is the nub of
my argument against MI, developed at much greater length in the
following chapter.

Macdonald and Pettit might object that what stops Spartacus from
leaving the school, and what ends the slave revolt he leads is nothing
but the action of other individuals – the guards, Roman soldiers and
so on. But this objection is bootless. The acts which destroyed the
slave revolt and whose possibility buttressed power-relations within
every slave barracks involved large-scale co-ordination and organization depending on the exercise of powers by individuals such as the
consul M. Licinius Crassus, which reflected their position within the
Roman state and more generally within prevailing social relationships.
Nor will it alter matters one whit to say that these relationships are
themselves the consequences of individual actions. For these actions
themselves involved the exercise of powers determined at least in part
by the social relations prevailing at the time they were performed.
However far one pushes back to story, action-explanation will still
involve both individuals' beliefs and desires and the structures on
which their powers partly depend. I shall try and make this strong
claim more plausible in section 2.5.

Another objection might be that in my account of what Spartacus
did (or didn't) do I assume the truth of historical materialism, since
the structures I invoke are clearly relations of class exploitation. This
is no real objection, since my concern in this book is to offer a
Marxist account of agency which does not collapse into MI. But in
any case other forms of social theory are likely to involve a similar
form of explanation. If, for example, we substitute a Weberian form
of legitimate domination for the slave mode of production, social
relations would still play an essential part in explaining why
Spartacus couldn't just leave the gladiators' school and go home to
Thrace.

I conclude that Macdonald and Pettit are wrong. The explanatory
autonomy of social structures is not inconsistent with the orthodox
conception of agents, since action-explanations involve a hidden
premiss, (4), ascribing to agents the power to perform the action
explained. To establish a formal consistency is, however, not enough.
The case made out for MI by 'rational-choice' Marxists such as Elster
turns on the supposed inadequacies of non-individualist versions of
historical materialism. Let us turn, then, to the questions raised by
Marx's theory of history.

CHAPTER 2

STRUCTURE AND ACTION

2.1 THE CONCEPT OF SOCIAL STRUCTURE

Why think of societies in terms of the structures they possess? Various considerations might lead one in this direction. First, there is what Anthony Giddens describes as 'the degree of interdependence of action, or "systemness"' that societies evidently display.[1] Secondly, and closely connected, societies persist in time. We can follow Giddens in refusing to regard them as self-reproducing organisms and still refuse to apply the term 'society' to any set of human relationships which showed no capacity to continue across generations. Thirdly, it is a characteristic of social relations that their nature and existence do not depend on the identity of the particular agents involved in them. Social relations are sets of empty places.[2] Fourthly, social relations often involve regularities which occur with the agents involved in them not understanding, or even necessarily even being aware of them. In this respect social life involves processes which go on, as Hegel put it, behind the backs of human agents. Finally, to say that a society has a structure is to say that there are limits to the extent to which it may vary without becoming an instance of a different kind of society.

Rather than offer a formal definition of social structure, I shall try to indicate some of the issues addressed by explanations that mention entities falling under this concept. A good place to start is the distinction drawn by David Lockwood btween 'social integration' and 'system integration'. The former concept is central to what he calls the 'normative functionalism' of Talcott Parsons and his followers, an approach characterized by 'first, the emphatic role attributed to "common value elements" in the integration of social action; and second, the unwarranted assumption that the study of social stability must precede the analysis of social change'. Parsons' critics, for example Ralf Dahrendorf and John Rex, emphasized instead the existence of conflicting interests and values, an approach which highlighted the problem of social change, itself explained as 'a result of the shifting balance of power between conflict groups': 'Now while social change is very frequently associated with conflict, the reverse does not necessarily hold. Conflict may be endemic and intense in a social system without causing any basic structural change. Why does some conflict result in change while other conflict does not?'[3]

Conflict theorists such as Dahrendorf and Rex have no answer to this question, a limitation which reflects their sharing with Parsons the problematic of social integration. Overcoming this weakness requires formulation of the concept of system integration: 'Whereas the problem of social integration focuses attention upon the orderly or conflictual relationships between the *actors*, the problem of system integration focuses on the orderly or conflictual relationship between the *parts* of a social system'. Lockwood uses Marx to illustrate the latter concept: 'One might almost say that the "conflict" which in Marxian theory is decisive for change is not the *power* conflict arising through the relationships in the productive system, but the *system* conflict arising from "contradictions" between "property institutions" and the "forces of production." '[4]

Giddens suggests that we should further distinguish between social system and structure, the latter being conceived as 'an absent set of differences, temporally "present" only in their instantiation, in the constituting moments of social systems'.

> Social systems involve regularized relations of interdependence between individuals or groups, that typically can be best analysed as *recurrent social practices*. Social systems are systems of social interaction . . . Systems, in this terminology, have structures, or, more accurately, have structural properties. Structures are necessarily (logically) properties of systems or collectivities, and *are characterized by the 'absence of a subject'*.[5]

Underlying this distinction seems to be the thought that the role of the concept of social structure is to explain 'the binding of time and space in social systems'.[6] One way of putting it (though Giddens might reject this gloss) is that structure and system are respectively the *explanans* and the *explanandum* of social theory. How do human actions involve persisting (and changing) patterns of social inter-action? The concept of structure should be seen as helping us to answer that question. Better than abstract reflection on this concept, however, is consideration of attempts to formulate concrete accounts of social structures. Historical materialism offers one such account (section 2.2). I shall consider two apparently very different statements of the relationship between structure and action within this tradition, respectively G. A. Cohen's 'orthodox historical materialism' (section 2.3) and the 'rational-choice' Marxism of Jon Elster and others (section 2.4), before setting out a more adequate account of the relationship (section 2.5) and considering its implications for Marxism (section 2.6).

2.2 THE BASIC CONCEPTS OF HISTORICAL MATERIALISM

Historical materialism can be seen as making a distinctive claim about the *kinds* of structures which have primacy in explaining social systems, namely that these are the forces and relations of production. But before considering these concepts let us first note that Marxism can also be taken as distinguishing between two kinds of social *system* as well. These are modes of production and social formations. Étienne Balibar writes: '*Capital*, which expounds the abstract theory of the capitalist mode of production, does not undertake to analyse concrete social formations which generally contain *several* different modes of production, whose laws of co-existence and hierarchy must therefore be studied.'[7]

This distinction should not be conflated with that between economic base and ideologico-political superstructure. To quote Nicos Poulantzas, 'a mode of production, as Engels stated schematically, is composed of different levels or instances, the economic, political, ideological, and theoretical.'[8] The difference between mode of production and social formation is rather one between different levels of abstraction: the former refers to certain basic combinations of forces and relations of production along with the other structures which may be inferred from each such combination, while a social formation typically 'presents a particular combination, a specific overlapping of several "pure" modes of production (as Lenin demonstrated in *The Development of Capitalism in Russia*)'.[9] The distinction is not made explicitly by Marx, Lenin or any of the other classical figures, but by Althusser and his followers: however, the concept of social formation is one that can be put to good use in historical writing.[10]

The fundamental concept of historical materialism is, in any case, that of mode of production. To specify the character of a mode of production is to give an account of the specific combination of the forces and relations of production it involves. There has been much discussion of these concepts in recent years, as a result of the attempts by Althusser and by Cohen to reconstruct a coherent theory of historical materialism from Marx's own evolving and often inconsistent usage. What follows draws on both this discussion and Marx's writings, especially *Capital*.

Because of Marx's own inconsistencies and ambiguities, much turns on which parts of his writings one chooses to focus on. Thus Cohen takes the famous 1859 Preface to *A Contribution to the Critique of Political Economy* as the bench-mark of his interpretation. By contrast, I prefer the following summary of historical materialism:

> The specific economic form, in which unpaid surplus-labour is pumped out of direct producers, determines the relationship of rulers and ruled, as it grows directly out of production itself and, in turn, reacts upon it as a determining element. Upon this, however, is founded the formation of the economic community which grows out of the production relations themselves, thereby simultaneously its specific political form. It is always the direct relationship of the owners of the conditions of production to the direct producers – a relationship always naturally corresponding to a definite stage in the development of the methods of labour and thereby its social productivity – which reveals the innermost secret, the hidden basis of the entire social structure, and with it the political form of the relation of sovereignty and dependence, in short, the corresponding specific form of the state.[11]

In this passage Marx does three things. First, he claims that exploitation – 'the specific economic form, in which unpaid surplus-labour is pumped out of direct producers' – explains the particular form of political domination. Secondly, exploitation itself is grounded in the relations of production, 'the direct relationship of the owners of the conditions of production to the direct producers'. Thirdly, the relations of production are conceived as 'naturally corresponding to a definite stage in the development' of the productive forces, i.e. 'the methods of labour and thereby its social productivity'. It is tempting to see these three points as representing the sort of hierarchical structure which Cohen assigns to a mode of production: at the top the ideologico-political superstructure, then the 'economic structure' on which it rests, the relations of production and finally the productive forces whose development provides history with its dynamic.[12]

Starting at the basement, so to speak, let us consider the production forces. Cohen thinks of these as a list of elements contributing to production: 'To qualify as a productive force, a facility must be capable of use by a producing agent in such a way that production occurs (partly) as a result of its use, and it is someone's purpose that the facility so contribute to production.' Subtle and illuminating though Cohen's discussion of the constituents of the productive forces is, it is not unfair to say that his primary concern is with their development. He argues that 'the development of the productive forces may be identified with the growth in the surplus they make possible, and this in turn may be identified with the amount of the day that remains after the labouring time required to maintain the producers has been subtracted.'[13]

This approach does not, however, capture an important feature of Marx's own usage. Göran Therborn points out that the concept of productive forces (*Produktivkräfte*) originated as Marx's translation of 'productive powers' in the writings of Smith, Ricardo and other classical economists. However, Therborn argues:

> In Marx's theory, 'forces of production' was transformed into a new concept. Not only is its role in Marxist theory quite distinctive, and vastly more important (in relation to other concepts) than in classical economics; it also acquires a wholly new referent. The Marxist concept refers to the connection between different types of technical organization of labour and different types of economic and social system. . . . The concept of forces of production has no doubt something to do with productivity. But it refers not, as with Smith and Ricardo, simply or even primarily to productivity or productive capacity as such. Its primary reference is rather to the *different ways in which productivity is ensured*. Productive capacity is no longer merely a quantitative phenomenon: the dominant concern is no longer with its quantitative improvement, but with the qualitatively different technical forms of labour.[14]

This interpretation is supported by the passage already cited above, where Marx refers to the productive forces as 'the *methods* of labour and *thereby* its social productivity' (emphasis added). What he means by 'methods of labour' is made clear in chapter 7 of *Capital* volume I, where the capitalist process of production is conceived as a combination of the 'labour process' and the 'process of valorization'. The valorization process (*Verwertungsprozess*) consists of the extraction of surplus-value, the mode of exploitation specific to capitalism. By contrast,

> the labour-process is purposeful activity aimed at production of use-values. It is an appropriation of what exists in nature for the requirements of man. It is the universal condition for the metabolic interaction between man and nature, the nature-imposed condition of human existence, or rather it is common to all forms of society in which human beings live.

The labour process consists of three elements: '(1) purposeful activity, that is work itself, (2) the object on which that work is performed, and (3) the instruments of that work'. (2) and (3) – raw materials and instruments of labour respectively – reduce to one category, the means of production, counterposed to labour-power, the capacity to work embodied in human beings.[15]

Cohen also treats the productive forces as consisting primarily in the means of production and labour-power.[16] However, viewing them as a labour-process *combining* these elements introduces an additional, very important nuance, suggested by Balibar when he argues that the productive forces should not be thought of as 'a *list*'. Rather they, 'too, are a connexion of a certain type within the mode of production, in other words, they, too, are a *relation of production*'.[17] One sense in which this is so arises simply as a consequence of the fact that labour is, for Marx, a social activity. Co-operation, a social relationship between actors, is a necessary feature of the labour-process as the 'nature-imposed condition of human existence'. Thus Marx endorses the view that 'hunting was the first form of co-operation.'[18]

Cohen indeed distinguishes between '*material and social relations of production*', where 'a description is social if and only if it entails an ascription to persons . . . of rights and powers *vis-à-vis* other men.' However, he excludes 'material relations of production' from the productive forces. This seems to reflect Cohen's insistence that 'the familiar distinction between forces of production and relations of production is, in Marx, one of a set of contrasts between nature and society.'[19] It does not sit well with Marx's claim in *The German Ideology* that the 'mode of co-operation is itself a "productive force" '.[20]

How is the labour-process, conceived as a structured relationship between labour-power and the means of production, to be distinguished from the relations of production proper? Marx argues that:

> It is not only what is made but how, and by what instruments of labour, that distinguishes different economic epochs. Instruments of labour not only supply a standard of the degree of development that human labour has attained, but they also indicate the social relations within which men work.[21]

Althusser suggests the following interpretation of this passage:

> One of the three constitutive elements of the labour-process . . . is therefore dominant: the *means of labour*. . . . The 'means of labour'

determine the typical form of the labour-process considered: by establishing the 'mode of attack' on external nature subject to transformation in economic production, they determine the *mode of production*, the basic category of analysis (in economics and history); at the same time, they establish the level of *productivity* of productive labour.[22]

Althusser's gloss requires two qualifications. First, his ascription of dominance to the instruments (or means) of labour to some degree reflects his anti-humanist predilections. Instruments of a certain kind require labour-power possessing specific skills to operate them. Furthermore, the construction of such instruments requires particular sorts of knowledge. Cohen rightly includes the 'productively relevant parts' of science within the productive forces.[23] Secondly, it remains to be seen in what sense the instruments of labour 'determine the *mode of production*'. Marx does not, contrary to what he says in this passage, distinguish 'different economic epochs' according to the instruments of labour they involve. As their names suggest, modes of production such as slavery, feudalism and capitalism differ according to their relations of production. Nevertheless, Althusser's basic point seems right. The labour-process is a particular technical organization of production, combining certain kinds of means of production and labour-power, and, as a consequence, achieving a certain level of productivity.

The relations of production also involve a specific combination of labour-power and means of production. While discussing the purchase of both these constituents of the labour-process by capital, Marx argues that behind this transaction 'lies . . . distribution; not distribution in the ordinary meaning of a distribution of articles of consumption, but the distribution of the elements of production itself, the material factors of which are concentrated on one side, and labour-power, isolated, on the other'. As Marx of course shows in his famous discussion of 'primitive accumulation' in Part Eight of *Capital* volume I, the separation of labour-power from the means of production is a social condition arising from a historical process, the expropriation of the peasantry. Here he makes the same point, but as a general claim about the relations of production:

Whatever the social form of production, labourers and means of production always remain factors of it. But in a state of separation from each other either of these factors can be such only potentially. For production to go on they must unite. The specific manner in which this union is accomplished distinguishes the different economic epochs of the structure of society from one another.[24]

One might put it like this. The labour-process, 'the nature-imposed condition of human existence', involves a particular way of combining labour-power and means of production in order to produce use-values. But whether this combination actually occurs depends on the historically specific social relations determining the distribution of the means of production among members of society. Marx is quite emphatic about the importance of this kind of distribution:

> before distribution can be the distribution of products, it is: (1) the distribution of the instruments of production, and (2), which is a further specification of the same relation, the distribution of the members of the society among the different kinds of production. (Subsumption of the individuals under specific relations of production.) The distribution of products is evidently only a result of this distribution, which is comprised within the process of production itself and determines the structure of production.[25]

The relations of production are constituted by this distribution of the means of production, which determines who controls not simply the means themselves, but also labour-power itself (this is partly what is meant by Marx's treating as a consequence of the distribution of the means of production the 'subsumption of the individuals under specific relations of production'). If we remember that by 'productive forces' Cohen means labour-power and the means of production rather than their combination in the labour-process, then we can accept the following definition he offers: 'Production relations are EITHER relations of ownership by persons of productive forces or persons OR relations presupposing such relations. By *ownership* is meant not a legal relationship but one of *effective control*.'[26]

This last point, that relations of production involve ownership in the sense of effective control, or, as Barry Hindess and Paul Hirst put it, 'effective possession', cannot be stressed strongly enough.[27] One of Marx's main criticisms of Proudhon was that he conflated production relations with the 'metaphysical or juridical fiction' of legal property forms. Elsewhere he endorsed the political realism of such thinkers as Machiavelli, Boudin and Hobbes who 'regarded *might* as the basis of right [*Recht*, which also means 'law'] . . . If power is taken as the basis of right, as Hobbes etc. do, then right, law, etc., are merely the symptom, the expression of *other* relations upon which state power rests'.[28] Failure to observe Marx's distinction between production relations and juridical property forms had led many of his followers into enormous confusion, notably as a result of their tendency to identify socialist relations of production with state ownership of the means of production.

Robert Brenner does not make this identification, so it is surprising to see him use the expression 'property relations' to refer to what Marx calls the relations of production:

> By property relations, I mean the relationships among the direct producers, among the class of exploiters (if any exists), and between the exploiters and producers, which specify and determine the regular and systematic access of the individual economic actors (or families) to the means of production and to the economic product.

Brenner denies that these are, 'in any useful sense, understandable as relations of production *per se*'. His reason seems to be that Marx in *The German Ideology* conceives the relations of production as both 'socio-technical relations within the unit of production' (roughly, the labour-process) and property relations determining 'the distribution of the social product among the social classes'. The result is a form of technological determinism, in which the development of the division of labour is treated as the motor of historical change.[29]

Now it is certainly true that *The German Ideology* involves what I have elsewhere called 'a persistent confusion of technical and social relations', particularly but not solely in its treatment of the division of labour.[30] However, as Therborn points out, Marx does not use the concept of the relations of production in this work. Rather, 'the concept that accompanies the forces of production is *Verkehr* or *Verkehrsform*, a much broader term meaning approximately communication, commerce or intercourse.' The concept of the relations of production (*Produktionsverhältnisse*) only 'emerges in *The Poverty of Philosophy*, in close relation with the concept of property, to denote a specific totality of economic relationships'.[31] Far from perpetuating *The German Ideology*'s conflation of social and technical relations, this concept allowed Marx to distinguish sharply between them, for example in his discussion of the labour-process and the valorization-process in *Capital* volume I. When discussing Brenner's work I shall, therefore, treat his use of 'property relations' as referring to production relations in the sense given here.

So identifying the relations of production primarily (though not, as we shall see below, exclusively) with the mode of effective control over the means of production has recently been challenged by Chris Harman:

> It seems to me to limit the notion of the 'social relations of production' far too much. Much of the power of Marx's account of history lies in the way in which it shows how small changes in the forces of production lead to small cumulative changes in the social relations arising directly at the point of production, until they challenge the

wider relations of society. These small changes might involve new property relations, but in many, many important cases do not.[32]

Harman seems to agree with Cohen in interpreting the productive forces narrowly, as the material elements of production, but then defends a conception of production relations wide enough to include the labour-process. This gives rise to the following dilemma: either changes in the productive forces arise from changes in production relations (*qua* labour-process), a view which Harman would reject since he is committed to treating the productive forces as the dynamic element in the historical process, or the organization of work changes in response to the development of the productive forces, a pretty extreme form of technological determinism. His very broad conception of production relations has the effect that social contradictions (see section 2.3) occur solely between different social relations. Thus 'small changes in the forces of production lead to small cumulative changes in the social relations . . . of production, until they challenge the wider relations of production.' Harman identifies this conflict with that between base and superstructure: 'The distinction between base and superstructure is a distinction between social relations which are subject to immediate changes with changes in the productive forces, and those which are relatively static and resistant to change.'[33] So, far from, as Marx had argued, production relations furthering or fettering the productive forces, they are the aspect of social relations which are most responsive to changes in the productive forces. Quite aside from the unsatisfactory theory of the superstructure that Harman's account involves (see section 4.5), my version has the virtue of following Marx's mature usage, particularly in assigning centrality to the contradiction between the forces and relations of production.

Cohen distinguishes between four main modes of production on the basis of their ownership structures (see table 2.1). Jon Elster criticizes this table because it omits the 'Asiatic mode of production' mentioned by Marx in the 1859 Preface and discussed in the *Grundrisse*. Cohen's reason for doing so has much to do with the devastating historical criticisms of the Asiatic mode by Perry Anderson and others.[34] The result is that pre-capitalist relations of production in Asia are reduced to 'a sub-variety of serfdom', itself conceived very widely so that it embraces all cases where surplus-labour is extracted from a smallholding peasantry. Elster objects that while 'from the point of view of the immediate producers, the two [i.e., the Asiatic and feudal modes of production] may be indistinguishable', nevertheless 'the nature of the non-producing owners would presumably enter importantly into any analysis of the furthering or fettering of the productive forces by the relations of production.'[35]

TABLE 2.1 OWNERSHIP STRUCTURES

Direct producer	His labour-power	The means of production he uses
Slave	None	None
Serf	Some	Some
Proletarian	All	None
Independent producer	All	All

Source: G. A. Cohen, *Karl Marx's Theory of History* (Clarendon Press: Oxford, 1978), p. 65

Support for Elster's argument is provided by Chris Wickham in two very important recent articles. He argues that we must, in order to account for the specific historical trajectories of East and West, distinguish between the feudal mode, 'tenants paying rent to (or doing labour service for) a monopolistic landowning class', and what he calls the 'tributary mode of production', 'a state bureaucracy taxing a peasantry'.[36]

The two modes involve different forms of surplus-extraction, namely rent and tax: 'both are modes of surplus-extraction based on peasant production, individual or collective. Seen existentially from the peasant standpoint, there might seem not to be a lot of difference between them in that they are both unnecessary outgoings enforced, ultimately, by extra-economic coercion of various kinds.' Nevertheless:

> States do not only tax peasants; they characteristically tax landlords too, at least in that they take a percentage from the surplus the landlord has extracted. . . . One arena in which tax is thus very definitely opposed to rent lies in the structural antagonism there is between the state (unless it is a feudal state) and the landed aristocracy.

Wickham argues that pre-capitalist Asian social formations combined the tributary and feudal modes, with the former dominant. The distinctiveness of Western Europe lay in the fact that the collapse of the Roman Empire involved the gradual establishment of feudalism as the dominant mode of production.[37]

This analysis backs up Elster's argument that the relations of production include both 'the relation of the producers to the means of production and their own labour-power' and 'the nature of the non-producing owners, if any'.[38] Only such a definition can capture one very important aspect of Marx's analysis of capitalism, namely the claim that 'capital exists and can only exist as many capitals, and its self-determination therefore appears as their reciprocal interaction with one another.' The form this interaction takes is competition, and it is by virtue of competition that capitals are compelled to extract and accumulate surplus-value. 'Competition is nothing more than the way in which the many capitals forced the inherent determinants upon one another and upon themselves' so that 'the influence of individual capitals on one another has the effect precisely that they must conduct themselves as *capital*.'[39] No account of capitalist relations of production which does not take note of the division of the exploiting class into competing capitals will therefore be adequate.

The relations of production also include a third element – the form of exploitation – in addition to the relationship of the direct producers to the means of production and their own labour-power and the nature of any non-producing owners. Effective possession of at least some means of production and perhaps even of labour-power itself enables non-labourers to exploit the direct producers. Exploitation is the appropriation of surplus-labour, that is, it consists in compelling the direct producers to work longer than is necessary to produce the means of subsistence for themselves and their dependents: 'Wherever a part of society possesses the monopoly of the means of production, the worker, free or unfree, must add to the labour-time necessary for his own maintenance an extra quantity of means of subsistence for the owner of the means of production.' Modes of production can be distinguished according to the particular mode of appropriation of surplus-labour each involves: 'What distinguishes the various economic formations of society . . . is the form in which this surplus-labour is in each case extorted from the immediate producers.'[40]

Whether or not we choose strictly to include classes in the relations of production, they undoubtedly possess a conceptual connection to exploitation. As G. E. M. de Ste Croix puts it, 'class . . . is essentially the way in which exploitation is reflected in a social structure.'[41] Marx's own discussion of the concept of class is notoriously unsystematic. In Althusser's words: 'The reader will know how Volume Three [of *Capital*] ends. A title: *Classes*. Forty lines, then silence.'[42]

This is not to say that it is impossible to reconstruct a coherent account of class from Marx's writings. Ste Croix's attempt to do so seems to me so successful that I shall merely quote it:

Class (essentially a relationship) is the collective social expression of the fact of exploitation, the way in which exploitation is embodied in a social structure. By *exploitation* I mean the appropriation of part of the product of the labour of others. . . . A *class* (a particular class) is a group of persons in a community identified by their position in the whole system of social production, defined above all according to their relationship (primarily in terms of the degree of ownership or control) to the conditions of production (that is to say, the means and labour of production) and to other classes. . . . The individuals constituting a given class may or may not be wholly or partly conscious of their own identity and common interests as a class, and they may or may not feel antagonism towards members of other classes as such.[43]

So connecting exploitation and class implies a further link to class struggle. Erik Olin Wright states the premises providing the link, which Marx would certainly have endorsed, namely that class structure, based as it is on relations of exploitation, involves 'an *intrinsic* antagonism', and that 'manifest class behaviour is fundamentally determined by class structure.' Given these premises, 'then class struggle itself becomes an intrinsic rather than a contingent consequence of the structure of class relations.'[44]

Ste Croix goes further, apparently to equate class struggle and exploitation: 'I use the expression *class struggle* for the fundamental relationships between classes (and their respective individual members), involving essentially exploitation, or resistance to it. It does not necessarily involve collective action, and it may or may not include activity on a political plane.' Ste Croix takes this course because he wishes to insist, rightly, against ancient historians and modern sociologists that both classes and class struggle may exist even where they do not involve '*class consciousness* and *active political conflict*'.[45]

The further step of identifying exploitation and class struggle might be justified by arguing that the exploiters must always organize to extract surplus-labour, and that the exploited will always resist this extraction. This thought is half right. Exploitation does not take place automatically, and it will tend to evoke resistance, if only in such molecular forms as sabotage and ca'canny, but it does not follow that we should therefore say that exploitation *is* class struggle. There may be situations where the balance of forces is so favourable to the exploiters that surplus-extraction is a routine process and resistance minimal or non-existent. It would seem better to say that exploitation *explains* class struggle, where the latter consists in some actual conflict, even if the combatants lack class consciousness.

One may then summarize the preceding discussion. Every mode of production involves a particular combination of the forces and relations of production. The productive forces are the labour-process, the particular technical combination of labour-power and means of production employed in order to transform nature and to produce use-values, thereby determining a particular level of productivity. The production relations comprise the relationship of the direct producers to the means of production and their labour-power, the nature of any non-producing owners and the mode of appropriation of surplus-labour from the direct producers by any such owners. This mode of surplus-extraction, or exploitation, in turn determines the class structure, so that classes are defined relationally, by their objective relationship both to the means of production and labour-power and to other classes. Exploitation in turn gives rise to class struggle. Social formations typically comprise elements of more than one mode of production, with one mode, however, dominant.

2.3 ORTHODOX HISTORICAL MATERIALISM

One might reasonably ask what the point is of this elaborate apparatus of concepts, to whose clarification Marxist philosophers and historians have devoted so much attention in recent years. Ste Croix provides the answer when polemicizing against Weber's account of classes and status groups, which lack 'any *organic relationship* with one another', and so 'are not dynamic in character but merely lie side to side, so to speak, like numbers in a row'. The Marxist theory of classes, where the latter are conceived as necessarily in relation to one another by virtue of their roots in exploitation, is concerned by contrast not to describe social gradations, but to explain '*social change*'.[46]

Marxism does more than seek to account for historical transformations. As Andrew Levine and Elliott Sober put it, it does so

> historically, by reference to processes that are endogenous to the very historical systems it identifies as its proper domain. In this regard, it is a radically historical theory, different in kind from [Darwinian] evolutionary theory and also from rival accounts of historical change which, like evolutionary theory, conceive historical change as the effect of exogenous variables on historical communities.

In this sense, 'historical materialism retains the radical historicity of the Hegelian view of history, while, at the same time, maintaining, unlike its Hegelian predecessor, the explanatory objectives of modern science.'[47]

There are two respects in which Hegel's thought is inconsistent with 'the explanatory objectives of modern science'. First, it treats the world, natural, social and mental, as the self-realization of the Absolute Idea. Secondly, this process of self-realization has a triadic structure, that of determinate negation, in which antagonisms are first developed and then reconciled in the negation of the negation, which is the culmination and the goal of both reality as such and of each particular stage in its development. These two aspects are connected conceptually: the Absolute is nothing other than the dialectical process of original unity, first negation and the negation of negation. Both are incompatible with historical materialism. There is no materialist dialectical 'method' which can be extracted from Hegel's idealist 'system'. Equally, the dialectic of nature developed by Engels and other Marxists is nothing but the speculative projection of Hegelian categories onto the physical world – at best irrelevant, at worst an obstacle to the scientific understanding of that world.[48]

There is, however, a limited sense in which historical materialism can be said to be 'dialectical'. It is plausible to regard Marx as believing that contradictions exist in social reality. But contradictions of this kind have nothing to do with either Hegelian determinate negation or logical contradictions of the form $(p.-p)$. Rather they are antagonisms intrinsic to a social structure. Such a structural contradiction exists if and only if:

(1) a relationship exists between two or more social entities;
(2) the social entities are constituted by virtue of their being terms of the relationship;
(3) the entities are mutually interdependent by virtue of the relationship;
(4) the entities are potentially in conflict by virtue of the relationship.

The main types of social entities I have in mind here are structures, for example, production relations and productive forces, and collectivities such as classes. The paradigmatic case of a structural contradiction is indeed that between the forces and relations of production, of which more below. Some commentators, for example, Therborn and Ste Croix, argue mainly on the basis of Marx's own usage that 'it is possible to speak of a contradiction between the forces and the relations of production, but not between classes.'[49] This approach seems too restrictive, failing to consider why one might wish to locate structural contradictions. As Elster suggests, 'the notion of a social contradiction has the theoretical function of identifying causes of instability and change.'[50] Such a view accords well with Marx's criticism of Proudhon for dividing contradictions into separate 'good' and 'bad' sides. Proudhon thus fails to recognize that 'dialectical movement is the coexistence of two contradictory sides, their conflict and their fusion into a new category' and that 'it is the bad side that produces the movement which makes history by providing a struggle.'[51] There seems to be no good reason not to include exploitation and class-relations among the structural contradictions which give rise to the 'bad side' of history and hence to struggle and change. In the case of the capitalist mode the competitive interaction of 'many capitals' also seems to fulfil the conditions of a structural contradiction. Finally, it should be noted that such a contradiction should not be equated with actual conflict (see condition (4) above), but thought of rather as a tendency towards such conflict.[52]

The central difficulty with historical materialism is how the two principal contradictions, those between the forces and relations of production, and between classes, relate to one another to bring about social transformations. One answer, that the development of the productive forces is the motor of historical change, is given by Marx in the 1859 Preface:

> At a certain stage of development, the material productive forces of society come into conflict with the existing relations of production. . . . From forms of development of the productive forces these relations turn into their fetters. Then begins an epoch of social revolution. The changes in the economic foundation lead sooner or later to the transformation of the whole immense superstructure.[53]

On the basis of this passage a version of Marxism has been developed – what Levine and Sober call 'orthodox historical materialism' – which gives an account:

> (a) of necessary (material) conditions of change (where what is possible depends on the level of development of productive forces); (b) of the *direction* of change (since economic structures change to maximize the level of development of productive forces and are therefore cumulative and irreversible); (c) of the *means* through which change is achieved (class struggle); and finally (d) of sufficient conditions for change (since what is possible is, in the long run, necessary).[54]

Orthodox historical materialism (hereafter OHM) has played a not unimportant part in the history of the workers' movement. It is associated particularly with the Marxism of the Second International, of Kautsky, Plekhanov, Labriola and the like, for whom the class struggle served to effect the inevitable social revolutions commanded by the development of the productive forces and, in a much vulgarized form, with Stalinist Diamat. Today, however, OHM is identified with Cohen's highly sophisticated statement and defence of Marx's theory of history and it is naturally on this, the strongest formulation of OHM, that I shall concentrate.

Cohen's version of OHM turns on two propositions:

(a) The productive forces tend to develop throughout history (the Development Thesis).
(b) The nature of the production relations of a society is explained by the level of development of its productive forces (the Primacy Thesis proper).[55]

If true, these claims would together account for historical change, since according to them the continuous development of productive forces will compel the transformation of production relations whenever the prevailing set ceases to maximize the growth of these forces.

Let us consider first the Primacy Thesis. Cohen's originality lies not in holding this to be true, since it is essential to any version of OHM, but in claiming that the relationship between the productive forces and production relations is one that can be accounted for only by means of functional explanation:

> We hold that the character of the forces *functionally* explains the character of the relations. . . . The favoured relations take this form: *the production relations are of kind R at time t because relations of kind R are suitable to the use and development of the productive forces given the level of development of the latter at t.*[56]

Cohen gives a widely discussed account of functional explanations where they are a sub-type of 'consequence-explanations'. A consequence law invoked in such explanations has the following form:

> IF it is the case that if an event of type E were to occur at t1, then it would bring about an event of type F at t2
> THEN an event of type E occurs at t3.

A consequence-explanation is thus one where, '*very roughly*, . . . the character of what is explained is determined by its effect on what explains it.' It is not, however, a teleological explanation, in which an event is explained by some future event which it will bring about (the goal or purpose of the first event, Aristotle's final cause). For, '*it is the fact that were an event of a certain type of occur, it would have a certain effect*, which explains the occurrence of an event of the stated type.' Consequence-explanations appeal to some 'dispositional fact' of the form given by the hypothetical sentence relating events of type E and F in the consequence law, not to some future state of affairs. 'A functional explanation is a consequence-explanation in which the occurrence of the *explanandum* event [one of type E in the consequence law] . . . is functional for something or other, whatever "functional" turns out to mean.'[57]

In the case of historical materialism, 'functional' means crucially 'tending to promote the development of the productive forces' (although Cohen also believes that the superstructure is functional to the relations of production in the sense of tending to stabilize the latter). This reinterpretation of OHM is ingenious. One standard criticism of the Primacy Thesis has always been that Marx in *Capital* treats capitalist relations of production as preceding and making possible the productive forces characteristic of this mode, above all machinofacture. Thus he distinguishes between the 'formal and real subsumption of labour under capital'. The former involves the introduction of capitalist relations with a productive base consisting in handicraft methods inherited from the feudal mode. This is the phase of manufacture, which is followed by the 'real subsumption' which occurs when the labour-process is transformed as a result of the large-scale introduction of machinery.[58] How, ask the critics of OHM, can this analysis be made consistent with the claim that the development of the productive forces explains the nature of the production relations?

Cohen's answer, effectively, is that it cannot, so long as we think of the relation between the forces and relations of production as a simple causal one, in which the former's development causes changes in the latter. Once, however, we see the relations as *functional* to the force's development then the problem vanishes. As Cohen puts it, 'the bare fact that economic structures develop the productive forces does not prejudice their primacy, for forces select structures according to their capacity to promote development.'[59] The capacity of capitalist relations of production to revolutionize the labour-process does not contradict the Primacy Thesis, for it is precisely this capacity, that is, their tendency to develop the productive forces, which explains their existence.

Cohen's defence of the Primacy Thesis is an elegant one. It is vulnerable, however, to objections to his reliance on functional explanations. This issue has been central to the debate between Cohen and Elster following the publication of the former's book. Elster argues that functional explanations are legitimate in biology.

Here the properties of organisms are explained functionally, in terms of their tendency to maximize the reproductive capacity of the organisms concerned. Such explanations are not teleological, since the maximization of reproductive capacity is not the consciously adopted or objectively required goal of organisms, but is enforced on them by the mechanism of natural selection, a blind and purposeless process whose structure can only be captured by probabilistic laws, and which consists in the interaction between populations of organisms and their environment.[60]

Elster argues that functional explanation has, however, a much more limited role to play in social theory. He tries to bring this out by giving 'a valid, if rarely instantiated, form of functional explanation' of the social world:

> An institution or a behavioural pattern X is explained by its function Y
> for group Z if and only if:
> (1) Y is an effect of X;
> (2) Y is beneficial for Z;
> (3) Y is unintended by the actors producing X;
> (4) Y – or at least the causal relation between X and Y – is unrecognized
> by the actors in Z;
> (5) Y maintains X by a causal feedback loop passing through Z.[61]

The crucial condition is (5). If we take (1) and (2) together to be the rough counterpart of the sort of 'dispositional fact' which, according to Cohen, consequence-explanations invoke, then (5) specifies the mechanism which accounts for this fact. (5) demands that we should find some mechanism comparable to natural selection in biology. Elster claims that 'functionalist sociologists argue *as if* (which is not so say *that*) criterion (5) is automatically filled whenever the other criteria are.' The result is 'an objective teleology, a process that has no subject, yet has a goal'. He argues that Marx and his successors are often guilty of this conflation and that indeed 'Marxist social scientists tend to compound the general functionalist fallacy with another one, the assumption that long-term consequences can explain their causes even when there is no intentional action or selection.'[62]

Cohen commits neither of these fallacies. However, in effect he denies that specifying the mechanism whose existence is required by (5) is a necessary condition of a valid functional explanation. The reason is that 'a consequence-explanation may well be confirmed [in the sense that 'instances satisfying its major antecedent and consequence' are found to exist] in the absence of a theory as to *how* the dispositional property figures in the explanation of what it explains.' Therefore a functional explanation 'may be offered without an elaboration, that is, an account of *how* the functional fact contributes to explaining what it does'.[63] As Elster observes:

> Cohen's defence of functional explanation rests on epistemological considerations, not a substantive sociological theory. He argues that while knowledge of a mechanism is a sufficient condition for a successful explanation, and the existence of a mechanism a necessary condition, the knowledge is not a necessary condition.[64]

This is a very weak defence of functional explanation. Thus, as Elster observes, Cohen provides no criterion for distinguishing between 'explanatory and non-explanatory correlations'.[65] In other words, events of type X may accompany those of type Y, which have beneficial consequences to group Z, without there being a 'dispositional fact' linking them. To assert otherwise is to commit the functionalist fallacy. Cohen concedes this, but argues that the comparable 'fallacy *post hoc ergo propter hoc* does not disqualify causal explanations.'[66] No, but the latter fallacy does suggest the need to identify the underlying mechanisms responsible for genuine causal regularities. Surely we should require the same of purported functional relationships. Much of the difficulty with Cohen's defence of functional explanation seems to derive ultimately from an empiricist conception of science where to explain is to isolate regularities linking types of events.[67]

This is not to say that there may not be ways of rescuing Cohen's functionalist interpretation of the Primacy Thesis. Thus Philippe van Parijs offers an elaborate account of functional explanations as specifying the equilibrium states towards which certain complex systems tend. On this basis he takes the Primacy Thesis to claim that there are laws of correspondence between particular sets of productive forces and production relations such that the relations adapt to the level of development of the forces more rapidly than they promote the expansion of the forces.[68] But to assert that there are such laws is not to say what they are. Van Parijs leaves us still wondering what the specific mechanisms are which account for the alleged fact, asserted by him as well as Cohen, that certain production relations exist *because* they tend to promote the development of the productive forces.

Andrew Levine decomposes 'the case for the Primacy Thesis, in Cohen's reconstruction . . . into a number of distinct theses' which do not rely on functional explanations:

> (1) *The Compatibility Thesis*: A given level of development of the productive forces is compatible with only a limited range of relations of production.

'Compatibility' here has a precise sense: forces and relations of production are compatible whenever the relations of production allow for the further development of the productive forces, and whenever productive forces help to strengthen and reproduce existing relations of production . . .

(2) *The Development Thesis*: Productive forces tend to develop throughout history . . .

(3) *The Contradiction Thesis*: Given [(1) and (2)] . . . the productive forces will develop to a point where they are no longer compatible with – where they *contradict* – the relations of production under which they had previously developed . . .

(4) *The Transformation Thesis*: Where forces and relations of production are incompatible (as they are bound to become so long as class society persists), [then, given (1) and (3)] the relations will change in a way that will re-establish compatibility between forces and relations of production . . .

(5) *The Optimality Thesis*: When a given set of relations of production become fetters on the further development of the productive forces and are transformed, [then, given (2) and (4)] they will be replaced by relations of production that are functionally optimal for the further development of the productive forces . . .

(6) *The Capacity Thesis*: Where there is an 'objective' interest in progressive social change, the capacity for bringing that change about will ultimately be brought into being.[69]

The two key theses are (2) and (6). The Development Thesis imparts an asymmetry to the relation between the forces and relations of production, which generates situations where the latter fetter the former. The Capacity Thesis predicts that contradictions of this kind will be resolved by social revolutions which introduce relations of production compatible with the productive forces. The reason why this will happen is that the fettering relations of production involve a class with both an interest in, and the capacity to effect such a transformation. Levine says that the Capacity Thesis is implied by the Primacy Thesis, but surely it is better seen as specifying the mechanism demanded by Elster, which brings it about that production relations exist because they promote the development of the productive forces. This mechanism is the class struggle. If (2) and (6) were true, then, given also (1), OHM would be true.

Cohen himself offers the following argument for (2).

A measure of acceptance of the Development Thesis may be motivated
by reflection on three facts:
(c) Men are . . . somewhat rational.
(d) The historical situation of men is one of scarcity.
(e) Men possess intelligence of a kind and degree which enables them
to improve their situation.

Rational beings who know how to satisfy compelling wants they have
will be disposed to seize and employ the means of satisfaction of these
wants . . . (e) tells us that men are disposed to reflect on what they are
doing and to discern superior ways of doing it. Knowledge expands,
and sometimes its extensions are open to productive use, and are seen
to be so. Given their rationality ((c)), and their inclement situation
((d)), when knowledge provides the opportunity of expanding productive power they will tend to take it, for not to do so would be
irrational.[70]

Cohen is by no means wholly confident of this argument, but still
recommends it because it helps to explain 'the notable lack of
regression' of the productive forces. Confronted with one notable
case of such regression, the collapse of classical antiquity in the West,
he comments: 'If we would devise a concept of a normal society
comparable to that of a normal organism, we could then distinguish
between historical theory and historical pathology, and we could
enter the Development Thesis within the former.'[71]
This passage has always struck me as quite outrageous. Modern
European historiography virtually originates in Gibbon's attempt to
describe and explain the disintegration of the Roman Empire. In
recent years the problem is one that has attracted the attention of
some of the best Marxist historians – among them Anderson, Ste
Croix and Wickham. Cohen himself describes historical materialism
as 'a theory about epochs': how can he then exclude from its purview
one of the most important epochal changes in world history?[72] The
distinction he draws here between 'historical theory' and 'historical
pathology' not only has precisely the sort of biologistic overtones
which Elster, Giddens and others rightly want to exclude from social
theory, but bears a suspicious resemblance to the kind of 'conventionalist strategems' which Popper condemned because of their use to
rescue hypotheses from refutation by empirical counter-examples.
One reason why Cohen's discussion of regression is so unsatisfactory is that empirical support for the Development Thesis is not as
strong as he implies. There is, for example, the immensely important
case of China, which between 1300 and 1800 experienced first
decline and then stagnation of the productive forces.[73] Joshua Cohen
observes that, for Cohen, 'blocked development' of this kind 'is

counter-evidence to the Marxist theory of history'. He suggests that we should rather regard such cases as pointing to a central flaw in Cohen's argument from premises (c), (d) and (e) to the Development Thesis, namely that it abstracts from agents' conflicting class interests:

> The fact that individuals have an *interest* in improving their material situation, and are intelligent enough to devise ways of doing it, does *not* so far provide them with an interest in *improving the forces of production*. Only under *specific structural* conditions is the interest in material advantage tied to an interest in a strategy of productivity-enhancing investment.[74]

Brenner argues in a highly provocative recent article that these 'structural conditions' do not exist in *any* pre-capitalist agrarian societies:

> In all of these societies, the property relations had two defining traits:
> *First:* the direct producers held direct (i.e. non-market) access to their full means of subsistence, that is the tools and land needed to maintain themselves . . .
> *Second*: in consequence of the direct producers' possession, the members of the class of exploiters (if one existed) were obliged to reproduce themselves through appropriating a part of the product of the direct producers *by means of extra-economic coercion.*[75]

Consequently,

> in allowing both exploiters and producers direct access to their means of reproduction, pre-capitalist property forms . . . freed both exploiters and producers from the *necessity to buy* on the market what they needed to reproduce, thus of the necessity to produce for exchange, thus of the necessity to sell competitively on their market their output, and thus of the necessity to produce at the socially necessary rate . . . In consequence, both producers and exploiters were relieved of the necessity to cut costs so as to maintain themselves, and so of the necessity constantly to improve production through specialization and/ or accumulation and/or innovation.

In such conditions, 'economic growth in agriculture will, by and large, take the form of the multiplication of units of production on already existing lines', while 'the long-term developmental trend will be toward stagnation, if not crisis.'[76]

'Modern economic growth', the intensive development of the productive forces involving what Joshua Cohen calls 'productivity-

enhancing investment' exploiting technological innovations is likely
to occur only under capitalist property relations, 'where all the direct
producers are separated from their means of subsistence, and where
no exploiters are able to maintain themselves through surplus-
extraction by extra-economic coercion'. It is only here that

> all the economic actors have no choice but to adopt as their rule for
> reproduction the putting on the market of their product ... at the
> competitive, i.e. lowest, price. It is only in such an economy that all
> economic actors are perpetually *motivated* to cut costs. It is only in
> such an economy that there exists a *mechanism of natural selection* (i.e.
> competition on the market) to eliminate those producers who are not
> effectively cutting costs.[77]

Brenner's argument can be defended exegetically. See, for example,
Marx's praise of capitalism in the *Communist Manifesto*: 'the
bourgeoisie cannot exist without constantly revolutionizing the
instruments of production ... Constant revolutionizing of production, uninterrupted disturbance of all social conditions, everlasting
uncertainty and agitation distinguish the bourgeois epoch from all
earlier ones.'[78] Brenner's historical perspective of long-term stagnation
and crisis in pre-capitalist social formations seems to offer some
explanatory purchase, not just on the decline of classical antiquity
and blocked development in China, but also on the terrible cycle of
population growth followed by holocausts of famine, plague and war
traced by Guy Bois in later medieval France.[79]

Note, however, that Brenner does not claim that there was no
growth in the productive forces before the emergence of capitalist
relations of production, but rather that it took primarily an extensive
form, through the settlement of new land gained by conquest or
reclamation – processes which certainly loomed large in the economic
history of pre-industrial Europe and China. But his argument is
incompatible with Cohen's claim that the development of the
productive forces is a consequence of 'enduring facts of human
nature' – human beings' rationality and capacity to innovate leading
to such development in circumstances of scarcity.[80] This is not so
much to deny, for example, that actors are 'somewhat rational' but
rather to assert that *what* it is rational to do will depend on their
specific position in the relations of production. The development of
the productive forces arises not from some transhistorical principles
of human conduct. Rather, as Balibar puts it, 'the *rhythm* and *pattern*
of their development' are dictated by 'the nature of the relations of
production, and the structure of the mode of production'.[81]

The Primacy Thesis, and with it OHM, could only be salvaged in some recognizable form if the Capacity Thesis were true. Cohen seems to believe something like it. Defending himself against the criticism that the Primacy Thesis leaves no place for the class struggle, he writes: 'I do not wish to deny that class struggle is always essential for social transformation.' But (and it is a big but)

> if we want to know why class struggle effects this change rather than
> . that, we must turn to the dialectic of forces and relations of production
> which governs class behaviour and is not explicable in terms of it, and
> *which determines what the long-term outcome of class struggle will*
> *be.*[82] [my emphasis]

This last, italicized clause implies that social revolutions are inevitable. Indeed Cohen has recently sought to make this thesis consistent with the fact that human action is required to bring about epochal social changes by arguing that:

> the ground of the Marxian claim that the advent of socialism is
> inevitable is that a sufficient number of workers are so placed that the
> rational thing for them to do is to strive to bring socialism about. When
> capitalism is in decline, and socialism is possible, there are bound to be
> so many workers who have good reasons for joining the fight against
> capitalism that a successful socialist revolution will inevitably ensue.

Cohen is chiefly concerned, in the paper cited, with the issue of whether it is rational to participate in revolution (see section 5.3 below), but he is also committed to the idea that revolution is inevitable *because* it is rational. The only alternative to socialism is the unacceptable one of barbarism, and 'people are too rational to allow barbarism to occur when they can choose socialism.'[83]

This argument places quite unendurable strain on Cohen's reliance on the assumption that human beings are 'somewhat rational' to explain historical change. Given that the exploited class has an interest in social revolution, it does not follow, as the Capacity Thesis asserts, that it has the means to act on this interest. As Levine urges, 'class capacities for struggle – the organizational, ideological and material resources available to class agents – are not *identical* to class interests in the *outcomes* of struggles.' Thus slaves undoubtedly have an interest in overthrowing their masters, but have generally been unable to do so: the only successful slave rising was made possible by the French Revolution. Therefore, as Levine puts it, 'there is no necessary connection between the development of an objective interest in epochal social change and the development of class capacities for bringing about epochal transformations.[84] The Capacity Thesis, and with it the Primacy Thesis, must therefore be rejected.

Even where the exploited class has both an interest in, and the capacity to accomplish social revolution, as is true of the modern proletariat, it does not follow that the overthrow of capitalism is inevitable. To assert otherwise is to ignore the experience of the international workers' movement since the outbreak of the First World War in August 1914. The grim succession of defeated revolutions and the lengthy incorporation of the Western proletariat into the capitalist order suggest that the objective interests and capacities of the working class are not necessarily translated into the conscious struggle for political power. This historical experience does not imply that socialist revolution is impossible, but it does underline the perversity of Cohen's adherence to the kind of Second International Marxism whose belief that 'the dialectic of forces and relations of production . . . determines what the long-term outcome of class struggle will be' foundered forever in August 1914. His argument for the inevitability of revolution is almost a *reductio* of OHM and I conclude that Cohen's recasting of Marxism is untenable.

2.4 RATIONAL-CHOICE MARXISM

Is the fact that OHM is indefensible fatal to historical materialism? Cohen thinks so: 'I believe that historical materialism's central explanations are unrevisably functional in nature, so that if functional explanation is unacceptable in social theory then historical materialism cannot be reformed and must be rejected.'[85] Here Elster parts company with him. Elster agrees that there are large portions of Marxist thought which are not simply functionalist but teleological. Thus, 'in Marx's philosophy of history . . . *humanity* appears as a collective subject whose inherent striving towards full realization shapes the course of history. Within the theory of capitalism, *capital* plays a similar role.' At the same time, 'Marx was also committed to methodological individualism, at least intermittently. The German Ideology, in particular, rests on a strong individualist and anti-teleological approach to history.'[86] Elster proposes, in effect, that we resolve this ambiguity by salvaging from the ruins of OHM a consistently methodological individualist version of Marxism.

I shall in the next section defend a *via media* between OHM and what has come to be known as 'rational-choice' Marxism. But I wish first to explore the genealogy of Elster's proposed reconstruction, to consider a predecessor, to examine the kinds of reasons which might lead one towards it, to trace some of its consequences. It is appropriate to do so because, whether or not we accept Cohen's restatement of historical materialism as good exegesis and/or true theory, it is a version of Marxism with a well-established pedigree going back, if not to Marx himself, at least to the following generation, that of Kautsky and Plekhanov. But an individualist Marxism is a new thing.

Or rather, almost new. The one precedent for rational-choice Marxism is Sartre's chaotic and unfinished masterpiece, the *Critique of Dialectical Reason*. Here Sartre sought, as a contribution to the process of de-Stalinization following Krushchev's 1956 secret speech and amid the terrible tumults and passions of the Algerian Revolution, to free Marxism from the naturalistic ontology which the 'dogmatic dialectic' of Diamat had imposed on it. To do so required taking individual agents as the initial premiss of historical materialism:

> If we do not wish the dialectic to become a divine law again, a metaphysical fate, it must proceed first *from individuals* and not from some kind of supra-individual ensemble . . . the dialectical movement is not some powerful unitary force revealing itself behind History like the will of God. It is first and foremost a *resultant*; it is not the dialectic which forces historical men to live their history in terrible contradictions; it is men, as they are, dominated by scarcity and necessity, and confronting one another in circumstances which History or economics can inventory, but which only dialectical reason can explain.[87]

To hold that '*the entire historical dialectic rests on individual praxis*' is not, however, to regard human beings as in control of their own history. On the contrary, their union with 'matter', that is, the labour they perform to meet their needs, is what Sartre calls 'the passive motor of History', which takes 'a particular and contingent form, since the whole of human development, at least up to now, has been *scarcity*'. The particular sense in which the dialectical movement is a result of individual actions can only be understood by means of 'a study of the type of passive action which materiality as such exerts on man and his History by returning a stolen *praxis* to man in the form of a counter-finality'. Sartre here has in mind what he believes to be the general property of human action that the pursuit of individual goals is typically self-defeating, leading to undesired consequences. The example he gives is of Chinese peasants who, by clearing land, bring about deforestation and thereby cause floods. Thus, 'in being realized, human ends define a field of counter-finality around themselves.'[88]

The *Critique*, despite its tortuous prose and dense and often repetitive argumentation, is a much richer and more interesting work than anything yet produced by rational-choice Marxism. Nevertheless, there is an important conceptual similiarity between Sartre's theory and that propounded by Elster and his co-thinkers. After all, methodological individualism involves treating social structures as the unintended consequences of individual actions. Elster suggests that we take counter-finality as characterizing the *negative* unintended consequences of our actions. He tries to give a perspicuous account of counter-finality as involving the fallacy of composition, namely: 'what is possible for any single individual must be possible for all of them simultaneously.' He suggests that counter-finality consists in '*the unintended consequences that arise when each individual in a group acts upon an assumption about his relations to others that, when generalized, yields the contradiction in the consequent of the fallacy of composition, the antecedent of that fallacy being true.*' Thus a Chinese peasant commits the fallacy of composition when he clears land in the belief that because his doing so alone will not cause floods his doing so together with all other peasants will also not cause floods. Elster holds that counter-finality thus understood is the only valid instance of social contradiction.[88]

Sartre's aim was, having analysed the structure of human action by means of tools such as counter-finality in the first volume of the *Critique*, published in 1960, 'to establish', in the long-unavailable second volume, 'that there is *one* human history, with *one* truth and *one* intelligibility'.[90] Perry Anderson suggests, in a sympathetic discussion of both volumes, that the attempt is a failure. Why this is so, Anderson argues, is clear from the extended discussion of the fate of the Russian Revolution, which forms the focus of the second volume, where 'Sartre was unable to demonstrate how the ravaging struggles of the time generated an ultimate structural unity', falling back onto the implicit assumption that 'Soviet society was held together by the dictatorial force wielded by Stalin, a monocentric sovereignty imposing a repressive unification of all the praxes within it.'[91] Such an analysis evidently contradicts Sartre's view of history as a 'totalization without a totalizer', a unified and intelligible process which, however, lacks either an individual or collective subject.[92]

Anderson argues (and this view is shared by other commentators such as Ronald Aronson) that Sartre's abandonment of the incomplete second volume of the *Critique* reflected this theoretical impasse. He implies that this failure counts against any attempt to base historical materialism on the individual subject. Indeed it may, but it should be stressed that the theoretical inadequacies of the *Critique* are closely connected to pervasive features of Sartre's thought. Thus counter-finality is a general property of human action, not because, as Elster suggests, human beings tend to commit the fallacy of composition, but because their practice involves working up 'matter' in order to meet their needs in conditions of scarcity: 'matter alienates in itself the action which works it . . . because its inertia allows it to absorb the labour-power of Others and to turn it back against everyone.' Counter-finality occurs by virtue of 'matter' and involves human action assuming the properties of 'matter':

> The first thing that is necessary for counter-finality to exist is that it should be adumbrated by a kind of *disposition* of matter (in this case the geological and hydrological structure of China). . . . Second, human *praxis* has to become a fatality and to be absorbed by inertia, taking on *both* the strictures of physical causation *and* the obstinate precision of human labour. . . . Last, and most important, the activity must be carried on *elsewhere*: peasants *everywhere* must burn or uproot the scrub.[93]

Note that only the third condition refers to the fallacy of composition on which Elster bases his account of counter-finality. That it is the 'most important' of the three may be doubted in the light of the extended analyses which follow, where Sartre treats social structures, the unintended consequences of action, as the 'practico-inert', '*inverted praxis*', that is, practice which has taken on the properties of 'matter'. Thus, by virtue of counter-finality, 'worked matter . . . becomes, *by* and *for* men, the fundamental force of History.' It is the 'practico-inert', the materialized consequences of their practice, which unifies human actions so that, for example, '*class-being*' is 'the practico-inert statute of individual or common *praxis*', '*inert collective being*, as the *inorganic common materiality* of all the members of a given ensemble'. And such unification depends on the 'practico-inert' because human beings, in circumstances dominated by scarcity, relate to one another as 'radically Other – that is to say, as threatening us with death'. The possibility of class antagonisms arises from the fact that 'the relations of production are established and pursued by individuals who are always ready to believe that the Other is an anti-human member of an alien species.'[94]

At the core of this way of thinking about social relations is the conception of an isolated self confronted with an inert and alien world. That is, the *Critique* presupposes the metaphysics of *Being and Nothingness*, the conflict between an essentially Cartesian subject and the material world on which it is dependent by virtue of the fact of its being an embodied self – but which it is compelled to negate if it is to be a subject, and not just to become swallowed up in the inert matter surrounding it. In the *Critique* this account of the relation between self and world is projected onto history, so that the subject is constantly baffled by the transformation of its practice into the 'practico-inert'. The possibility of co-operative social relations, and indeed of relations which allow us collectively to control the objective environment of our actions seems ruled out a priori. As Aronson puts it, 'in the analyst of scarcity we once again meet the philosopher of "hell is other people".'[95] There are other continuities. So deeply embedded was Sartre's metaphysical individualism that throughout his career he could only actually comprehend history as totalization through the study of an individual life – from his discussion of Wilhelm II in the *War Diaries*, through that of Stalin in the *Critique*, to the gargantuan attempt to discover 'what we can know about a man these days . . . Gustave Flaubert, for instance' in *The Family Idiot*.[96]

The importance of identifying the philosophical underpinnings of the *Critique* lies in the fact that is by no means obvious that methodological individualism requires this kind of metaphysical individualism. It seems perfectly coherent to see human beings as embodied agents involved in social relations that are as much co-operative as antagonistic and still to assert that the structures present in these relations are merely the unintended consequences of individual actions. MI is a claim about valid social explanations and not (necessarily) a theory which conceives human beings as isolated and competitive monads. Therefore the failure of the *Critique* does not of itself count against attempts to formulate an individualist version of historical materialism. The rational-choice Marxists may just have come up with something better.

If the *Critique* represented Sartre's tortured attempt to construct a view of history as 'totalization without a totalizer' while keeping the faith with his metaphysical individualism, what were the reasons for the formulation of rational-choice Marxism? Elster tends to emphasize the liability of Marxists to commit the functionalist fallacy of explaining social phenomena by their beneficial consequences.[97] Another factor was the impact of the 'neo-Ricardian' critique of Marxist economic theory developed by Ian Steedman and other followers of Piero Sraffa in the 1970s. I know of no analytical Marxist, Cohen included, who accepts the law of the tendency of the rate of profit to fall, which is central to Marx's theory of crises in *Capital* volume III, and of only one, Brenner, who still holds the labour theory of value expounded in volume I to be true. The inadequacies of the latter theory led John Roemer to replace the

Marxist notion of exploitation as the appropriation of surplus-labour with his 'game-theoretic definition of exploitation in which property relations, not the labour theory of value, is the central concept.'[98]

It is difficult to overstate the importance of analytical Marxism's rejection of the labour theory of value (LTV) and of the law of the tendency of the rate of profit to fall (TRPF). For these two theories – in conjunction with the theory of surplus-value derived from the first and the account of the capitalist mode as a system of competitive accumulation presupposed by the second – form the core of Marx's account of the laws of motion of capitalist social formations, of the dynamic processes which drive them forward and recurrently into crisis. The nexus of relationships which this corpus of concepts identifies possess a solidity, an internal logic which it is at worst implausible, at best unhelpful to treat as the unintended consequences of human actions. Rejecting the LTV and the TRPF therefore removes a major obstacle to accepting methodological individualism.

We can see this clearly enough in Wright's case. In a paper originally given at a 1978 conference on value, he conceded one basic point made by the Sraffian critics of Marx, namely that the LTV is not needed to determine the rate of profit. He continued to hold, however, that the amount of surplus-value set limits to the possible variations in the level of profits. In this respect, the LTV provided 'a theory of the social determination of profits, in particular a theory of the systematic linkage between class structure, class struggle, and profits'. Consequently, 'the central research question immediately becomes: what are the social processes which influence the amount of surplus-labour performed?' The LTV would therefore encourage researchers to pursue the kind of study of the capitalist production process inspired by Harry Braverman's *Labour and Monopoly Capital*, of which Wright's own theory of contradictory class locations is an important example.[99]

By the time his essay, along with some of the other main contributions to the conference, was published in 1981, Wright had had second thoughts. He now described his 'analysis of limits' imposed by surplus-value on profits as 'largely formal in character', lacking any account of 'the causal mechanisms operative between surplus-value and profits'. He also conceded the claim of one Sraffian, Geoff Hodgson, that neo-Ricardian economics was perfectly consistent with 'a production-level, relational concept of class'.[100] Wright defended such a conception of class against Roemer's reconceptualization of exploitation when the latter was first published in 1982. Or rather, while not contesting Roemer's account of exploitation, he argued that the existence of classes requires, not just exploitation, but also 'domination directly within the social organization of production itself'.[101] In a book published in 1985, however, Wright abandoned this position and indeed argued that his earlier identification of class relations with 'relations of domination rather than exploitation' and the resulting 'marginalization of exploitation' was at the root of a series of anomalies in his theory of contradictory class locations. He sought therefore to develop a theory of class based on Roemer's 'central message ... that the material basis of exploitation lies in inequalities in the distribution of productive assets, usually referred to as property relations'. Wright interpreted productive assets very widely, so that they include not just labour-power and the means of production but also skills and what he called 'organization assets'. The result is that 'the actual class structure of given societies will be characterized by complex patterns of intersecting exploitation relations', where some classes may be both exploiters and exploited, (see section 5.2 below.)[102]

Wright is a very thoughtful scholar whose theoretical evolution must be seen as a series of responses to various conceptual anomalies and empirical problems. But it is difficult not to feel that his metamorphosis from one-time Althusserian into rational-choice Marxist had something to do with his initial starting-point. Wright's defence of the LTV had little to do with the understanding which it and the theories that can be derived from it might provide into the dynamics of capitalist development: even in his most orthodox days Wright seems to have been sceptical about the TRPF.[103] Rather it was concerned chiefly with the encouragement the theory might offer to studying the capitalist production process as a form of class domination. Even when he began to doubt the worth of the LTV Wright hung on to an identification of class relations with relations of domination, even at one point defining exploitation as '*a social relationship within which surplus-labour is appropriated through the domination of labour and the appropriation of surplus products*'.[104]

Thus to equate class and/or exploitation with domination is to be liable to efface the distinction between Marxism and other forms of social theory (usually influenced by Nietzsche or Weber) for which class is merely an instance of the more pervasive and fundamental phenomenon of domination.[105] But one of Marx's central claims is surely that exploitation *explains* domination, that, as he puts it in the passage from *Capital* volume III cited at the beginning of section 2.2, the 'specific economic form, in which unpaid surplus-labour is pumped out of direct producers, determines the relationship of rulers and ruled.' This claim extends, not simply to political domination, but also to domination within production. That is, 'the domination of labour' by the exploiters occurs when it is a necessary condition for the appropriation of surplus-labour to take place. Roughly speaking, domination within production is such a necessary condition in the capitalist mode, but not in the tributary and feudal modes. In any case, it is exploitation that requires such domination in some cases and not others, rather than being identical to it. One merit of Roemer's work is to have insisted on the logical independence of exploitation from domination.[106] Since Wright's whole theory of exploitation and class had previously tended to identify these with domination, once he ceased to make this identification there was no obstacle to rethinking class theory in Roemerian game-theoretical terms.

Of course, to say that Wright saw the LTV primarily as a tool in analysing class domination rather than as the key to Marx's analysis of capitalist development (and so was vulnerable to the sort of challenge which Roemer made to identifying exploitation with domination) is not to show that either the LTV or the TRPF are true. Defenders of the two theories have had a bad press recently. Rational-choice Marxists and neo-Ricardians (two sets with a large intersection) tend to denounce them as 'obscurantists' and to accuse them of being hostile to the use of mathematical techniques in economic theory, a crime which the accusers plainly see as being on the same level as claiming that the earth is flat.

This rhetoric has obscured the existence of a set of very powerful arguments for both the LTV and the TRPF and against the neo-Ricardian reconstruction of Marxist economic theory which is offered in their place.[107] These arguments suggest that far from being redundant and outdated the LTV and the TRPF are absolutely indispensable to the scientific understanding of capitalism, not just in abstract or historical terms but as a world system currently undergoing massive and highly disruptive transformations. This book is not about Marxist economic theory and so I shall not enter into the value debate in any depth. It is, however, necessary to indicate the sorts of considerations involved in the controversy.

Consider the following remark by Elster: 'Marx went wrong [in economics], largely because he believed he could discuss verbally problems that can only be handled by quantitative techniques which allow us to sort out the net effect of the many opposed tendencies at work.' (Elster is given, as in this passage, to treating Marx like a rather backward student. Thus *Capital* volume II is 'one of the most strikingly boring works written by a major author'; Marx suffered from an 'inherent lack of intellectual discipline'; and Paul Samuelson was right to dismiss his economic writings as the work of a 'minor post-Ricardian'. The idea is presumably to establish Elster's tough-mindedness and perhaps also *épater les orthodoxes*, but the general effect is to remind one of the philistine heyday of analytical philosophy, when Plato or Spinoza could be dispatched for committing elementary mistakes in the course of an afternoon's seminar.)[108]

The quantitative technique which, I think, Elster chiefly has in mind here is simultaneous equations. The use of simultaneous equations is essential to the neo-Ricardian critique of *Capital*. Employed to correct Marx's own 'transformation' of values, reflecting conditions of production in specific firms or industries, to prices of production, which arise from the equalization of profit rates across the economy, the method produces the result that prices of production can be determined without resort to values. Again, the TRPF is based on Marx's claim that the dynamic growth of the productive forces under the capitalist mode causes a rise in the organic composition of capital, the ratio between constant and variable capital, that is, capital invested in the means of production and in labour-power respectively, and hence to a fall in the rate of profit. But once the relationship of the different variables is translated into a set of simultaneous equations, we find that the same rise in labour productivity which causes a rise in organic composition will also cheapen the elements of constant capital, tending therefore to compensate for this rise and to prevent a fall in the rate of profit. Thus, the LTV turns out to be redundant and the TRPF not to be a tendency at all.[109]

Exponents of what is best described as the sophisticated defence of Marx have pointed out the limitations of the sort of mathematical techniques employed by the neo-Ricardians, namely that they have been constructed and employed primarily in order to characterize conditions of static equilibrium. As John Weeks puts it:

> The approach is one of comparing static equilibria, which is ill-designed by its nature to analyse the dynamic passage from one equilibrium to the next. In comparing static states, the question of the stability of the equilibria is not treated, but rather subsumed under the rubric of competition. This use of equilibrium analysis has the consequence of excluding time from the model, except in a purely formalistic way. The treatment of time is formalistic in that the past, present and future are perfectly interchangeable. The 'time' sequence of the different equilibria can be altered merely by changing the subscripts on the equations.[110]

These properties of neo-Ricardian models (which are, incidentally, highly reminiscent of the deterministic systems of classical physics now increasingly challenged by developments in fields such as thermodynamics)[111] make them of little use in resolving the problem confronted by Marx in *Capital* volume III, namely that of analysing dynamic processes of change in an economic system where control of the means of production is divided among competing capitals. As Alan Freeman says of Sraffa's model of a commodity economy:

> A system has been created in which the economy has no means for reaching its ideal state. It has no economic mechanisms: only economic results. It is therefore incapable of studying the economic mechanism most characteristic of industrial capitalism, the most central feature of the 'production of commodities by means of commodities', namely the pursuit of differential profit derived from advances in labour productivity occasioned by technical advance.[112]

The upshot of this kind of criticism is not so much to impugn the mathematical results reached by neo-Ricardian critics of the LTV and TRPF, but rather to use different techniques of analysis better suited to the explanatory problems which solution Marx had pursued and in the process to throw a different light on these results. Thus a result mathematically equivalent to that of the neo-Ricardian version of the transformation from values into prices of production can be reached using an iterative procedure which effectively generalizes Marx's own method of transformation. This approach has two virtues. First, it much more closely approximates the competitive interactions of 'many capitals', which cause the equalization of profit rates. Secondly, it makes possible an explanation of the apparent anomalies which arise in the simultaneous-equations version of the transformation, the fact that, for example, surplus-value is no longer equal to profits and that the rate of profit in luxury industries no longer participates in the formation of the general rate of profit.[113]

Similarly, defence of the TRPF has focused, not on denying that higher labour productivity will cheapen the means of production, but rather on the processes through which such devaluation of fixed capital actually takes place. The neo-Ricardians' reliance on simultaneous equations leads them to treat the devaluation as occurring instantaneously. As Freeman points out:

> A series of bizarre consequences follow, not the least of which is that capitalists would be obliged almost instantaneously to liquidate their entire stock of fixed capital almost at will in order to embark on a new technique of production without regard either to the time it takes to supply the new fixed capital required – that is, the rate of investment – or the effect on the profits of suddenly liquidating old factories, tools and stocks which have not yet realized their value.[114]

In reality, the typical form in which fixed capital is devalued and the tendency of the rate of profit thereby offset, is the sudden and catastrophic shape of crises, where large-scale bankruptcies permit the liquidation of outdated means of production. The Marxist theory of crises thus involves analysing the manner in which the interaction of the tendency of the rate of profit to fall *and* its counteracting tendencies brings about the cycle of boom and slump.[115]

Note that the sophisticated defence of Marx does not resort either to 'dialectical' dismissals of 'bourgeois' mathematics or to a conventionalist reinterpretation of *Capital* designed to rescue it from refutation. Not only can it be defended exegetically but it is concerned with the explanatory tasks of Marxist economic theory, namely the analysis of the causal processes through which the competitive accumulation of capital and the consequences of that accumulation occur. Marxists sharing this sophisticated understanding of *Capital* have been able to develop illuminating analysis of contemporary capitalism. Ten years after the neo-Ricardian assault on Marx was launched we are still awaiting the Sraffian equivalents.[116]

Acceptance of the neo-Ricardian critique of *Capital* has had two important consequences for analytical Marxism. First, as Hector Guillén Romero points out, 'for Marx, exploitation is the extraction of surplus-labour in the production process. For the neo-Ricardians, it only has to do with the mode in which the social product is distributed.'[117] The clearest example of this treatment of exploitation as a distributional phenomenon is in Roemer's work. In the first part of his *A General Theory of Exploitation and Class* he constructs a series of models in which exploitation is treated as arising from unequal exchange. One of these models even shows exploitation taking place through the market where there are no differential ownership of the means of production and hence no classes. Such results are possible because Roemer defines exploitation non-relationally, so that one producer is an exploiter and another exploited simply because they work less and more respectively to earn the same bundle of goods. Whatever formal interest Roemer's models may have, they have little to do with either Marx's or common-sense conceptions of exploitation, which treat it as a relationship between persons or groups. Roemer's distributional focus naturally leads him to reduce the theory of exploitation to a principle of justice, since the typical tasks of such principles include defining a fair distribution of the social product.[118]

Secondly, the belief that *Capital*, because of its reliance on value theory, fails to construct an acceptable account of the laws of motion of the capitalist mode, has led most analytical Marxists to abandon the search for such laws of motion governing this, or any other mode. Thus Cohen's account of historical materialism relies entirely on two transhistorical principles, the Primacy and Development Theses, justified respectively by an account of functional explanation and by arguments drawing on certain general characteristics of the human condition – rationality, scarcity etc. Now I do not wish to argue that reliance on such principles and forms of argument is as such mistaken. However, to rely exclusively on them involves impoverishing historical materialism, in that it omits consideration of the *specific* characteristics of particular modes of production which explain (in conjunction with the type of considerations on which Cohen's reconstruction of OHM rests) the patterns of development of the social formations in which they prevail.

To put it another way: Levine and Sober describe historical materialism as 'a radically historical theory' in that it explains events 'by reference to processes that are endogenous to the very historical systems it identifies as its proper domain'. This is, however, not true of Cohen's version of OHM, which explains events by reference to processes that are indeed endogenous to human society as such, but which manifest themselves in, rather than being specific to, particular social systems. An implication is likely to be that Marxism will treat each mode of production as instantiating some general pattern of change. But this conflicts with the direction taken by some of the best Marxist historical research, which has, for example, been concerned with arguing that bourgeois revolutions do not have the same structure as proletarian revolutions, in that the bourgeoisie typically is not a self-conscious actor on the historical stage but gradually achieves dominance by means of a variety of molecular processes and often by means of a compromise with the old feudal landowning class.[119]

Instead of exploring the *differentia specifica* of particular modes of production, analytical Marxists tend to focus on what they see as Marx's views of the universal mechanisms of historical change. Thus Elster has on a number of occasions discussed the problem of how production relations fetter the development of the productive forces. Do they prevent actual development of the productive forces, thereby causing stagnation? Or do they rather impede the *optimal* development of the productive forces, so that by overthrowing the prevailing mode we will permit a faster rate of development than at present? Or is it that prevailing production relations prevent us making the best possible *use* of the existing productive forces? Elster argues, on exegetical grounds correctly, for the second interpretation, so that 'it is quite posible for technical progress during the later phase of capitalism to be *both increasing and lower than what it would have been under a socialist regime starting at the same technical level.*' The trouble with this is that the theory is then 'too abstract as a basis for action. If one could point to a declining performance over time, this might be an incentive to change the system', but people are unlikely to undergo the risks and discomforts involved in taking part in a revolution merely to achieve a faster rate of growth.[120]

Elster's discussion of this issue proceeds as if Marx did not think that fettering of the productive forces by production relations would take the form of a structural crisis of the mode of production, involving, in the case of capitalism, severe slumps creating certainly 'a basis for action' by the working class, although by no means making the outcome of such action in socialism inevitable. The reason Elster does not do so is that he believes the TRPF to be false and 'the other theories of capitalist crisis scattered around in [Marx's] . . . writings . . . to be trivial, or rambling and repetitive, or obscure'.[121]

The result is effectively to excise from historical materialism the concern with the specific dynamics of different modes of production. I have suggested that this move is unjustified as far as Marx's theory of crisis in *Capital* is concerned. It has lead to discussion of Marx's theory of history degenerating into the offering of different glosses on the 1859 Preface. Such abstract speculation is hardly likely to encourage empirical research. Certainly analytical Marxism has yet to bear fruit in the form of the kind of historical writing which Althusser's work stimulated. The one major exception is Brenner's very important analyses of the transition from feudalism to capitalism, but these are hardly representative. As we have seen, the thrust of his work is to emphasize the *differences* between pre-capitalist and capitalist modes and therefore the absence of any general form of development of the productive forces. In the absence of any analysis of capitalism's laws of motion, even Cohen's 'orthodox' version of analytical Marxism is likely to become little more than a variant of Utopian socialism, able to make a moral critique of the injustice and irrationality of bourgeois society but incapable of identifying the conditions of socialist revolution.[122]

2.5 STRUCTURAL CAPACITIES AND HUMAN ACTION

The previous section has been devoted largely to considering the kind of Marxism which Elster and his co-thinkers have sought to develop. Let us now turn to its philosophical underpinnings. Elster argues that the only way to avoid the teleological proclivities of Marx's quasi-Hegelian philosophy of history is to espouse methodological individualism (MI), 'the doctrine that all social phenomena (their structure and change) are explicable only in terms of individuals – their properties, goals, and beliefs'. This involves 'a search for microfoundations of Marxist social theory', deriving its theorems from premisses which mention only individuals and their attributes. The explanation of social events should take the form of 'mixed causal-intentional explanation – *intentional understanding* of the individual *actions*, and *causal explanation* of their *interaction*'.[123]

On the basis of this general conception of social science, Elster particularly recommends game theory, which he characterizes as involving 'strategic' interactions, i.e. those where 'each actor has to take account of the intentions of all other actors, including the fact that their intentions are based upon their expectations concerning his own.'[124] The standard work on game theory treats it as a generalization of neo-classical economics concerned particularly with analysing conflicts of interests as situations of individual decision-making in conditions of risk – i.e., conditions where the outcome of a particular game (or set of decisions) cannot be predicted with certainty, but where each outcome has a known probability. Some of the chief premisses of game theory originate in neo-classical economics. Thus it is assumed that each player's preferences can be represented by a linear utility function and that he or she will act rationally in the sense of always choosing the alternative with the greater utility. The most famous result in game theory is the Prisoner's Dilemma, where the optimal outcome for the two players requires both to co-operate in circumstances where they have good reason not to co-operate, so that equilibrium is reached only where the solution is sub-optimal for both players, even though the decision each player makes is rational for that player (see also section 5.3).[125]

Elster argues that 'game theory is invaluable to any analysis of the historical process that centres on exploitation, struggle, alliances, and revolution.'[126] Roemer makes use of game theory in order to redefine exploitation so that it exists where there is some hypothetically feasible society such that one group – the currently exploited – would be better off and the remainder – the exploiters – worse off. But even in the earlier parts of his book, where Roemer uses unequal-exchange models of exploitation, he observes the tenets of MI. Thus he comments on his proof of what he calls the Class Exploitation Correspondence Principle, according to which all labour-hirers are exploiters and all labour-sellers are exploited: 'in this model both exploitation status and class position emerge endogenously as a consequence of individual optimization in the face of a constraint determined by one's ownership of productive assets.'[127] As I indicated in the previous section, I do not find the case for Roemer's reconceptualization of class and exploitation at all compelling but this does not dispose of the argument for MI.

Consider the following statement by Elster: 'The basic premisses of rational choice theory [i.e. game theory and neo-classical economics] are (1) that structural constraints do not completely determine the actions taken by individuals in a society, and (2) within the feasible set of actions compatible with the constraints individuals choose those they believe will bring the best results.'[128] (1) is undoubtedly true. (2) I shall consider in the following chapter, but will accept here as true for the purposes of argument. Certainly some assumption about agents' rationality is essential. However, (1) and (2) are not equivalent to, nor do they entail MI. But let us consider first the reasons for accepting (1) in particular.

There are at least three such reasons. First, the orthodox conception of agents and the theory of human nature in which it is embedded would be, if not false, certainly empty if agents did not have more than one outcome between which genuinely to choose. There would be little point in ascribing beliefs and desires to agents if their course of action were structurally determined in advance.

Secondly, to regard human actions as so structurally determined is inconsistent with Marxism. While it is true that on occasions Marx treated the socialist revolution as inevitable, what is entailed by his theory of history is better captured by the passage from the *Manifesto* where he declares that the class struggle can end 'either in a revolutionary reconstitution of society at large, or in the common ruin of the contending classes'.[129] Unlike Cohen, Marx does not seem to have believed that socialism is inevitable because, faced with the choice between socialism or barbarism, people, being rational, will choose socialism. More generally, the leading figures in the revolutionary Marxist tradition which followed him – Lenin and Trotsky especially – were insistent that the overthrow of capitalism was not inevitable and that the system would not collapse by virtue of its economic contradictions so long as workers are prepared to pay the price involved in temporarily alleviating these contradictions.[130]

The third reason, or kind of reason, for accepting (1) is negative. It springs from reflection on the alternative, on the sorts of social theories which do treat individual actions as structurally determined in that the structural context of action permits only one outcome. Typically such theories do not do so explicitly but rather indirectly, by treating agents as 'cultural dopes', the bearers of social norms and values which dictate their actions, so that, as Adam Przeworski puts it, 'the society becomes internal to individuals who manifest this internalized society in their actions.'[131]

The prime example of this approach is, of course, Parsons' 'normative functionalism' but there is no shortage of Marxist versions. The result, all too often, is a kind of vulgar functionalism where every action, particularly by members or representatives of a ruling class, reveals some hidden pattern, is explicable as part of some long-term project somehow corresponding to deep-rooted changes in the structure of capitalism. (As this suggests, the transition from functionalism to a conspiratorial view of history is all too easy.) One effect is that such concepts as 'error' and 'miscalculation' cease to have any application in the explanation of social events. But this is absurd. It is one thing to say that Algerian independence and the establishment of the institutional regime of the Gaullist Fifth Republic fitted the requirements of French capitalism as it was evolving in the late 1950s and early 1960s. It is quite another thing to say that this relationship *explains* why these events happened. And it would be ridiculous to claim that mistake – for example, the belief of the supporters of *Algérie Française* that de Gaulle was their man – and accident – the availablility of a political figure with the character and standing of de Gaulle – are not essential features of an explanation of the bloody and hazardous transition from the Fourth to the Fifth Republic. There are sophisticated exponents of the cock-up theory of history – A. J. P. Taylor is the prime example among historians, whose books often expose with mastery the role played by chance in great events. But one does not have to be one to insist that social events do not simply conceal a hidden meaning which subsumes them.

This argument might seem to open the door to a view of history which attributes explanatory primacy to the actions, not of individuals generally, but of a few decisive individuals. Such a 'great man theory' is clearly antithetical to any version of historical materialism. The classic Marxist discussion of 'the role of the individual in history' is, of course, Plekhanov's. He makes two fundamental points. First, 'individuals often exercise considerable influence upon the fate of society, but this influence is determined by the internal structure of that society and by its relation to other societies.' Secondly:

> It has long been observed that great talents appear whenever the social conditions favourable to their development exist. This means that every man of talent who *actually appears*, every man of talent who becomes a *social force*, is the product of *social relations*. Since this is

the case, it is clear why talented people . . . can change only individual features of events, but not their general trend; *they are themselves the product of this trend*; were it not for that trend they never would have crossed the threshold that divides the potential from the real.[132]

But it is in fact not clear at all why it should follow from two undoubtedly true propositions – namely that the opportunities individuals have to influence events depend on the structure of social relations and that these individuals themselves are shaped by social relations – that such influence cannot affect the 'general trend' of events. Plekhanov's entire discussion seems permeated by Hegel's concept of the 'world-historic individual', whose greatness depends precisely on the way in which he fulfils the needs of History in his epoch. Recently Ernest Mandel, aside from Cohen perhaps the most notable contemporary exponent of Second International Marxism, has sought to develop Plekhanov's account by analysing the 'selection mechanisms' through which a class assures that it has an appropriate leadership:

> In bourgeois society, these institutions include the patriarchal nuclear family, the education system (including religious instruction and other 'ideological apparatuses'), the various state institutions through which the individual seeks power, and, finally, the particular matrix of partisan organizations which selectively promote promising candidates (parties, corporations, power networks, employers' associations, etc.). It is a truism that no individual can escape the influence of these powerful institutions, and it is the specific contention of historical materialism that they exercise the *decisive* influence in the formation of social leadership, moulding talents and dispositions into certain directions and not into others. They are, in other words, the powerful sources of social conformism, producing personalities which conform to the needs of social classes or their major fractions. They generate personalities who assure the defence and reproduction of a given social order, inasmuch as they 'internalize' the basic values which correspond to the structure and interests of that order.[133]

Mandel is quite right to stress the importance of these mechanisms. While he focuses on the case of the bourgeoisie, one can identify similar processes at work within the proletariat, practices which range, depending on the historical circumstances, from underground work to trade-union organizing and which select a layer of individuals capable of playing a leadership role. What Mandel does not show is that such individuals necessarily 'conform to the needs' of the class whose interests they claims to represent. Indeed, he concedes that 'no automatic law ensures that a social class chooses the leadership it needs.'[134] One reason is that no class is by virtue of its mere existence a collectivity capable of so co-ordinating its actions as to select leaders consciously (see section 4.1). Selection mechanisms are often molecular processes involving the unintended consequences of uncoordinated actions. Even when more conscious selection does occur, the time-lag between the circumstances in which leading individuals are formed, and those which they have the opportunity to influence, may undermine them. German Social Democracy, shaped during the years of peaceful, gradual growth before 1914, was ill-suited to coping with the storms which followed the Kaiser's fall.

It is in times of political crisis that individuals can play an especially decisive part. Trotsky argues in his great *History of the Russian Revolution* that Lenin was indispensable to rapidly winning the Bolshevik Party to the strategy of replacing the provisional government with soviet power:

> Lenin was not a demiurge of the revolutionary process . . . He merely entered into a chain of objective historic forces. But he was a great link in the chain . . . Is it possible . . . to say confidently that the party without him would have found its road? We would by no means make bold to say that. The factor of time is decisive here, and it is difficult in retrospect to tell time historically. Dialectic materialism at any rate has nothing in common with fatalism. Without Lenin the crisis would have assumed an extraordinarily sharp and protracted character. The conditions of war and revolution, however, would not allow the party a long period for fulfilling its mission. Thus it is by no means excluded that a disoriented and split party might have let slip the revolutionary opportunity for many years. The role of personality arises before us here on a truly gigantic scale. It is necessary only to understand that role correctly, taking personality as a link in the historic chain.[135]

Lenin was 'a link in the historic chain', albeit 'a great link', in two crucial respects. Firstly, he was a product of specific selection mechanisms, and in particular of the Russian revolutionary movement, from the terrorism of Narodya Volya, through Plekhanov and the Emancipation of Labour Group, to the split with the Mensheviks, the 1905 Revolution and the efforts to keep the Bolsheviks together in the period of retreat which followed. Secondly, Lenin was able to win the debate inside the party following his return to Russia in April 1917 because, as Trotsky shows, he articulated the aspirations of the Bolshevik rank and file and of many middle-layer activists. When Trotsky's biographer, Isaac Deutscher, invoked Plekhanov's authority against this appraisal of Lenin's decisive role, Alasdair MacIntyre commented that at stake here are two different conceptions of history, one in which 'history from time to time presents us with real alternatives where my actions can make all the difference', the other in which 'I am . . . just part of an inevitable historical progress.'[136] Unless Marxism is to be a teleological philosophy of history, in which human beings are blind victims of the Hegelian Ruse of Reason, then we must accept that sometimes what an individual does 'can make all the difference'.

These considerations lead to two conclusions. First, the only entities to which purposes may properly be assigned are intentional systems, the bearers of beliefs and desires, i.e., for present purposes, human agents. More particularly, social systems do not have purposes. Nor is it proper to regard them as having needs, if this leads, as functionalism suggests, to the claim that these needs are necessarily fulfilled. (An all-too-common version of this kind of reasoning among Marxists is as follows:

1 A social formation requires certain conditions for its reproduction.
2 These conditions exist.
3 These conditions exist *because* they are necessary to the reproduction of that social formation.

The underlying assumption which justifies this inference is that social formations will necessarily be reproduced. This is a strangely static view of society for Marxists to accept.) It does not follow, as Giddens (one of the most vehement contemporary critics of functionalism) sometimes suggests, that it is therefore wrong to speak of functions *tout court*. It is often an important step in explanation to identify some social phenomenon which has beneficial consequences for some group and/or consequences which contribute to the reproduction of the social formation, provided that one does not, without specifying a feedback mechanism of the kind required by Elster, proceed to explain the phenomenon by these consequences.[137]

Secondly, the demand for 'microfoundations' cannot simply be rejected. If human agency is an irreducible aspect of social events, then no explanation of these events is tenable which does not make claims about the intentions and beliefs which actors have and how these will issue in action. Such claims may be of quite a high order of generality – they may involve the sorts of premisses on which Cohen bases the Development Thesis, namely that human beings are 'somewhat rational' and capable of improving their knowledge. Given that the intentional activity of human beings is not structurally determined, then no explanation which does not contain premisses specifying how they will behave or are likely do behave in the situation under consideration, can be a genuine *explanans*. To the extent that those demanding 'microfoundations' are simply saying this, they are clearly correct. But of course they are saying something stronger, namely that the explanation of social events is *nothing but* providing 'microfoundations'. Not only is this claim false, but it does not follow from (1) and (2), according to Elster the premises of rational-choice theory, respectively the denial that human conduct is structurally determined and the rationality principle.

Consider Elster's description of the alternative to MI: 'Methodological collectivism – as an end in itself – assumes that there are supra-individual entities that are prior to individuals in the explanatory order. Explanation proceeds from the laws of self-regulation or of development of these larger entities while individual actions are derived from the aggregate pattern.[138] This position, as Elster goes on to argue, leads naturally to functionalism. So, if Elster is right, we seem stuck with the choice between MI and functionalism.

To see why he is wrong, we need only reflect on the definition he gives of 'methodological collectivism', where 'individual actions are *derived* from the aggregate pattern' (my emphasis). If Elster is claiming that the denial of MI entails this doctrine, then he is quite mistaken. For 'methodological collectivism' is the contrary of MI, not its contradictory. MI says that structures must be explained in terms of individuals. To deny this is just to say that structures can*not* be explained in terms of individuals, not to say that individuals must be explained in terms of structures. All methodological collectivists (in Elster's sense) deny MI, but all those who deny MI are not *ipso facto* methodological collectivists.

All that the opponent of MI has to say is that social structures have explanatory autonomy in the sense given by Graham MacDonald and Philip Pettit (see section 1.2 above). To say that social structures have explanatory autonomy is to say that they cannot be eliminated from the explanation of social events. It is *not* to say that individuals and their attributes can, or should be eliminated. The model of social explanation which I began to outline in section 1.5 was one in which *both* individuals and structures figure irreducibly in the premises of explanations of social events. 'Methodological collectivism', in which individuals are the 'bearers' of 'supra-individual entities', is a red herring and I shall have nothing more to say about it.

Of course, to show that denying MI does not entail accepting 'methodological collectivism' is not of itself to give a reason for denying MI (although it does remove an obstacle to taking this step). Why not, if we can, use Ockham's razor and reduce structures to individuals? The answer is that we can't. I suggested in section 1.5

that 'individualist' explanations typically have structures concealed about them. Often the structures lurk in the *ceteris paribus* clause, or in the description of the situation in which the individual is trying rationally to optimize. But they may appear openly in the premises of the supposedly individualist explanation.

An example of the latter is provided by Roemer when he seeks to prove the Class Exploitation Correspondence Principle for a dynamic capitalist economy. He makes the following assumption: 'all agents are accumulators, seeking to expand the value of their endowments (capital) as rapidly as possible.'[139] This axiom merely introduces, in individualese, one of the main structural properties of the capitalist mode for Marx, namely the fact that capitalists tend to reinvest the surplus-value extracted from workers in further production rather than consuming all of it. Why they should do so is left unexplained by Roemer. Marx himself accounts for the accumulation of capital in terms of the competitive pressure of capitals on one another (see section 2.2.). It is perfectly legitimate for Roemer simply to place capital accumulation among the premises of his proof of the Class Exploitation Correspondence Principle but it does not alter the fact that the proof only appears to conform to MI, assuming as it does a structural property of the capitalist mode of production.

The sleight of hand through which Roemer turns this property into an attribute of individuals seems to me typical of the way in which adherents to MI seek to conceal the reliance of their explanations on structures. I claim that this reliance is not a contingent feature of some explanations, but that the explanation of social events necessarily involves premises referring to both structures and individuals. This is a much stronger claim than merely showing, as I did in section 1.5, that invoking structures is consistent with the orthodox conception of agents. To make it out requires a consideration of the relationship between the two irreducible components, structures and individuals.

The most illuminating recent discussion of these issues is to be found in Giddens's writings. He suggests that we think of structures as 'the unacknowledged conditions and unanticipated consequences of human action'. Such a perspective, he argues, will resolve the long-standing 'dualism' of structure and action. It will allow us to focus on what he calls 'the duality of structure', that is, the fact that 'the structural properties of social systems are both the medium and the outcome of the practices that constitute those systems.' More specifically, structures are to be thought of not simply as constraining action, but also as enabling: '*Structure is thus not to be conceptualized as a barrier to action, but as essentially involved in its production.*'[140]

The duality of structure can only be understood once the conceptual connection between power and action is grasped. Action involves the exercise of 'transformative capacity', the ability to bring about some alteration in the course of events. Structures consist in the rules and resources which make possible, *inter alia*, the exercise of the more specific form of power which Giddens calls domination and which involves actors compelling others to comply with their wants. The dualism of agency and structure typical of contemporary discussions of political power, for example, can be overcome only

> if it is recognized that power must be treated in the context of the duality of structure: if the resources which the existence of domination implies and the exercise of power draws upon, are seen to be at the same structural components of social systems. The exercise of power is not a type of act; rather power is instantiated in action, as a regular and routine phenomenon. It is a mistake moreover to treat power *itself* as a resource as many theorists of power do. Resources are the media through which power is exercised, and structures of domination reproduced.[141]

Giddens now seems to me to be fundamentally on the right track. This is, however, obscured by certain specific features of his argument. First, to say that structure is the 'medium' of action is different from describing it as the 'condition' of action. In practice, Giddens tends towards the first and weaker version. This is brought out, secondly, by his conceiving of structure as consisting of rules and resources. Rules, as Wittgenstein argues in the *Philosophical Investigations*, cannot constitute practice, while resources, as Giddens says, can only be thought of as media of action. They only condition action in the weak sense of being necessary conditions of action, but Giddens's general formula is surely meant in a stronger, causal sense of structures *conditioning* action. Thirdly, his account of power is hopelessly confused by the claim that the concepts of transformative capacity – which seems little more than a synonym for 'causal powers' – and domination are logically connected. The overall effect is a position much closer to methodological individualism than Giddens's general account of structure would suggest. I have discussed these and other defects of Giddens's theory of structuration at length elsewhere and shall not repeat that discussion here. However, these defects perhaps prevented me from acknowledging more emphatically the two great strengths of the theory.[142]

These strengths are, first, the definition of structure as both unacknowledged condition and unanticipated consequence. This encompasses the dimension of structure accepted by proponents of

MI, the unintended consequences of individual actions but at the same time recognizes what they deny, namely that structures also causally govern actions. The second strength of Giddens's account is the way in which he conceptualizes this governing of action by structure. Structures do not simply constrain action. They do not simply act as inert limits, restricting the alternatives open to agents. They are also enabling and are thus present in the actions actually pursued by individuals or groups. This move is possible because of the connection which Giddens establises between structures and power. 'Power', he says, 'is instantiated in action', but agents' powers cannot be understood without an analysis of structure. The fact that power is instantiated in action is crucial to rendering the claim that structures govern action consistent with the orthodox conception of agency. For, as we saw in section 1.5, action-explanations implicitly contain a premiss to the effect that the agent has the power to do the action believed to be a way of realizing his or her desire. The crucial issue concerns precisely how power and structure are related.

Giddens argues in the passage cited above that power should not be identified with structure, or rather with the resources in which structure partially consists. Rather, these resources are the media through which power is exercised. This seems wrong to me. It leaves open the question of the nature of agents' capacities. Now some of these are natural, in the sense that any normal, adult human organism will have them. But:

(1) the exercise of even these natural capacities often depends on agents' position within the relations of production;
(2) agents in addition have capacities which are derived from their position within the relations of production.

The truth of (1) is easy to establish. I am (more or less) capable of meeting my needs through some form of labour. Whether I am able to do so, however, depends typically in the capitalist mode on whether or not I can sell my labour-power.

More to the point, however, are the capacities specified in (2), structural capacities. This expression derives from Wright, who in his pre-Roemerian phase distinguished between the '*structural capacities of a class . . .* which are generated directly by the structural developments of capitalist society', and '*organizational capacities . . .* which are constituted by the conscious organization of the members of that class'. Wright argued that 'we can treat the structural capacities as shaping, or setting limits upon, the organizational capacities.'[143] I am using 'structural capacity' in a more general sense, to refer to any capacity which derives from an agent's position within the relations of production. (This is not to say, however, that the distinction drawn by Wright is not a useful one, but for present purposes my usage of 'structural capacity' embraces both structural and organizational capacities as he defines them.)

Examples of structural capacity might be the ability to make an investment or to go on strike. The exercise of such capacities involves the exercise also of natural capacities (to speak, move etc.) but this does not affect the distinction between the two *kinds* of human capacities. As the second example suggests structural capacities can often only be exercised collectively and not by individual agents. This raises issues which will be pursued further in subsequent chapters. For the present we need simply note that the dependence for their exercise of certain structural capacities on the formation of collective agents is a consequence of a general feature of production relations, namely that they involve large numbers of individual agents *sharing* the same relationship to the means of production and to labour-power.

Let me now consider a possible objection to this way of thinking about structures from proponents of MI, namely that agents choose their position in the relations of production. The argument is put by Przeworski, who invites us to consider the case of Mrs Jones, 'a lady who owns some land, is married to a machinist, is a mother of a prospective accountant, and is white and Catholic.' Mrs Jones becomes a salesperson in a department store. But: 'Many workers eventually do succeed in owning their own business. Why could not Mrs Jones? . . . Mrs Jones becomes a worker because she *chooses* to become a worker.'[144]

Przeworski defends this claim as follows:

> Clearly, I do not mean that people decide to be workers at their pleasure, offended by a life sparkled by diamonds and rocked only by yacht decks. What I mean is the following. Mrs Jones has some goals; for example, she seeks, with the assistance of her family, to maximize the current value of her consumption stream when she becomes a widow, which as a wife of a worker she is likely to become. She also has resources: her labour-power, the unused labour-power of her husband and son, some social connections . . . and some credit . . . She now sits around a table with her family and friends and thinks how to realize her objective given the constraints of family resources. She enrolls in an optimization course and upon graduation she decides that the best thing for her to do is to become a worker. She has objectives and resources: she chooses to become a worker. Her objectives and her resources do not classify her as a worker; she decides to become a worker given her objectives and resources.[145]

Does Mrs Jones really choose to become a wage-labourer? The question is discussed and answered in an article of surpassing elegance by Cohen. He suggests that 'a worker is forced to sell his or her labour-power ... if and only if the constraint is a result of standard exercise of the powers constituting relations of production', where being forced means having 'no *reasonable* or *acceptable* alternative course', not that there is 'no alternative whatsoever'. This way of understanding 'force' means that it is not an objection to the claim that workers are compelled to sell their labour-power that the alternative is not starving to death but going on the dole, if being on the dole is an unacceptable alternative (which it is).[146]

The serious objection to the idea that workers are forced to sell their labour-power is, as Cohen observes, the existence of 'persons who, initially possessed of no greater resources than most, secure positions in the petty bourgeoisie and elsewhere, thereby rising above the proletariat.' The particular example he gives is that of the petty and sometimes bigger capitalists who have emerged among Asians in Britain but there are others. The fact that people can thus escape from the working class suggests that workers are generally not forced to sell their labour-power, since they could always choose to try to enter the petty bourgeoisie. The fact that only a few can actually succeed in the attempt is no real objection:

> The number of exits from the proletariat is, as a matter of objective circumstance, small. But more proletarians are not trying to escape, and, as a result, *it is false that each exist is being actively attempted by some proletarian.* Therefore for most proletarians there exists a means of escape. So even though necessarily most proletarians will remain proletarians, and will sell their labour-power, perhaps none, and at most a minority, are forced to do so.[147]

A worker's freedom to escape, however, depends on the over-whelming majority of other workers not actually seeking to exercise their own similar freedom. Were they to do so, all available exits from the proletariat would rapidly be used (indeed blocked by those struggling to reach them). Each worker's freedom is conditional on the others not exercising their own conditional freedom. Thus, 'though each is individually free to leave, he suffers with the rest from what I shall call *collective unfreedom*', where 'a group suffers collective un-freedom with respect to a type of action A if and only if performance of A by all members of the group is impossible.' So, 'although most proletarians are free to escape the proletariat, and indeed, even if every one is, the proletariat is collectively unfree, an imprisoned class.'[148] Mrs Jones is free not to become a worker, but the entire class to which she belongs as a wage-labourer is not.

Cohen's argument is framed to deal with the specific case of the working class. But if the proletariat is collectively forced into the class position they occupy then it seems very unlikely that the exploited in other modes of production – where what Marx calls 'direct extra-economic force' rather than the 'silent compulsion of economic relations' (i.e. the absence of any acceptable alternative to the sale of one's labour-power) is essential to the extraction of surplus-labour – are any less unfree.[149] It is true that the capitalist has a genuine alternative to being a capitalist, namely selling his or her labour-power, but there can be little doubt which course of action the best use of his or her endowments will require. This reasoning will apply *a fortiori* to the case of other ruling classes. The sense in which class positions are chosen is therefore a very limited one and does not undermine the general account of structure given above.

My claim that structures have explanatory autonomy thus comes down to the assertion that agents' powers are partly dependent on their position in production relations. This thesis need not be formulated in Marxist terms, so long as one accepts that agents' ability to realize their goals is determined to a significant degree by their place in social relations, whether one thinks of these relations as structures, institutions, or whatever. Note that the argument does not depend on any claim about individuals' beliefs being about, or shaped by structures. Elster himself emphasizes that 'methodological individualism holds only in extensional contexts . . . People often have beliefs about supra-individual entities that are not reducible to beliefs about individuals.'[150] MI is about what structures *are*; it is perfectly consistent with people having (according to MI) false, because collectivist, beliefs about structures. Equally my argument for the ineliminability of structures turns not on people's beliefs about structures, but on the powers that they *have* (and indeed may have without knowing that they have them).

Elster's response would, I imagine, be to argue that structures empower only in so far as they are themselves the properties of individuals. Such at any rate is the impression conveyed by some recent, highly compressed comments on the claim that 'structures . . . have causal efficacy', where a structure is a 'set of relations defined in abstraction from the specific relata': 'I disagree. . . . In extensional contexts, what has causal efficacy is a relation with its relata or, as I put it, individuals with their relational properties.'[151] Elster gives no reasons for this claim that structure conceived as a set of empty places can have no causal efficacy, while a relationship between specific individuals does. Either Elster is ignoring the salient historical truth that human beings usually find themselves in patterned, persisting relationships to whose basic character their individual actions can generally make little difference, in which case it is hard to take him seriously, or he is engaged in a purely verbal manoeuvre, calling structures the properties of individuals, in which case he has still to come up with an argument to show that these disguised structures have no causal efficacy. Lurking behind Elster's admittedly obscure remarks may be the belief that structures, where not conceived as the unintended consequences of individual actions, must be some sort of mysterious quasi-organic or spiritual entity. But this belief is false. A perfectly acceptable definition of structure is provided by Roy Bhaskar, who, like Giddens, conceives structure as 'both the ever present *condition* (material cause) and the continually reproduced *outcome* of human agency'.[152] (Note that this formulation does not suffer from the sort of ambiguity between cause and medium towards which Giddens tends.)

Bhaskar offers the following definition: 'Society . . . is an articulated ensemble of tendencies and powers which, unlike natural ones, exist only as long as they (or at least some of them) are being exercised; are exercised in the last instance via the intentional activity of men; and are not necessarily space-time invariant.' This definition is intended to encourage us to see society as continuous with nature, which also involves powers and tendencies, but also stresses the peculiarity of social structures, namely that they exist 'only in virtue of [the] . . . activity' of a certain class of intentional systems, namely human agents.[153]

While I agree with Bhaskar's characterization of social structures, I must confess to a certain impatience with the demand that some such account of their ontological status must be given. Quine has taught us to relativize ontology to the sciences, so that what exists is simply those types of objects to which our theories refer. The only question then becomes whether we can reduce one such kind to another.[154] If social structures have explanatory autonomy, as I have argued, then they cannot be reduced to individuals and we are stuck with them if we wish to explain social events. No dark suggestions about the 'mystical' nature of social entities are of any interest, any more than were Cartesian objections to the concept of universal gravitation because it required the possibility (ruled out by Descartes' metalphysics) of action at a distance. Defences of MI only too easily degenerate into attempts by philosophers to legislate for social theory. There is no reason why this should be any more acceptable than it is in the physical sciences.

The intrusion of metaphysical as opposed to methodological individualism is most evident in the case of the objection, already dismissed in section 1.5, that any given structure is the consequence of human action. Indeed it is, but that action will itself have taken place under conditions which themselves included structures. Pushing the causal sequence back makes no difference to the question of the explanatory autonomy of structures. What presumably would justify the attempt is the existence of some state of affairs in which individuals brought structures into existence without their actions themselves being conditioned by structures. Did such an 'original situation' ever exist? I doubt it. It seems far more likely that human beings have always lived in social systems which embodied specific structures. But the search for the origins of structure is highly revealing. Gaston Bachelard once said: 'Philosophers believe that by studying origins they can discover creations.'[155] The creation in this case is that of structures by individuals. Surely we have here a case of the 'philosophy of subject', the conception first rigorously formulated by Descartes according to which the self has epistemological (and, in some versions, ontological) priority? The Cartesian subject underpins Sartre's metaphysical individualism. It also lurks behind the kind of defence of methodological individualism which rests on the idea that if we push history back far enough we shall find a society without structures.

2.6 WHAT'S LEFT OF HISTORICAL MATERIALISM?

We can now return to the question posed at the beginning of section 2.4. What is left of Marxism once orthodox historical materialism (OHM) is shown to be untenable? That section and the following were devoted to considering the alternative proffered by rational-choice Marxism, which we have now dismissed. What then remains of historical materialism? The answer is: a great deal.

Levine and Sober describe what's left as 'weak historical materialism', i.e. 'the orthodox theory without the unlikely and unwarranted claim that what is necessary for epochal historical change is ultimately also sufficient'.[156] That is, it consists in items (a), (b) and (c) of their definition of OHM – respectively the necessary conditions of change (the level of development of the productive forces), the direction of change (towards maximizing the development of the productive forces) and the means of change (the class struggle) – but excludes item (d), effectively the Primacy Thesis (the forces of production will select the production relations which will promote their further developments) (see section 2.3).

Levine writes elsewhere:

> Reduced to its rational kernel, historical materialism is a theory of
> *possible* production relations, an account of what can be placed on the
> historical agenda, *in view of the level of development of productive
> forces* . . . [It] will not by itself explain historical change; nor will it
> predict the outcomes of class struggles. But it does give an account of
> the conditions for the possibility of change and of the options available
> to classes in struggle.[157]

This is, I think, to understate the strengths of the 'rational kernel'
of the Marxist theory of history. Nor shall I call this theory, minus the
Primacy Thesis, 'weak', but rather what it is, *classical* historical
materialism. For, as I have argued above, neither Marx and Engels
nor the other great Marxists – Lenin and Trotsky, Luxemburg and
Gramsci – consistently treated social revolution as the inevitable
consequence of the development of the productive force (see section
2.5).

Levine effectively reduces historical materialism to the Compatibility Thesis, that is, to the claim that 'a given level of development of
the productive forces is compatible with only a limited range of
production relations' (see section 2.3). Then, inasmuch as the
productive forces develop, they will tend to come into conflict with
the prevailing relations of production, so that the Contradiction
Thesis to that extent also holds true. But, given that the Capacity
Thesis is false, there is no guarantee that the class struggle will install
production relations permitting the optimal development of the
productive forces. While I agree with all this, I believe that we can add
three more things.

First, I think we can say, with Wright, that there is at least a 'weak
impulse' for the productive forces to develop through history.[158]
Other things being equal, the direct producers will adopt innovations
which reduce the burden of toil. Of course, as Brenner argues, other
things are often not equal and only the capitalist mode places
exploiters and exploited under systematic pressure to develop the
productive forces. We should not forget, though, that in two of the
three main pre-capitalist forms of class society, the feudal and
tributary modes of production, the productive forces are broadly the
same, since both involve a labour-process based on peasant
households which partially control the means of production and
labour-power (note that the Compatibility Thesis states that a given
level of development of the productive forces is compatible with only
a *limited range* of production relations, not [necessarily] only one set

of production relations).[159] To the extent that peasant direct producers have partial control over the production process they will have the opportunity to and sometimes an interest in introducing innovations which reduce the burden of labour on them (whether they have such an interest will depend on various factors – for example, the precise form taken by surplus-extraction: if the surplus is a fixed quantity then peasants can, by increasing productivity, lighten their labour and/or increase their own consumption). Equally, the exploiter may have an interest in taking advantage of innovations which will increase *his* consumption – for example, grain mills, of which feudal lords usually had a monopoly. Factors of this kind would not give rise to the intensive growth of the productive forces characteristic of the capitalist mode, but they are sufficient to make the Development Thesis true in this qualified sense: the productive forces indeed tend to develop throughout history, but there are powerful counter-tendencies which may override this tendency.

Secondly, even if the fettering of the productive forces by the production relations does not necessarily lead to the establishment of more progressive production relations, it is likely to lead to actual social crisis. The point is made well by Lockwood (albeit in a rather opaque sociological vocabulary):

> The actualization of the latent social relationships of the system [which include production relations more compatible with the productive forces than the prevailing ones] will depend on the success with which groups having vested interests in the maintenance of the institutional order [i.e. the prevailing production relations] are able to cope with the dysfunctional system in the case of particular exigencies. . . . If the exigencies lead to an intensification of the functional incompatibility of the system, and if compensating measures by vested interest groups lead (unintentionally) to a further actualization of the potential social relationships of the system, a vicious circle of social disintegration and change of the institutional order is under way. If, on the other hand, compensating measures are effective, the institutional order will remain intact, but the focal point of strain [i.e. the fettering of the productive forces] will continue to be evident so long as the functional incompatibility of the system persists.[160]

What Lockwood describes here is well captured by Gramsci's concept of an 'organic crisis':

> A crisis occurs, sometimes lasting for decades. This exceptional duration means that incurable structural contradictions have revealed themselves (reached maturity), and that despite this, the political forces that are struggling to conserve and defend the existing structure itself

are making every effort to cure them, within certain limits, and to overcome them.[161]

Such an organic crisis need not eventuate in social revolution. The ruling class may succeed in 'curing' the underlying contradiction, temporarily at least – as it did in the case Gramsci had in mind, Europe after the Russian Revolution. It seems to me that classical historical materialism is committed to asserting the following:

(1) Inasmuch as the productive forces actually develop, they will come into conflict with prevailing production relations.
(2) Such cases of fettering will take a specific form depending on the nature of the mode of production (see sections 2.4 and 5.5).[162]
(3) The result will be an organic crisis as Lockwood and Gramsci characterize it, in which the underlying contradictions 'mature', forcing the ruling class to struggle to 'cure' them, or at least to limit their effects, faced with the constant threat of 'social disintegration', or even revolution, if it fails.
(4) The outcome of such an organic crisis will depend on the class struggle, which is in any case likely to be exacerbated by the material hardships involved in the crisis.

Now the falsehood of OHM turned crucially on the fact that the class struggle cannot be relied on to produce progressive social change. But – and this is the third respect in which classical historical materialism goes beyond a theory of possible modes of production – it does not follow that the outcome of the class struggle is simply indeterminate. On the contrary, in the first place historical materialism specifies the structural capacities possessed by agents by virtue of their position in production relations, i.e. their class position. Secondly, it claims that these capacities, and also the class interests which agents share, have primacy in explaining their actual behaviour. This second claim is not equivalent to the Capacity Thesis: that is, it does not assert that these interests and capacities are sufficient to achieve progressive social change. But it does imply that whether or not such change occurs is to be explained primarily in terms of structural capacities and class interests, as well as in terms of the concepts used to specify the nature of the organic crisis which provides the objective context of the class struggle. This is a strong claim.

These three elements – the existence of a weak tendency for the productive forces to develop, the consequent likelihood of organic crises and the primacy of structural capacities and class interests in explaining social action – make of classical historical materialism a theory of history, a theory, that is, which claims to account for the dynamic processes through which social systems are transformed. It is also one in which human agency plays a pivotal role – in the terrible, bloody struggles which unfold in a period of organic crisis. How it does so is inseparable from undoubtedly the most controversial of the three elements necessary to turn historical materialism into a genuine theory of history, namely the claimed primacy of capacities and interests. Much of the remainder of this book will be devoted to rendering this claim plausible and to exploring, in its light, some of the ways in which human beings make history.

CHAPTER 3

REASONS AND INTERESTS

3.1 EXPRESSIVISM AND THE HERMENEUTIC TRADITION

We must now, in a sense, retrace our steps. The debate between proponents of methodological individualism and functionalism, which was one of our main concerns in the previous chapter, is one variant of a much more fundamental argument over the extent to which the explanation of social events differs from that of natural events. This issue has dominated reflection on the status of social theory for the past century.

The starting-point for this debate is provided by the fact that human action must be interpreted. In order to characterize an action *as action* rather than mere physical movement we must think of it as performed for reasons whose content can be specified by assigning beliefs and desires to the agent. This irreducible element of interpretation has been seized on by a succession of thinkers who argue that it introduces an essential difference between social theory and the physical sciences. Perhaps the first to offer a systematic argument to this effect was Wilhelm Dilthey, whom Hans-Georg Gadamer describes as 'justifying the human sciences epistemologically, by conceiving the historical world as a text to be deciphered'. Or, as Dilthey himself put it: 'Life and history have meaning like the letters of a word.'[1] The reliance of social theory on interpretation was held to be inconsistent with what is usually called the deductive-nomological model of explanation in the physical sciences, where an event is explained if and only if it can be deduced from the conjunction of a general law and certain initial conditions (this is what Graham Macdonald and Philip Pettit call 'nomothetic explanation': see section 1.2).[2] Thus Weber argues that the deductive-nomological model involves 'criteria the satisfaction of which excludes the possibility of an immediately understandable "interpretation" of concrete historical structures', and that, 'phenomenologically "interpretation" simply does not fall under the category of subsumption under generalizations.'[3] And so there arose the contrast between the interpretive understanding (*Verstehen*) of human action and the deductive-nomological explanation of physical events.

Discussion of the issue was for long bedevilled by the tendency of both proponents and opponents of the view of social theory as *Verstehen* (whom I shall henceforth call methodological anti-naturalists and naturalists respectively) to conceive of interpretation as a subjective identification of interpreter with interpretand. As Jürgen Habermas put it, Dilthey tends to think of the role of the interpreter as one of '*empathy*, of basically solitary reproduction and re-experiencing' rather than as '*participation in communication learned in interaction*'.[4] Weber shared this conception of *Verstehen*: ' "intellectual understanding" includes "inner participation" and therefore "empathy".'[5]

The historic contribution of Gadamer to the debate was to reject this subjective conception of understanding and instead, following Heidegger, to think of understanding as transcending the distinction between subject and object, 'the original character of the being of human life itself'. And because *Dasein* necessarily involves both a relationship to others and to past and future, 'understanding is not to be thought of so much as an action of one's subjectivity, but of the placing oneself within a process of tradition, in which past and present are constantly fused.' The objectivity of understanding is provided by the fact that it is a relation to tradition, but not one that consists in merely the mechanical transmission of past thought, but its active, transformative appropriation within the context of our own purposes, so that 'understanding . . . is always the fusion of [the] . . . horizons' of past and present. This encounter can only occur in language, the 'central point where "I" and the world meet or, rather, manifest their original unity'.[6]

Gadamer thus embeds methodological anti-naturalism in the hermeneutic tradition. Charles Taylor, perhaps the most important contemporary exponent of this viewpoint among English-speaking philosophers, describes it as 'the triple-H theory' because it originated in the Romantic philosophy of language developed by Herder and Humboldt and was continued in a somewhat different form by Heidegger. Taylor argues that this conception involves the doctrine of 'expressivism'. That is, it implies that the 'representative function' of language, by means of which our utterances refer to objects, is not, as both the philosophers of the seventeenth-century scientific revolution and analytical philosophers influenced by Frege think, its most fundamental dimension. Rather, reference presupposes the 'expressive dimension' of language, which has three aspects. First, 'through language we can bring to explicit awareness what we formerly had only an implicit sense of.' Secondly, 'language enables us to put things in public space.' Thirdly, it 'provides the medium through which some of our most important concerns, the characteristically human concerns, can impinge on us all'. All three are different ways of 'disclosure, of making things plain.'[7]

What is disclosed by language expressively used is the context of speech:

> This context is made up both of the horizon of concerns which is further articulated by the term in question, and also by the practices connected with them. The practices are an inseparable part of the horizon, not only because the concerns will have to do with certain practices . . . but also because some concerns are most fully expressed in social practices and institutions, those precisely which lack some explicit articulation of the values involved.

Therefore, language is fundamentally

> a pattern of activity, by which we express/realize a certain way of being in the world, that of reflective awareness, but a pattern which can only be deployed against a background which we can never fully dominate, and yet a background that we are never fully dominated by, because we are constantly reshaping it.[8]

The nub of expressivism, then, is that language cannot be separated from that which is expressed in it. As Gadamer puts it, 'to be expressed in language does not mean that a second being is acquired. The way in which a thing presents itself is, rather, part of its own being.'[9] The hermeneutic view of language has major implications for social theory. These are spelled out by Hubert Dreyfus, who argues that the 'inherited background of practices' implicit in our speech but never fully articulated by it 'cannot be spelled out in a theory', because '*what makes up the background is not beliefs*, either explicit or implicit, but habits or customs, embodied in the sort of subtle skills which we exhibit in our everyday interaction with things and people.' If social theory models itself on the physical sciences and ignores this background, seeking instead to establish generalizations according to the deductive-nomological schema, then it leaves out of account 'the unique feature of human behaviour, the human self-interpretation embodied in our everyday know-how (*Vorhabe*)'.[10]

Does the 'triple-H' philosophy of language rule out the possibility of social *theory*? In other words, does it deny that the explanation of social events can (or indeed must) invoke the structural properties of social systems as we suggested in the last chapter? Does it imply that all the investigator can do is to characterize the self-understanding of agents, indeed of necessity relying on the very conceptual vocabulary they themselves use to articulate this self-understanding, as Peter Winch argued in *The Idea of a Social Science*? I shall consider one unsuccessful attempt to accommodate the role of interpretation within the framework of methodological naturalism (section 3.2). The reasons for its failure lead on to consideration of Donald Davidson's philosophy of language, which offers a theory of interpretation superior to both expressivism and Jürgen Habermas's hermeneutics of communicative action (section 3.3). Davidson's theory crucially involves the assumption that agents are rational; the content of such an assumption is further explored by examining the utilitarian conception of action accepted by rational-choice theorists (section 3.4). Although the utilitarian theory is found wanting, it has a rational kernel, namely the claim that agents are moved by interests, consideration of which returns us to the concept of structural capacities introduced in the previous chapter (section 3.5).

3.2 INTERPRETATION AND SOCIAL THEORY

One contemporary thinker who denies that hermeneutics and social theory are incompatible is Anthony Giddens. He argues that understanding is '*the very ontological condition of human life in society as such*'. Any purely interpretive sociology fails, however, to take into account the intrinsic connection between human action and power and the dependence of the latter on the resources which, as we saw in the last chapter, Giddens regards as constitutive of structure. He therefore advocates a 'hermeneutically informed social theory', one that does not eschew structural analysis, but which also makes irreducible reference to 'practical consciousness', that is, to 'tacit knowledge that is skilfully employed in the enactment of courses of conduct, but which the actor is not able to formulate discursively'.[11]

Giddens's work can be seen as an attempt to transcend the opposition between hermeneutics and positivism, that is, between those who respectively affirm and deny the relevance of interpretation to social theory. W. G. Runciman similarly described the recent first volume of his *Treatise on Social Theory* as an attempt to steer 'a safely manageable course between the Scylla of positivistic empiricism and the Charybdis of phenomenological hermeneutics'.[12] His attempt to do so is worth considering in some detail, since it illuminates some of the difficulties involved.

Runciman's thesis is that 'there is no special problem of explanation in the human sciences, only a special problem of description'. He distinguishes between four main tasks of social theory – reportage, explanation, description and evaluation, which consist in answering the questions 'what?', 'why?', 'what like?' and 'how good or bad?' respectively. To report an action is simply to characterize it as a specific action by ascribing beliefs and intentions to the person performing it. To explain it is to establish a causal connection between some other event and the *explanandum*, which is itself an instance of a relationship accounted for by a set of broader sociological generalizations. To evaluate it is to pass moral judgement on the action. All three are distinct from one another. Reportage and explanation in principle share the logical structure of their counterparts in the physical sciences. Description, however, is unique to social theory. To describe an action in this sense is 'to understand . . . what it was like to do it'. Its role is 'to bridge a presumptive divide between the culture of those whose thoughts, words or deeds are being described and that of the presumptive reader and/or the sociologist himself'. The worth of a description must be judged by 'the responses of those whose experiences have been described'. However, it 'necessarily involves more than the mere repetition of what "they" say about their experiences', and so consists in '*re*interpreting the meaning to "them" of the experiences so described'. Descriptions are not so much true or false as 'authentic' or 'inauthentic'. Description, however, is in principle an infinite process, in which authentic redescriptions of the same experience are not mutually incompatible but rather complement one another.[13]

Runciman's account of description undoubtedly captures an important feature of social theory. It is often noted how anthropologists seek to understand an alien culture and to characterize the way in which the world is experienced by members of that culture. But much the same is often true of historians. Some of the most memorable pieces of historical writing do not so much either tell a story or explain events but show what it was like to be a member of a particular society, to live at a certain time, to be present on some occasion. Runciman says that 'description in sociology calls for an exercise of imagination on the sociologist's part, which is not involved in reportage or explanation or, therefore, in the practice of natural science at all.'[14] And some historical writing does have a distinctly literary character. This is not so much a matter of style as of the nature of what is being done. Art invites us to experience the world in a particular way. So too does social theory when it attempts to answer the question 'what like?'

At the same time, Runciman does not reduce social theory to the imaginative reconstruction of how particular actors experience the world. Rather: 'Explanatory, descriptive and evaluative sociology, however closely combined in practice, are always distinguishable in principle.'[15] The idea is to characterize the distinctiveness of social theory in such a way as to allow full scope for explanation in the same sense as in the physical sciences. The difficulties which Runciman's account of the methodology of social theory runs into, however, concern not so much description as explanation and reportage.

The first difficulty arises from an important disanalogy between the explanation of social and physical events. Alastair MacIntyre argues that 'the salient fact' about social theory is 'the absence of the discovery of any lawlike generalizations'. Such generalizations as do exist 'coexist . . . with recognized counter-examples . . . lack not only universal quantifiers but scope modifiers', and 'do not entail any well-defined set of counterfactual conditionals', differing fundamentally in all these respects from scientific laws in the deductive-nomological model. MacIntyre identifies 'four sources of unpredictability in human affairs'. First, no discovery can be predicted since any such prediction would involve possession of the concept in whose elaboration the discovery consists. Secondly, I cannot predict action which depends in part on a course of action of my own on which I have yet to decide. Thirdly, 'the game-theoretic character of social life' introduces uncertainties arising from the interdependence of actors' decisions. Fourthly, there is 'pure contingency', the accidents which may have a large bearing on events, such as the length of Cleopatra's nose.[16]

It should be noted that these sources of unpredictability, with the partial exception of the fourth (since natural events such as earthquakes count as cases of 'pure contingency'), all arise from something we highlighted in the previous chapter, namely the fact that society exists only in virtue of the intentional activity of human agents. This fact is also crucial to Roy Bhaskar's discussion of social generalizations. Bhaskar argues that causal laws identify mechanisms which in certain conditions give rise to certain sequences of events (the constant conjunctions with which Humeans identify causal laws). These conditions do not, however, typically exist in nature. Rather, what we have is an 'open system', in which the interaction of underlying mechanisms produces the rather chaotic flux of events which we experience. Human intervention is necessary in order to create a 'closed system', i.e. one in which the conditions specified by the causal law are met, and one can therefore establish experimentally whether the constant conjunction predicted by the law actually occurs. Experimentation in the physical sciences typically involves interfering in nature in order to set up the conditions which allow us to test proposed causal laws.[17]

Things go differently in social theory, however. Because of the dependence of social structures on intentional activity, 'social systems are not spontaneously, and cannot be experimentally closed.' Bhaskar does not believe, however, that this makes the explanation of social events impossible:

> The real methodological import of the absence of closed systems is strictly limited: it is that the social sciences are denied, in principle, decisive test-situations for their theories. This means that criteria for the rational development and replacement of theories in social science must be *explanatory and non-predictive*.[18]

Bhaskar's analysis is illuminating. It captures the peculiarity of social generalizations. This is not that it is always open to the investigator, rather than to abandon a hypothesis in the face of refuting evidence, to explain away the evidence. The same move is available to physical scientists and is perfectly legitimate so long as the explanation is itself independently testable. The difficulty is rather the way in which social generalizations seem able to coexist indefinitely with recognized counter-examples, a situation which reflects the impossibility of establishing conditions where one remove the interference of those factors which, exponents of the generalization in question typically argue, are responsible for the counter-example.

The question then arises of how such generalizations can be tested, if at all. Runciman suggests that

> the mode of reasoning most appropriate to sociological explanation is neither deductive-nomological nor inductive-statistical but quasi-experimental; and if, accordingly, there is a directive to be framed it is to the effect that practising sociologists should normally be looking neither for regularities nor for probabilities but for suggestive contrasts – suggestive, that is, in that they may either test or extend a theory which has application over as much as possible of the range of events, processes or states of affairs which have been chosen for study.[19]

The precise import of this methodological injunction to search for 'suggestive contrasts' is not made wholly clear in either this passage or the extended discussion which follows it. The difficulty does not lie so much with the adjective 'suggestive' – Runciman has in mind the inability just referred to of social generalizations to deal decisively with counter-examples. The problem is rather the following: is the search for contrasts to guide the construction or the corroboration of our hypotheses? If it is the latter, then the comparison of different cases acts primarily as an empirical control on the generalization. An example might be Robert Brenner's account of the transition from feudalism to capitalism: he claims that the decisive variable in determining whether or not agrarian capitalism was likely to develop lay in the relative strengths of the two main feudal classes, the lords and the peasants. This claim is then put to the test by comparing the trajectories of English and French feudalism. Brenner argues that it was the relative weakness of the English peasantry which allowed the lords to establish absolute property in land and gradually to introduce capitalist relations based on wage-labour, while the strength of their French counterparts left them with access to their means of livelihood, leading to a very different resolution of the crisis of late-mediaeval feudalism, namely the centralization of lordly power in the absolute monarchy.[20]

If, however, our social generalizations are themselves to embody 'suggestive contrasts', then we are likely to be predisposed towards comparative sociology, that is, to a form of social theory which 'appeals either to the performance of similar functions by institutions dissimilar in structure or to the performance by institutions similar in structure of dissimilar functions'. That Runciman is inclined to make such a claim about the substance of social theory is suggested by a critical discussion of Perry Anderson's two books *Passages from Antiquity to Feudalism* and *Lineages of the Absolutist State*. He argues that 'Anderson's account of social evolution remains too closely constrained within a narrative framework', so that 'societies evolve . . . out of a process of internal contradictions and external pressures, and the way in which this comes about is analysed diachronically, case by case.' In fact, Runciman suggests, Anderson's genealogy of the modern state is better understood within a comparative framework, where societies involve differential combinations of invariant structures and functions.[21] This is, in effect, an argument against historical materialism *tout court*, since Marxism generally accounts for the development and transformation of social formations in terms of 'internal contradictions and external pressures'. But such a substantive claim could not, without much more argument, be derived from purely methodological considerations. Its effect would be to subordinate history to social theory rather than to unite the two. That this indeed is Runciman's aim is implied by such remarks as 'sociology . . . can best be regarded as psychology plus social history' and social 'explanation is typically by reference to psychological dispositions'.[22] Social theory is to concern itself on this view with the manifestations of an invariant human nature and of the social structures and functions to which it gives rise.

The conclusion I draw from this is not that we should reject Runciman's proposal that social theory should search for suggestive contrasts but that we should interpret it in the first sense distinguished above, that is, as a procedure for corroborating hypotheses rather than as a view about their substance. This is not, of course, to reverse Runciman's preference and rule out comparative explanations. It is, however, also to admit explanations which make reference to the structural properties of modes of production, that is, of distinct kinds of social systems, in the way in which Anderson does in his structural history of European state-forms.

The second and more fundamental difficulty with Runciman's proposed methodology lies in his account of reportage. To report an action is to ascribe a mental state to the actor, as is clear from the following: 'to specify an action in the ordinary way is to account for the bodily movements which, together with both the agent's intention and such features of the social context as are relevant, make the action what it is.' Reportage, Runciman claims, involves no pre-suppositions about the agent's rationality: 'At the level of primary understanding [i.e. reportage], behaviour is neither rational nor irrational as such.' Reportage is logically distinct from explanation, description and evaluation, providing in particular a means of characterizing social events which is neutral between rival explanations.[23]

It is important to specify this property of reportage, namely that the aim is to construct reports that do not prejudge the question of which is the best explanation of the event reported, because one might otherwise think that Runciman is suggesting that observational statements (of which reports are a subset) are independent of *all* theory. His claim is the weaker one, that the report is independent of the theories offered to account for the *explanandum* captured by the report. Nevertheless, the notion of reportage seems vulnerable to the following difficulty.

Runciman says that typically 'the intentions and beliefs of the agents themselves as they are reported by themselves' form a court of appeal by means of which to settle disputes over how to report a given action.[24] This brings out the basic thesis of the hermeneutic tradition, namely that understanding social action involves interpreting the agent's speech. This is not a simple task, for the reason given by Donald Davidson:

A central source of trouble is the way beliefs and meanings conspire to account for utterances. A speaker who holds a sentence to be true on an occasion does so in part because of what he means, or would mean, by an utterance of that sentence, and in part because of what he believes. If all we have to go on is the fact of honest utterance, we cannot infer the belief within having the meaning, and have no chance of inferring the meaning without the belief.[25]

One way out of the circle might seem to be to try to match an alien speaker's sayings with the observed context of their utterances. This attempt founders on the problem of the indeterminacy of translation set out by Quine in the famous first chapter of *Word and Object*. The problem is twofold. First, say we try to isolate a subset of the alien language consisting of 'observation sentences', i.e. those sentences on which all speakers of the language will pass the same verdict (of assent or dissent) when subjected to the same physical stimulation. This might seem to give us a secure empirical base. But it does not: for there is no single way in which an observation can be reported. *All* sentences, observation sentences as well as the most refined theories, are underdetermined by the evidence for them. So, relative to the physical stimulus associated with the alien's observation sentence, there will be more than one way of translating the sentence into our own language. Secondly, there is the question of the entities referred to by the terms composing alien sentences. We might think that if an alien utters 'Gavagai' while pointing to a rabbit, we can safely translate 'Gavagai' as 'rabbit'. We would again be wrong. For the way in which terms pick out entities depends on the specific grammatical apparatus of a language and we know nothing about how the alien language works. 'Gavagai' might mean 'rabbit-stage', 'rabbit-part', or even 'rabbit-hood' for all we know. This doctrine, that of the 'inscrutability of reference', implies that there is more than one way, given the evidence, of translating sentences containing 'Gavagai'.[26]

Davidson's contribution to the philosophy of language has been in large part to offer a way out of the indeterminacy of translation, but one which shares with Quine the idea that

> the theory for which we should ultimately strive is one that takes as evidential basis preferences between sentences – preferences that one sentence rather than another be true. The theory would then explain individual sentences of this sort by attributing beliefs and values to the agent, and meanings to his words.

But how can he begin to do this? Simply by adopting the following 'Principle of Charity': 'I propose that we take the fact that speakers of a language hold a sentence to be true (under observed circumstances) as *prima facie* evidence that the sentence is true under those circumstances.'[27]

Davidson characterizes this approach thus:

> This method is intended to solve the problem of the interdependence of belief and meaning by holding belief constant as far as possible while solving for meaning. This is accomplished by assigning truth-conditions to alien sentences that make native speakers right when plausibly possible, according, of course, to our own view of what is right. What justifies the procedure is the fact that disagreement and agreement alike are intelligible only against a background of massive agreement.[28]

As Quine observes, 'Davidson proposed that the speaker is always right, in order to separate belief from meaning, until we have enough of a system so that we can start including error.'[29]

At the same time, Davidson emphasizes that the Principle of Charity is not a falsifiable empirical hypothesis: 'If we cannot find a way to interpret the utterances and other behaviour of a creature as revealing a set of beliefs largely consistent and true by our own standards, we have no reason to count that creature as rational, as having beliefs, or as saying anything.'[30] If Davidson is right, then reportage is not the unproblematic practice which Runciman thinks it is. The possibility of interpretation presupposes a substantive theory of rationality. Let us now consider what that theory might be like.

3.3 CHARITY, TRUTH AND COMMUNITY

Davidson introduced the Principle of Charity as part of a much broader philosophy of language. The link is provided by the claim that 'all understanding of the speech of another involves radical interpretation.' That is, the problems of indeterminacy of translation and inscrutability of reference arise even where we seek to interpret the utterances of other speakers of the *same* language. This makes the strategy of radical interpretation an aspect of a more general theory of meaning, conceived, following Frege, as the attempt to explain how it is that speakers understand an indefinite number of unfamiliar sentences. Davidson proposes, again following Frege, that we regard the sense of a sentence as consisting in its truth-conditions. He adopts Tarski's semantic conception of truth, according to which '*p*' is true if and only if *p*. The sentence '*p*' figures twice in this truth-sentence: it is first mentioned and then used in order to state its truth-conditions. The apparent triviality of this definition is removed once we

appreciate that Tarski explains truth in terms of the more fundamental semantic concept of 'satisfaction', the relationship between
predicates and the sequences of objects of which they are true. To give
a Tarskian theory of truth for a natural language is to reveal its
structure by showing how the basic expressions of the language figure
in a potentially infinite number of sentences. What such a truth-
theory does not do, however, is determine the meaning of individual
sentences. Tarski himself simply took for granted that '*p*' and *p* are
identical in meaning, and used this synonymy in defining truth.
Davidson, however, wants to use truth in order to characterize
meaning. It is here that radical interpretation comes in. For the
Principle of Charity provides us with a means of giving the meaning
of particular sentences by relating speaker's willingness to assent or
dissent from them to specific features of the world, judged in the light
of what *we* the interpreters hold true. We thus have an empirical
constraint allowing us to match up the speaker's beliefs and
utterances. The principle also underlines that a language can only be
understood holistically, since it gives a procedure for interpreting
sentences which involves attributing to the speaker a *system* of
beliefs.[31]

Davidson's theory of meaning can be called realist in two senses.
First, it bases meaning on a version of the classical conception of
truth, according to which our sentences are true or false in virtue of
the state of the world. Davidson writes:

> The semantic conception of truth developed by Tarski deserves to be
> called a correspondence theory because of the part played by the
> concept of satisfaction; for clearly what has been done is that the
> property of being true has been explained, and non-trivially, in terms
> of a relation between language and something else.

Secondly, Davidson's conception of radical interpretation is realist in
the sense that the Principle of Charity involves 'reference to the
objective features of the world which alter in conjunction with
changes in attitude towards the truth of sentences'.[32] Davidson's
work has been at the heart of contemporary debates among analytical
philosophers of language, many of whom (perhaps most notably
Michael Dummett) object to identifying the sense of a sentence with
its truth-conditions, since it may well be impossible for speakers to
establish whether or not these conditions are met. The ensuing debate
between realists and 'anti-realists' is, however, less relevant from our
point of view than two other criticisms.

The first is directed to the very notion of radical interpretation
itself. Taylor attacks 'Quine's notion [shared by Davidson] that any

understånding of one person's language by another is the application of a theory'. Radical interpretation involves conceiving understanding as a relationship between a detached observer and an independent reality:

> Now this may work for the domain of middle-size dry goods, the ordinary material objects that surround us, and are likely to be salient both to observer and native, in virtue of their similarity as human beings. Perhaps depictions of these can be understood by offering truth-conditional formulae in our language.

> But when it comes to our emotions, aspirations, goals, our social relations and practices, this cannot be. The reason is that they are already partly constituted by language, and you have to understand this language to understand them.[33]

Behind this argument is, I think, the fundamentally Wittgensteinian idea that one learns a language as part of a community of speakers where correct usage is determined by the shared practices of speakers. As Dummett puts it, 'to take the social character of language seriously is to recognize that, in using the language, a speaker intended to be taken as responsible to, and only to, those linguistic practices agreed on by all members of the linguistic community.' It follows that 'the linguistic dispositions peculiar to a single speaker do not have, even for him, the same status as do those accepted by all speakers.'[34] Understanding another speaker of the same language does not consist in constructing a theory about the meaning of his utterances in the light of the Principle of Charity but rather depends on our sharing the same linguistic practices. The problem of radical interpretation may arise when we are trying to interpret the utterances of an alien speaker but even then, Taylor seems to imply, interpretation is only likely to succeed through our making ourselves part of the community of alien speakers.

At one level the argument is well taken. It does seem wrong to assimilate understanding one's native language to interpreting a foreign language and some of those influenced by Davidson have conceded this point.[35] But the problem posed by Quine remains: how can we come to understand the utterances of an alien speaker? If Davidsonian radical interpretation errs in treating this problem as definitive of understanding *tout court*, Taylor and the hermeneutic tradition generally seem to commit the reverse error, that of reducing interlinguistic understanding to the understanding of a language by a native speaker. Thus Gadamer treats interpretation as a relation to tradition, which is both continued and transformed in being appropriated. But this 'fusion of horizons' seems to assume the existence of a persisting shared culture which unites both the living members of that culture and previous generations. But how does understanding occur when no such culture exists? The problem does not arise simply in the case of interpreting an alien speaker. It may also arise for the historian studying a society different in fundamental respects from his or her own. The hermeneutic tradition seems to condemn us in these cases to a sort of linguistic solipsism, in which members of different cultures confront one another in a relation of mutual incomprehension. Taylor does not seem to deny that we can understand an alien language but he offers no account of how this is possible.

It is in this light that we can appreciate the importance of the Principle of Charity since it offers us a procedure by means of which to interpret the utterances of an alien speaker. The second criticism of Davidson concerns this principle. Davidson has two arguments for trying to maximize agreement between the alien and ourselves. The first is that to do otherwise is to treat the alien as irrational, the second that assuming that the bulk of his beliefs are true provides a basis for then interpreting his utterances. But, as Colin McGinn observes, the second argument will be satisfied just as well if we assume systematic falsity rather than truth, while 'you appreciate the reasonableness of an action by putting yourself into its agent's shoes, not by forcing him into yours.'[36] Considerations of this kind have led to a refinement of the Principle of Charity, the Principle of Humanity which, according to Macdonald and Pettit,

> says that the interpreter should not so much maximize agreement, whatever the cost, as minimize a certain sort of disagreement which we find unintelligible. Where charity would have us recoil from the ascription of any disagreement or, as we are going to see it, error, humanity would only have us do so when we cannot explain how such disagreement or error could have come about.[37]

As its name suggests, the Principle of Humanity involves the notion of a common human nature. David Wiggins argues that

> one must take into account not only what the world presents to the experience of subjects but also their interests and their *focus* on the world. How else can we guess what the world *presents* to them? . . . But then we can only break out of the circle of belief, affect and meaning if, in advance of any particular problem of radical interpretation, we think we know more than nothing not only about the world but also about men in general.[38]

Wiggins elaborates on how the notion of human nature enters into radical interpretation:

> Presented with the human form we entertain immediately a multitude of however tentative expectations. We interpret the speech and conduct of the remotest human strangers in the light of the maxim that we should interpret them in such a way as to ascribe beliefs, needs and concerns to them that will diminish to the minimum the need to postulate *inexplicable* disagreement between us and them. We entertain the idea, unless we are irremediably conceited or colonialist in mentality, that there may be something we ourselves can learn from strangers about the true, the good and the rational. . . . In the absence of a belief in such a thing as human nature, I do not think that there is any idea of inexplicable error or disagreement that is available to us.[39]

This way of thinking about interpretation has a number of important implications. In the first place, it allows us to avoid the relativism which seems inherent in the hermeneutic conception of understanding. According to the Principle of Humanity, what makes understanding possible is not a background of practices which can never be fully articulated by a theory, but rather simply our common nature. Wittgenstein says: 'It is essential for communication that we agree in a large number of judgements.'[40] But this agreement springs from the contingent fact that human beings share certain fundamental characteristics. As Wittgenstein puts it, 'the common behaviour of mankind is the system of reference by means of which we interpret an unknown language.' Without such a reference point, springing from human beings' shared nature, there is no guarantee that communication is possible. Indeed, 'if a lion could talk, we could not understand him.'[41]

Secondly, Davidson's conception of interpretation is realist in the sense that, as we have seen, it starts from human sayings and doings in an objective world. This makes it preferable in fundamental respects to the account of understanding offered by Jürgen Habermas. Habermas sees his theory of communicative action as basic to a more general theory of rationality which will allow him to avoid the scepticism and pessimism of the early Frankfurt school – which by the 1940s had come to see reason itself as an instrument of domination – and the similar attitudes expressed by contemporary 'post-modernism' (Lyotard, Foucault, German neo-conservatives).[42]

Habermas argues that 'reaching understanding is the inherent telos of human speech.' But this implies a certain analysis of utterances (or, as Habermas calls them following J. L. Austin and John Searle, speech-acts). Specifically, 'only those speech acts with which a speaker connects a criticizable validity-claim can move a hearer to accept an offer independently of external force.' Therefore, 'a speaker can *rationally motivate* a hearer to accept his speech-act offer because ... he can assume the *warranty* for providing, if necessary, convincing reasons that would stand up to a hearer's criticism of the validity-claim.'[43]

Habermas elaborates what is involved in the idea that a speaker implicitly undertakes 'to redeem, if necessary, the validity-claim raised with his speech-act':

> When a hearer accepts a speech-act, an agreement comes about between at least two acting and speaking subjects. However, this does not rest only on the intersubjective recognition of a single thematically stressed validity-claim. Rather, an agreement of this sort is achieved simultaneously at three levels. We can identify these intuitively if we keep in mind that in communicative action a speaker selects a comprehensive linguistic expression only in order to come to an understanding *with* a hearer *about* something and thereby to make *himself* understandable. It belongs to the communicative intent of the speaker (a) that he perform a speech-act that is *right* with respect to the given normative context, so that between him and the hearer an intersubjective relation will come about which is recognized as legitimate; (b) that he make a *true* (or *correct*) existential presupposition, so that the hearer will accept and share the knowledge of the speaker; and (c) that he express *truthfully* his beliefs, intentions, desires, and the like, so that the hearer will give credence to what is said.[44]

This analysis of the presuppositions of communicative action confirms, Habermas believes, his claim that the aspiration to a rational society is implicit in our speech: 'What raises us out of nature is the only thing whose nature we know: *language*. Through its structure, autonomy and responsibility are posited for us. Our first sentence expresses unequivocally the intention of universal and unrestrained consensus.' Since such a consensus could only exist in an emancipated society, 'the truth of statements is based on anticipating the good life.'[45]

Habermas has a decidely odd conception of understanding. It seems to consist in the hearer's 'accepting' the speaker's 'offer' of a speech-act, resulting in an agreement between the two. In what does this agreement consist? Does the hearer accept the *truth* of the utterance? But this seems grossly implausible: it would imply that we cannot understand false sentences (or at least sentences which we reject as false). That Habermas does not have this in mind is suggested by formulations such as the following: 'The normative validity-claim is itself cognitive in the sense of the supposition (however counterfactual) that it could be discursively redeemed – that is, grounded in consensus of the participants through argumentation.'[46]

Understanding is the telos of the speech-act (here a moral judgement) in the sense of what would arise in an 'ideal speech situation' where discussion was motivated purely by the search for the truth. And truth itself seems to be identified with an ideal consensus, following Peirce's claim that

> the conception of reality ... essentially involves the notion of a COMMUNITY, without definite limits, and capable of a definite increase of knowledge. And so those two series of cognition – the real and the unreal – consist of those which, at a time sufficiently future, the community will always continue to reaffirm; and of those which, under the same conditions, will ever be denied.[47]

But such an identification of truth with ideal consensus is incoherent. For it is always possible, even 'at a time sufficiently future', to ask whether or not those sentences which 'the community ... continues[s] to reaffirm' are true. 'True' does not mean 'warrantedly assertible', however far into the future we project ourselves. It is precisely the objectivity of truth, its consisting in a relation between our sentences and the world independently of our ability to identify those sentences to which the predicate 'true' applies, which allows it to act as a regulative ideal for science, requiring us to revise the sentences we hold true when they clash with evidence.[48]

These difficulties aside, Habermas's account of understanding seems to imply that we can choose whether or not to understand an utterance – this, at any rate, is what is suggested by the idea that the hearer 'accepts' the speaker's 'offer'. A moment's reflection should be sufficient to make it clear that this view is drastically at odds with what happens in speech. No one who understands a given language can avoid understanding what is said in his or her presence in that language even if it is not addressed to him to her. The case of inattention is not a counter-example since this consists in, voluntarily or involuntarily, not listening to what is said, treating it as background noise. But, if we attend, we understand (though, of course, the use of unfamiliar jargon by the speaker may obscure certain parts of his or her speech).

Underlying this very peculiar treatment of understanding is what Michael Rosen calls a 'conventionalist' conception of language, according to which a set of tacit presuppositions involving, in this case, certain commitments on the part of the speaker to the hearer, is necessary for anything to be said.[49] Such a view of language is at odds with Wittgenstein's discussion of meaning and rule-following in the *Philosophical Investigations*, summarized by Colin McGinn thus:

> Understanding is not an inner process of supplying an interpretation of a sign which justifies one in reacting to the sign in a certain way; it is, rather, an ability to engage in a practice or custom of using a sign over time in accordance with one's natural propensities.

Thus viewing language as 'a form of natural behaviour', McGinn notes,

> is not incompatible with recognizing that language is in some sense 'conventional'. It is true (in some sense) that words mean what they do in virtue of the conventional relations between them and the world; but this does not imply that our nature makes no contribution to what we mean – indeed, one might well hold that our conventions are *underlain* by our nature.[50]

Davidson takes a similarly anti-conventionalist view of language, arguing that 'language is a condition for having conventions', rather than, as Habermas implies, the reverse.[51] Rather than to seek to identify the tacit presuppositions of speech which supposedly make it possible, the Davidsonian theory of interpretation claims that understanding depends simply on the fact that human beings share a common nature and live in the same world. We can interpret the utterances of an alien speaker, not because we implicitly posit an ideal speech situation in which the aspirations of German classical idealism towards freedom and reason are somehow realized, but because, in Wiggins's words, 'we know more than nothing not only about the world but also about men in general' and that by virtue of the fact that we are ourselves men and women in that world.

There is one respect in which the Habermasian and Davidsonian conceptions of understanding are at one. Each involves a theory of rationality. In the Davidsonian case it arises by virtue of the fact that interpretation involves ascribing beliefs to agents. As Macdonald and Pettit put it,

> Beliefs, like their propositional objects, are capable of being true or false and it would make no sense to ascribe beliefs to an agent without assuming that he was disposed to make moves appropriate to ensure that his beliefs were true. To assume this is to take it that the agent is attitudinally rational, where to make his utterances and actions as the rational issue of beliefs and desires was to assume behavioural rationality.[52]

It is in this sense that the truth of the orthodox conception of agents is a precondition of interpretation. Unless we assume that in this minimal sense agents are rational, their doings and sayings are unintelligible. The orthodox conception can therefore be said to be implied by the Principle of Humanity. We could treat this as a transcendental argument for the orthodox conception, as I suggested at the end of section 1.2. But the preceding discussion has underlined the dependence of the orthodox conception on a broader conception of human nature, to which the Principle of Humanity makes tacit appeal. In any case, the fact that the best available theory of interpretation issues in the orthodox conception of agents – which we have already seen in chapters 1 and 2 to be consistent with explanations of social events whose premisses mention structures – removes the threat that the indispensability of interpretation rules out generalizing social theory. Let us now consider ways of giving more content to the assumption that agents are rational.

3.4 THE UTILITARIAN THEORY OF ACTION

Consider utilitarianism, not as an ethical theory but as an account of human action. As such it has, Talcott Parsons suggests, four main characteristics, 'atomism, rationality, empiricism and randomness of ends'. Agents are conceived as being individual human organisms seeking to satisfy their wants. Rationality is understood as what Weber called *Zweckrationalität*, characterized by the optimizing principle mentioned in section 1.2: 'Action is rational in so far as it pursues ends possible within the conditions of the situation, and by the means which, among those available to the actor, are intrinsically best adapted to the end for reasons understandable and verifiable by positive empirical science.' Parsons notes that 'there is nothing in the theory dealing with the relations of the ends to each other, but only with the character of the means-end relationship.' Actions are instrumentally rational, in that they are the means best adapted to a given end. The givenness of ends, Parsons argues, implies 'the randomness of the ends, at least the ultimate ends, of actions'.[53]

The utilitarian theory of action has had an enormous influence on modern social theory. The various forms of rational-choice theory, such as neo-classical economics, game theory and public-choice theory, are essentially formalizations of its assumptions, so that agents are thought of as having an ordered and consistent set of preferences and of choosing that which will maximize utility for them as defined by these preferences. For rational-choice Marxists such as

John Roemer utilitarianism thus formalized is an immensely powerful means for transforming historical materialism into a deductive theory whose laws are proven theorems.[54] Equally there are those for whom the identification of rationality with optimization, if true, is profoundly problematic. Both Weber and the early Frankfurt school regarded modern civilization as the triumph of instrumental reason, a state of affairs which rendered the attainment of any substantive rationality, that is, of a rationality of ends rather than of means, impossible and which makes reason into the instrument of domination.[55]

The question I wish to pursue here is the following: does (or should) historical materialism involve the utilitarian theory of action? Parsons thought that it does, describing Marxism as 'a version of utilitarian individualism'.[56] This claim has been elaborated in a most interesting recent article by David Lockwood. He argues that Marx went beyond classical utilitarianism chiefly in introducing the notion of 'differential class rationality'. Capitalists are still thought of as *zweckrational*. Workers, however, possess ' "reason", in the sense of a capacity to understand that [instrumentally] rational action . . . can be self defeating'. Further, 'it is . . . through its exercise, under conditions created by capitalist [*sic*] accumulation, that the end-shift of the proletariat [i.e. their decision to overthrow capitalism and abolish class society] occurs.'[57]

Marx's reformulation of the concept of rationality still fails to distinguish, Lockwood argues, between two different forms of deviation from rational action. The first is 'irrational action', 'an integral part of utilitarian thinking', which is 'seen to be due either to the actor's inadequate knowledge of the facts of the situation, or to his imperfect understanding of the most efficient, that is, scientifically rational means of attaining his ends'. The second Lockwood calls, following Parsons and Pareto, '*non*rational action'. This is 'defined positively by the actor's conformity to rules or norms that he regards as obligatory because they embody some ultimate end or value'. Marxism, Lockwood argues, suffers from 'the lack of a clear distinction between irrational and nonrational action, which rules out the possibility of the rigorous analysis and empirical study of the conditions determining the institutionalization of values'. Consequently, the Marxist theory of ideology 'concentrates attention on the cognitive obstacles to revolutionary consciousness', while Marxist analyses of class tend to ignore 'the status order, the primary focus of the integration of the ends of class actors'.[58]

I shall discuss some of the issues raised by Lockwood's specific criticisms of Marxism in chapters 4 and 5. Here I wish to argue both that Marx rejected the utilitarian theory of action and that he was right to do so. The first claim is easy to establish. Marx devotes several pages of *The German Ideology* to a critical discussion of 'the theory of utility'. Thus he condemns Holbach because he

> depicts the entire activity of individuals in their mutual intercourse, e.g. speech, love, etc., as a relation of utility and utilization. Hence the actual relations that are presupposed here are speech, love, definite manifestations of definite qualities of individuals. Now these relations are supposed not to have the meaning *peculiar* to them but to be the expression and manifestation of some third relation attributed to them, the *relation of utility or utilization*.

Nevertheless, 'the apparent absurdity of merging all the manifold relationships of people in the *one* relation of usefulness, this apparently metaphysical abstraction arises from the fact that in modern bourgeois society all relations are subordinated in practice to the one abstract monetary-commercial relation'.[59]

Treating social relationships as instrumental, far from being a general feature of human action, is specific to the capitalist mode of production:

> All this is actually the case with the bourgeois. For him only *one* relation is valid on its own account – the relation of exploitation; all other relations have validity for him only in so far as he can include them under this one relation; and even when he encounters relations which cannot directly be subordinated to the relation of exploitation, he subordinates them to it at least in his imagination. The material expression of this use is money which represents the value of all things, people and social relations.[60]

While 'exploitation' is here used by Marx in a broader sense than he would give the term in *Capital*, where it refers to the appropriation of surplus-labour, the last sentence of the passage just quoted does point forward to one of the main themes of his mature economic writings, namely the manner in which competition brings about an equalization of different productive activities, reducing their distinct qualities to quantitative differences between units of abstract social labour.

That Marx rejects the utilitarian theory of action not just because it articulates a specifically bourgeois rationality but because it is profoundly wrong about the nature of human beings is clear from his denunciation of 'the arch-philistine Jeremy Bentham' in *Capital*:

> To know what is useful to a dog, one must investigate the nature of dogs. This nature is not itself deducible from the principle of utility.

Applying this to man, he that would judge all human acts, movements, relations, etc. according to the principle of utility would first have to deal with human nature in general, and then with human nature as historically modified in each epoch. Bentham does not trouble himself with this. With the driest naïveté he assumes that the modern petty bourgeois, especially the English petty bourgeois, is the normal man.[61]

Marx's objection to the utilitarian theory of action is that, by treating 'the modern petty bourgeois' as the 'normal man' it effectively homogenizes the qualitatively diverse abilities and dispositions of human beings and the 'manifold relationships' which these involves, to 'the *one* relations of usefulness' and thus misrepresents what 'human nature in general' is. At issue here are two different conceptions of human agency.

Charles Taylor argues that one characteristic of human agents is the ability to form 'second-order desires', that is, 'the power to *evaluate* our desires, to regard some as desirable and others as undesirable'. But there are 'two broad kinds of evaluation of desire.'

Thus someone might be weighing two desired actions to determine the most convenient, or how to make different desires compossible . . . or how to get the most overall satisfaction. Or he might be pondering to see which of two desired objects attracts him most, as one ponders a pastry tray to see if one will take an éclair or a mille feuilles.

But what is missing in the above cases is a qualitative evaluation of my desires; the kind of thing we have, for instance, when I refrain from acting on a given motive – say, spite or envy – because I consider it base or unworthy. In this kind of case our desires are classified in such categories as higher and lower, virtuous and vicious, more and less fulfilling, more and less refined, profound and superficial, noble and base. They are judged as belonging to qualitatively different modes of life: fragmented or integrated, alienated or free, saintly or merely human, courageous or pusillanimous and so on.[62]

Taylor calls these two kinds of evaluation 'weak' and 'strong' respectively. The crucial difference between them is that 'in weak evaluation, for something to be judged good it is sufficient that it be desired, whereas in strong evaluation there is also a use of "good" or some other evaluative term for which being desired is not sufficient.' 'Strong evaluation deploys a language of evaluative distinctions' such as those listed in the previous paragraph. And this leads to very different conceptions of agency. The subject of weak evaluation is 'a simple weigher of alternatives'. He is 'reflective in a minimal sense, that he evaluates courses of action, and sometimes is capable of acting out of that evaluation as against under the impress of immediate desire'. However, 'the reflection of the simple weigher terminates in the inarticulate experience that A is more attractive than B.' By contrast, 'for the strong evaluator reflection also examines the different modes of being of the agent. Motivations or desires don't only count in virtue of the attraction of the consummations but also in virtue of the kind of life and kind of subject that these desires properly belong to'.[63]

It should be plain that the 'simple weigher' is none other than the human subject as conceived by the utilitarian theory of action. Strong evaluation no longer treats the agent's desires, the ends of action, as given, random, but subjects them to critical examination. As Taylor makes clear, this position presupposes evaluative realism, that is, the thesis that 'concerning strong evaluations, there is a fact of the matter.'[64] In other words, seeing human agents as strong evaluators means treating their moral judgements as factual assertions capable of being true and false like all such assertions and rejecting the moral non-cognitivism, the treatment of value-ascriptions as a matter of irreducibly subjective choice, that is so deeply embedded in modern Western culture.

Now my claim is that Marx rejects the utilitarian theory of action because he believes human beings to be strong evaluators rather than simple weighers. There are, I think, two reasons for saying this. The first is what he contrasts to the 'principle of utility', namely 'all the manifold relationships of people', which are 'definite manifestations of definite qualities of individuals'. What we have here, *contra* Parsons, is an *anti*-utilitarian individualism, one which lays stress on the diverse and distinct characteristics of people and on the irreducibility of these characteristics. Secondly, there are the general arguments offered in section 1.4 above for attributing to Marx an Aristotelian moral theory concerned with establishing the (empirically ascertainable) conditions of human well-being.

Even if Marx did not reject the utilitarian theory of action, he should have done. It is interesting that Amartya Sen's criticisms of the theory should highlight its inability to cater for moral judgements. He considers the theory of revealed preference, which formalizes this conception of action, treating an agent's choices as indices of his underlying preferences and requiring of these preferences simply that they are consistent, so that if A chooses x rather than y, he must not, at some other time, choose y when x is also available. Sen comments: 'if you are consistent, then no matter whether you are a single-minded egoist, a raving altruist or a class-conscious militant, you will appear to be maximizing your utility in the enchanted world of definitions.'

What this way of thinking about action leaves out of account is the case of 'commitment', which Sen defines 'in terms of a person choosing an act that he believes will yield him a lower level of personal welfare than an alternative that is also available to him'. In this case the agent decides *not* to maximize utility. This concept helps to make sense of the fact that when confronted with situations having the form of the Prisoner's Dilemma 'people often do not follow the selfish strategy' – in other words, they do not take the instrumentally rational but collectively sub-optimal choice of confessing, even though by refusing to confess they run the risk of their least preferred solution, i.e. the maximum gaol sentence, if the other prisoner confesses, (see section 5.3 below). Sen argues that in such cases 'the person is *more* sophisticated than the theory allows', since he has been willing to 'consider the modifications of the game brought about through acting through commitment', i.e. through deciding not to confess come what may. Sen proposes that, rather than treat the agent as a 'rational fool decked in the glory of his *one* all-purpose preference ordering', we should ascribe to him, not one set of preferences but rather a 'meta-ranking' which expresses his preferences between different *sets* of preferences, expressing his evaluation, on moral, political or even class grounds, of different *kinds* of action.[65]

Why then do rational-choice Marxists espouse the utilitarian theory of action? Jon Elster cites Davidson in support of the idea that we should presume that agents are rational: 'irrational behaviour only makes sense against a background of rationality.' This justifies the methodological injunction that 'the social scientist should be prepared to spend time and imagination in thinking up rational explanations for the action he observes, and only after repeated failure should he tentatively label the action as irrational.'[66] But the sort of general considerations which Davidson advances do not entail the utilitarian theory of action, concerning which he has expressed some scepticism.[67] All that they compel us to accept is the Principle of Humanity and the assumption that agents are behaviourally and attitudinally rational, that is, that they act in the light of beliefs and desires which they are prepared to modify in the light of inconsistency or empirical counter-examples. This is not equivalent to saying that agents optimize. One can accept Elster's proposal that we presume agents are rational (indeed, if Davidson is right, we have no alternative to doing this if we are to understand them), without therefore preferring rational-choice explanations.

Indeed, much of Elster's substantive philosophical work has been concerned with the ways in which agents deviate from what is assumed about them in rational-choice models. Thus, he is led to weaken the identification of rationality with optimality, so that 'rationality sometimes must be understood as satisficing, i.e. as finding an alternative that is "good enough" for one's purposes rather than the "best".' Moreover, Elster is clearly aware of the more general inadequacies of the utilitarian theory of action as they are highlighted by Marx, Taylor and Sen:

> the notion of rational behaviour relative to *given* (and consistent) desires and beliefs is an extremely thin one. In addition to this formal rationality we want to have substantive rationality, in the twin forms of *judgement* and *autonomy*. . . . If people are *agents* in a substantive sense, and not just the passive supports of their preference-structures and belief-systems, then we need to understand how judgement and autonomy are possible. This, in my view, is the outstanding unresolved problem both in philosophy and the social sciences.[68]

It is also, one is inclined to comment, a problem that is extremely difficult to resolve if one takes the utilitarian theory of action as the bench-mark of rationality. Elster's worries about the theory make the question I asked above more pressing: why this underlying preference for rational-choice explanations? The answer is, I think, that they seem to embody a powerful theory, in which far-reaching consequences can be derived from a few extremely thin assumptions about what human beings are like (namely that they are Sen's 'rational fools'). The rational-choice Marxists' methodological individualism and their rejection of Marxist economic theory seems to leave them with no scope for social generalizations. The assumption that agents are optimizers provides them with a basis on which to formulate theories from which predictions can be derived. It meets a need, but only one which arises from their prior abandonment of classical historical materialism.

There are two final points to be made in this context. First, it should be noted that treating agents as strong evaluators is not vulnerable to the sort of objections which Parsons and Lockwood make to the utilitarian conception of action. For the agent *qua* evaluator acts in accordance with norms and values: their adoption is surely the outcome of a strong evaluation. The difference between this notion of agency and that implicit in the notion of non-rational action is that the first interprets value-ascriptions realistically, that is as either true or false; their acceptance is, in principle, a *rational* process, reflectively engaged in, so that one can dispute a particular evaluation as mistaken. This amounts, as Philip Pettit observes, to incorporating the ascription of value-judgements into the practice of radical interpretation: 'If one is an evaluative realist then one's ascription of evaluative beliefs will not be independent of one's assessment of those beliefs; this, because one will not normally want to ascribe beliefs which, on one's own assessment, there is no reason to maintain.' This does not rule out, of course, the possibility of 'radical insight or discovery', where 'the aliens recognize a real value in a case where we have not hitherto acknowledged a value, or have perhaps denied that there is any.'[69] One virtue of conceiving agents as strong evaluators is that it avoids one of the characteristic vices of sociology, namely that of treating actors as 'cultural dopes', the bearers of norms which they have passively ingested through a process of 'socialization'. Parsons' writings are merely the clearest example of this approach.

Secondly, while I think it is right to think of agents as strong evaluators, it would be a mistake therefore to treat social theory as a branch of moral philosophy. More particularly, to be a strong evaluator is not inconsistent with being an individual acting on interests which bring one into conflict with others. To see why this is so, consider Michael Sandel's recent critique of John Rawls's theory of justice. Sandel, heavily influenced by Taylor, concentrates his fire on the notion of agency present in the account which Rawls gives of the original position from which he derives his principles of justice. According to Rawls, Sandel argues,

> That we are distinct persons, characterized by separate systems of ends, is a necessary presupposition of a being capable of justice. What in particular our ends consist in, and whether in fact they happen to coincide or overlap with the ends of others is an empirical question that cannot be known in advance. This is the sense – epistemological rather than psychological – in which the plurality of subjects is given prior to their unity. We are distinct individuals first, and then (circumstances permitting) we form relationships and engage in co-operative arrangements with others.[70]

Sandel claims that this way of viewing agents is implicit in Rawls's account of the 'circumstances of justice', the situation typical of human society, involving such features as 'moderate scarcity' and 'mutual disinterest', which gives rise to the need for principles of justice to regulate conflict.[71] 'The assumption of mutual disinterest', Sandel says, 'is not an assumption about what motivates people, but an assumption about the nature of subjects who possess motivations in general'. One implication of this is that 'on Rawls's view, a sense of community describes a possible aim of antecedently individuated selves, not an ingredient or constituent of their identity.' Justice can therefore only provide a framework within which to regulate the conflicts among antecedently individuated subjects. Sandel proposes a different conception of agency, one in which people 'conceive their identity – the subject and not just the object of their feelings and aspirations – as defined to some extent by the community of which they are part'. This 'constitutive' sense of community implies that 'when politics goes well, we can know a good in common that we cannot know alone.'[72]

Sandel offers an attractive alternative to liberal theories of justice such as Rawls's. The trouble, from the point of view of social theory, which seeks to explain social events and not just to evaluate them, is that politics usually goes very badly. The community of which agents are part no doubt gives them much of their identity. Its structure is also usually such as to bring them into conflict with one another. No social theory which concentrates on what people share within a given social formation, on what unites them, is likely to be of much help in making sense of what happens in that society. Rawls himself writes:

> The postulate of mutual disinterest in the original position is made to insure that the principles of justice do not depend on strong assumptions. Recall that the original position is meant to incorporate widely shared and yet weak conditions. A conception of justice should not presuppose, then, extensive ties of natural sentiment. At the basis of the theory, one tries to assume as little as possible.[73]

Whether this is the right sort of constraint to put on a theory of justice is indeed disputable. But certainly no plausible social theory should rely on 'strong assumptions' perhaps to the effect that agents' strong evaluations involve a constitutive sense of community that units them. This is not to withdraw the idea that agents are strong evaluators rather than simple weighers. It is, rather, to say that we must also consider the way in which individuals' relations to social structures (in Marxist terms, their position in the relations of production) connect up with their beliefs and desires. That is, a *social* theory of agency must consider the question of the interests agents have, to which we now turn.

3.5 INTERESTS AND POWERS

The point of the concept of interests is to relate an agent's wants to the objective environment on which his or her opportunities for realizing those wants depend. William Connolly offers this analysis of the term 'interests':

To say that a policy or practice is in the interests of an individual or a group is to assert both that the recipient would somehow benefit from it and that there is therefore a *reason* in support for enacting that policy. Of course, the reason may be overridden by other considerations. But it is important to see that, as it is used in our society, 'interests' is one of those concepts that connects descriptive and explanatory statements to normative judgements.[74]

So, to say that doing x is in A's interests is to give A a reason for doing x. But why is this so? Connolly observes that 'although ["interests"] . . . has been variously defined, all definitions seriously advanced make an important reference to the wants, preferences, and choices of agents somewhere in the definition.'[75] Or, as Anthony Giddens more succinctly puts it, 'interests are logically connected with wants.'[76] But what is the connection? Is it that, simply, interests and wants are identical, so that, perhaps, doing x is in A's interests because A desires that p and believes that doing x will bring it about that p? This is what is sometimes called the subjective conception of interest. It bears an obvious relation to the utilitarian theory of action, in that the agent's interests are here identified with the ends he or she has choosen, reflecting his or her beliefs and desires. This way of viewing interests has had an important bearing on social theory, particularly in the shape of pluralist political science, which tacitly identifies interest with revealed preference, as is evident in Robert Dahl's insistence on treating as political issues only those which 'involve actual disagreement in preference between two or more groups.'[77]

Critics of pluralism have challenged this treatment of interests as revealed preferences, pointing out that the exercise of power does not simply arise in cases of overt conflicts of (subjective) interest, but is also present in the 'mobilization of bias', that is, in the elaboration of systems of evaluative beliefs which both alter the preferences of subordinate groups and prevent issues affecting them favourably from reaching the political agenda.[78] This kind of consideration suggests that an agent may not be aware of his or her interests and that his or her wants and interests may conflict. This inference is, in any case, licensed by ordinary usage. I may want to drink this cup of poisoned coffee, but it is not in my interests to do so. My drinking the coffee would be a consequence of, *inter alia*, my false belief that it is an ordinary, that is, non-poisonous, cup of coffee but also of the fact that I *want* to drink it. Again, I may know that smoking is bad for me, but still carry on smoking. Why? Because my desire for nicotine is stronger than my knowledge that it is not in my interests to smoke. The possibility of conflicts between wants and interests has led to the claim that interests are 'real' or 'objective'. And indeed, to assert that agents may be unaware of their interests is to suggest that the latter are objective in one standard sense, where something is objective when it exists even when subjects are not conscious of its existence. Pluralists object most strongly to the idea of objective interests, on grounds stated by Nelson Polsby: 'for pluralists, "false class consciousness" does not exist, for it implies that the values of analysts are imposed on groups in the community.'[79] On this view, to say that agents may be unaware of or mistaken about their interests (and in this sense have 'false consciousness') is to allow the social theorist arbitrarily to impose his or her views of what is right onto the agents. This objection amounts to saying that the notion of objective interests breaks the connection between wants and interests. An agent's interests now have nothing to do with his or her wants.

Various attempts have been made to deal with this objection by giving an account of objective interests as still bearing an essential connection to wants. Typically this is done by defining interests counterfactually, as the wants we would have in conditions of perfect information. Connolly, for example, proposes the following: 'Policy x is more in A's real interest than policy y if A, were he to experience x and y, would *choose* x as the result he would rather have for himself.' This involves, Connolly suggests, 'a choice between alternative experiences that is *fully informed* about the factors entering these experiences and helping to make each what it is'.[80] A perhaps more perspicuous version of the same kind of approach is offered by Elster, who defines class interests as, not 'the actual preferences and goals of the members' of the class, but rather 'goals that are somehow imputed to the members, such as the goals they would have if fully aware of the causes of, and possible remedies to, their situation'.[81]

The reason why the contrast between actual wants and counterfactual wants is a significant one is because of the existence of ruling ideologies preventing the mass of the population from having the requisite full knowledge of their situation. Thus Erik Olin Wright says that 'class interests in capitalist society are those potential objectives which become actual objectives of struggle in the absence of the mystifications and distortions of capitalist relations.'[82] In this way the definition seeks to capture the Marxist idea of workers often being misled about their interests (and in this sense having 'false consciousness') without breaking the connection between interests and wants.

There are two difficulties with this move. The first is that counterfactual wants do not easily play a causal role. My interests are unlikely to influence my action if they are what I would want were I free from the influence of bourgeois ideology. Conceiving interests as counterfactual wants does, in principle, allow us to measure the distance between what agents actually want and what they would want if armed with full knowledge of their situation but it does not allow us to predict what agents will do, except, I suppose, to say that, to the extent that agents approximate to full knowledge, they will act in accordance with their interests. There seems to be a tension here between two uses of 'interests', to appraise action and to explain it. The second difficulty with counterfactual wants is analogous to the objection I raised to Habermas's consensual conception of truth. It is simply this. Supposing that I have full knowledge and that I have considered the alternatives carefully, as Connolly requires us, which should I choose? Will what I know make it obvious what I should want? But then we seem in some danger of breaking the connection between interests and wants, since what I want can, in these circumstances, somehow be read off the objective situation. Or perhaps I have a genuine choice, but whatever course of action I pursue will not have harmful consequences; the difference lies in the degree to which I will benefit from the various outcomes. But this just seems implausible.

Just as in the case of truth identified with ideal consensus it is always open to us to ask of our most well-founded beliefs, are they true?, so in the case of interests defined as counterfactual wants, we can always ask, however full our knowledge, well, what should I want? If we are to conceive interests in this way, then some more definite account of how we would choose in the hypothetical condition of full knowledge seems required. Perhaps it is this kind of consideration which led Wright recently to propose the following approach:

> 'Deep down inside' people in general have a desire for freedom. In so far as the actual capacity that individuals have to make choices and act upon them − their real freedom − is shaped systematically by the class structure, they have objective class interests based on this real interest in freedom.[83]

This indeed solves the problem of how to give a content to our interests, but at the price of embedding them into a normative philosophical anthropology. This is to base our theory of action on 'strong assumptions' indeed. Moreover, once again we seem in danger of breaking the link between wants and interests, since the implication of the phrase 'deep down inside' is presumably that agents may not be articulately aware of having the desire for freedom which Wright imputes to them.

The sorts of difficulties I have outlined have led some writers to seek to get rid of the concept of interests completely. Göran Therborn, for example, describes it as 'an utilitarian residue in Marxism, which should be rejected, explicitly and decisively, once for all'. He elaborates:

> 'Interests' by themselves do not explain anything. 'Interest' is a *normative* concept indicating the most rational course of action in a predefined game, that is, in a situation in which gain and loss have already been defined. The problem to be explained, however, is how members of different classes come to define the world and their situation and possibilities in a particular way.[84]

Therborn's objection to interests, then, is that they play no explanatory role, providing no help in the task of explaining how agents consciously engage in social action. A more radical challenge, not simply to the concept of interests but also to the entire way of thinking about society involved in trying to distinguish these from agents' actual wants, was provided recently by Gareth Stedman Jones. He attacks the 'essentialist conception of class' shared by Marxist and non-Marxist historians of the British working-class movement:

> The implicit assumption is of civil society as a field of conflicting classes whose opposing interests will find rational expression in the political arena. Such interests, it is assumed, pre-exist their expression. Languages of politics are evanescent forms, mere coverings of an adequate, inadequate or anachronistic kind, through which essential interests may be decoded.[85]

This approach reckons without the 'non-referential' character of language. Stedman Jones takes Saussure and those influenced by him (the varieties of structuralism and post-structuralism) to have established 'the materiality of language itself, the impossibility of simply referring it back to some primal anterior reality, "social being", the impossibility of abstracting experience from the language which structures its articulation'. This requires reconceptualizing the relationships between agents' conscious experience and social structures:

> Language disrupts any simply notion of the determination of consciousness by social being because it is itself part of social being. We cannot therefore decode political language to reach a primal and material expression of interest since it is the discursive structure of political language which conceives and defines interest in the first

place. What we must therefore do is to study the production of interest, identification, grievance and aspiration within political languages themselves.[86]

Stedman Jones might be said to offer a discursive conception of interests, in which they are whatever our political language says they are. This view differs from the subjective conception, since interests are identified, not by revealed preference, but by the particular discourse through which an agent articulates his or her feelings and beliefs about how society is run. But involved in this is a more general challenge to Marxist theories of class. Stedman Jones is proposing that we treat class 'as a discursive rather than an ontological reality.'[87] Class, that is, is not an objective relationship defined by agents' position in the relations of production; rather, it is constructed within the political languages available to them.

Stedman Jones's argument for this conclusion seems to go something like this:

(1) Agents do not experience (social) reality in a direct and unmediated way;
(2) how agents articulate their experience depends on the particular forms of discourse they use;
(3) language is non-referential;
(4) we only have access to social reality through agents' experience of it.

This seems to be a sort of social Kantianism. Stedman Jones does not seem to deny that social systems exist, only that we can appeal to them in accounting for what agents do. In any case, the argument doesn't hold up. (4) is a very strong claim to make, unless 'experience' is defined so widely – embracing state papers, newspaper reports, official statistics, personal memoirs, popular songs, political pamphlets – as to be vacuous, since any investigator would have to examine these different sources critically and seek to find ways of resolving the numerous inconsistencies in and between them. (1) and (2) are true enough, but (3) is false. As Davidson's work shows (see section 3.3. above), a referential theory of language does not have to be atomistic, treating words as involving particular relations with specific items in reality. Davidson's is a holist theory of language, but one in which the ability of words to figure in an indefinite number of sentences is explained by means of the referential concept of satisfaction. Further, the case of radical interpretation shows that making sense of an agent's utterances is impossible unless we take account of their objective context.[88]

Therborn's approach has some similarity to Stedman Jones's. He is a fairly orthodox Marxist, in that he does not regard classes as discursive constructs but is concerned with how agents caught up in these relationships come to be conscious actors. He believes, however, that it is possible to do this without using the concept of interests, so that what people want is given simply by the conjunction of their actual preferences and the discourses they use to articulate their experience. The danger with this approach is that it can lead to a version of normative functionalism. Thus Therborn writes:

> The formation of humans by every ideology . . . involves a process simultaneously of subjection and qualification. The amorphous libido and manifold potentialities of human infants are subjected to a particular order that allows certain drives and capacities, and prohibits and disfavours others. At the same time, through the same process, new members become qualified to take up and perform (a particular part of) the repertoire of roles given in the society into which they are born, including the role of possible agents of social change.[89]

Compare this with Parsons' discussion of one of the two main mechanisms of social integration, namely, socialization, which has to cope with 'the "barbarian invasion" of the stream of newborn infants', and which seeks 'the integration of ego into a role complementary to that of alter(s) in such a way that the common values are internalized in ego's personality and their respective behaviours come to constitute a complementary role-expectation-sanction system'.[90] The similarities extend well beyond those of vocabulary (Therborn, for example, takes over Parsons' distinction between 'ego' and 'alter'). Both see agents as bundles of drives formed into coherent subjects through various social mechanisms which allocate to them a distinct role. Therborn indeed objects to role theory on the grounds that it treats 'social behaviour' as 'normatively defined', is static and downgrades social contradictions. All these points are well taken but it remains the case that for Therborn social actors are not *agents*, able to pursue their own goals, but are rather social constructs, the passive bearers of social relations which, it is true, may involve contradictions between the processes of subjection and qualification but of which the actors themselves are also mere effects.[91]

The difficulty is really the one around which this entire book revolves. How to think of the relation between structures and agents without dissolving the former into subjectivity, as Stedman Jones does, or reducing the latter to the 'supports' of a process without a subject in the way Therborn does? In the previous chapter we saw that part of the solution lay in understanding how action involves the exercise of structural capacities. There remains the question of how structures relate to agents' conscious experience. A great virtue of the notion of interests is that, properly understood, it allows us to connect the two *without* reducing either to the other. The same thought is expressed by Wright when he says that 'class interests . . . [are] the link between class structure . . . and class struggle.'[92]

It seems to me that the definition of interests which comes closest to meeting the sort of demand I have just placed on it is that given by Anthony Giddens:

> To say that A has an interest in a given course of action, occurrence or state of affairs, is to say that the course of action, etc. facilitates the possibility of A achieving his or her wants. To be aware of one's interests, therefore, is more than to be aware of a want or wants; it is to know how to go about trying to realize them.[93]

Note first that this is an objective conception of interests: 'Interests presume wants, but the concept of interest concerns not the wants as such, but the possible modes of their realization in given sets of circumstances; and these can be determined as "objectively" as anything in social analysis.' Secondly, these modes of realization will depend crucially on agents' structural capacities, that is, on the powers they derive from their position in the relations of production (see section 2.5). A worker and a capitalist will have very different ways open to them of realizing their respective wants. Determining a person's interests is thus not, on this definition, a merely technical exercise: it isn't like deliberating between fish and chips, the Indian take-away or a French restaurant, all conceived as different 'modes of realization' of my desire for supper when there's no food in the house. It depends on a rational assessment of the power that person has to realize his or her wants, and this power will largely turn on his or her position in the class structure. This leads directly to a third point. While, Giddens argues, groups do not have interests, since only persons can have wants, 'none the less actors have interests *by virtue of their membership of particular groups, communities, classes etc.*'[94] Why they do so is clear enough once we have the concept of structural capacity: agents may have different wants, but their ability to realize them will depend on their shared position in the relations of production. Only persons have interests, but they will share them with others in the same class position. Finally, and following from this last point, agents' interests are likely to conflict, since their different positions in the relations of production mean that they can only realize their wants by pursuing courses of action which cause them to clash. A capitalist, so long as he remains a capitalist, can only realize his wants by exploiting workers, while the latter's realization of *their* wants is likely to depend on collective organization against him.

Let us now consider two possible objections to this account of interests. The first is that it is a version of the utilitarian theory of action, in that it treats wants as given and concerns itself only with how to realize these wants. Note that it is not a reply to this objection to point out that interests are not here identified with revealed preference. For the kinship with utilitarianism lies elsewhere, in the 'randomness' of the ends of action, as Parsons would put it. Consideration of interests thus conceived, the objector might contend, is nothing but a case of instrumental rationality, in that reason is exercised only to the extent of deciding on the most appropriate 'mode of realization' of a given end.

There are, I think, two answers to this objection. The first is that Giddens's definition of interests makes no presumption that an agent's wants are given by his or her preference-set, as required by rational-choice theory, or even that a single preference-set can be given. If we simply say that an agent's wants consist in his or her desires, then these desires, given the conclusions reached in section 3.4, will include his or her first *and second*-order desires. That is, they will include the commitments the agent has made, both as a result of his or her being brought up in a particular group (Parsons' and Therborn's mistake was not that they talked of socialization, but that they made it constitutive of individual identity), and in consequence of the more reflective process which Taylor calls 'strong evaluation'. Thus this account of interests does not treat the ends of action as given *per se*, but only as far as the determination of interests is concerned.

Secondly, bracketing wants in this way is inevitable if social theory is to find a place for agency in its explanations. If we are to say that social action involves conscious choices, that these choices issue from agents' beliefs and desires and that their desires cannot be read off from the social structure or deduced from an ethical theory – and I think we must say all these things – then there seems no alternative than to consider the ways in which agents with fairly diverse wants may still benefit from certain common courses of action. Andrew Levine says that 'our true wants [i.e. our interests] . . . are our wants in so far as we are *prudent*.'[95] Levine treats interests as counterfactual wants and hence as reducible to wants. This is, as we have seen, mistaken. Nevertheless, the invocation of prudence in this context seems appropriate: agents who consider their interests, that is, the ways in which the realization of their wants depends on the powers they share with others in the relations of production, are indeed being prudent. This is not the only way in which reason governs action; it also enters into the selection of the ends of action. However, for some purposes we must treat these ends as given. If this is to collapse into the utilitarian theory of action, then it does not seem to me a terrible crime.

The second objection attacks the givenness of wants from another direction. Giddens's definition of interests supposes that we can treat wants as given and then consider their means of realization which, I have suggested, depends particularly on agents' structural capacities. But, the objectors ask, what if our wants partly depend on our powers? Consider one of the mechanisms of 'irrational preference formation' discussed by Elster:

> *Adaptive preference formation* is the adjustment of wants to possibilites – not the deliberate adaptation favoured by character planners, but a causal process occurring non-consciously. Behind this adaptation there is the drive to reduce the tension or frustration that one feels in having wants that one cannot possibly satisfy.[96]

Elster describes this as a case of 'sour grapes' – what one can't have, one doesn't want. For our purposes it doesn't matter whether adaptive preferences are formed consciously or unconsciously, rationally or irrationally. It is enough that they are formed, in other words, that people cut their wants to fit their powers. The result, the objection might run, is to remove the tension between wants and interests. Agents adjust their wants to the limited possibilities they see open to them. Consideration of interests will still enter into the picture, inasmuch as they seek to realize their restricted wants, but no very dramatic conflict between wants and interests is likely to arise.

One reply might be to suggest that wants are sticky downward. They will include certain basic needs into whose definition what Marx called 'a historical or moral element' may well enter, but whose denial or restriction agents are likely to resist.[97] In other words, there is a limit to the extent to which preferences are adaptive. Secondly, to what precisely do wants adjust? Is it to possibilities *tout court*, or rather to *what agents regard as possibilities*? Surely the latter is more plausible. Now one's view of what is possible partly depends on harsh experience – think of the people who take capitalism's promises of social mobility seriously, fail in their attempt to rise and then bitterly deride the success of others. Nevertheless, particularly concerning social action, it is also likely to be influenced by what ideologies say is

possible and here it will often be the case that what *is* possible and
what agents *think* is possible diverge greatly.

These considerations are important because the interaction between
wants and powers will often be a dynamic one, with both agents'
desires and their beliefs about what is possible changing and thus
mutually reinforcing or undermining one another. The American
labour historian David Montgomery seems to be using the (modified)
concept of adaptive preference when he says: 'What workers want is
a function of what they consider realistically they can get.'[98] What he
had in mind, I think, was the kind of spiral in which workers'
confidence in their bargaining strength encourages them to increase
their demands and the resulting victories further raise both their
confidence and their demands. The general escalation of workers'
struggles in Western capitalism at the end of the 1960s was an
illustration of this process. It can, of course, go in reverse, with
sagging confidence leading to more limited and increasingly defensive
demands and, when even these cannot be won, a further collapse of
morale: such, pretty much, has been the fate of the American working
class in the 1980s.

The class struggle is, in a sense, the process through which agents
discover their interests by exploring the extent of their powers. The
concept of interests acts is a hinge connecting conscious experience
and objective structures, since it refers to the way in which agents'
realization of their interests depends on their structural capacities. Do
not the kind of dynamic factors I introduced above mean that agents'
interests are likely to change much over time? Do American workers,
because of the defeats they have suffered, have different interests now
from those they had in the 1960s? Here we should recall the
distinction drawn by Wright between structural and organizational
capacities (see section 2.5 above). If structural capacities consist in the
powers agents have by virtue of their position in the relations of
production, then organizational capacities are those 'which are
constituted by the conscious organization of the members of that
class'.[99] It is on agents' structural capacities and not their organizational capacities that the realization of their wants fundamentally
depend. So the powers which American workers have by virtue of
their position in the relations of production (above all, the power to
paralyse production and to take collective control of it) have not
changed. What have undoubtedly declined are the organizational
capacities of the US proletariat, given the run-down of highly
unionized mass industries such as autos, steel and rubber. Therefore
(given the connection between interests and *structural* capacities),
American workers' interests have not changed.

So linking interests and structural capacities is a perfectly defensible move. In the first place, talk of interests is unlikely to be of much us unless they are relatively enduring. Moreover, it seems reasonable to think of a class's organizational capacities depending on and being limited by its structural capacities. The scope of the latter will generally be greater than the former, although at the limit they will coincide. Given the dependence of organizational on structural capacities, it seems appropriate to associate interests with the more fundamental capacity. But why make the realization of agents' wants depend on *class* capacities at all? The only answer can be the empirical claim that they are decisive in determining agents' abilities to realize their wants. This is not to say that there are no other ways of doing so. One is social mobility but the opportunities for rising are likely to be limited and in any case this move, if successful, simply involves changing one set of class capacities for another. But there are other bases of social power, for example, position in the state apparatus, or organization along ethnic lines. Do these generate distinct interests? The Marxist claim must be that these other forms of social power depend on the forces and relations of production, so that structural capacities are more fundamental to the realization of wants. This is an issue we shall consider in the next chapter, along with that, raised by the concept of organizational capacities, of how *collective* agents are formed. Considering these questions is part of a more general shift, in the final two chapters, towards examining how agents consciously experience and change the social world.

CHAPTER 4

IDEOLOGY AND POWER

4.1 COLLECTIVE AGENTS

So far I have talked only of *individual* agents. The extension of the term 'agent' has been restricted to individual human organisms. This usage flows from the account of agency given in chapters 1 and 3 above. To be an agent so far has been to be a human organism to which beliefs and desires can be ascribed on the basis of the Principle of Humanity. This understanding of agency is indeed basic. Insisting that this is so is essential as a corrective both to the post-structuralist abolition of the subject and to the functionalist tendency to treat society as itself an organism with its own needs. However, we must now consider *collective* agents as well. The main theme of the preceding chapters has been that agents draw their powers in part from structures (the forces and relations of production) which divide them into classes with conflicting interests. The fact, explored in section 3.5, that agents have shared interests by virtue of the structural capacities they derive from their position in the relations of production, makes it essential to consider to forms of collective organization through which they seek to pursue these interests.

Individual agents (or, as I shall henceforth tend to call them *persons*) are primary. It is they who form collectivities in order to pursue their objectives. To say this is to make no real concession to individualism, since the bases of collective action comprise not just agents but the structures from which they derive the power to realize their ends. *Collective action* may be defined simply as any attempt by persons to co-ordinate their actions so as to achieve some goal or goals. This is a very minimal conception of collective agency. Greater interest centres on patterned and enduring forms of collective action. Of these the most developed and formalized are *organizations*. Tom Burns defines an organization as 'an assembly of human resources equipped and directed according to rational principles as instruments for use in achieving specified ends'.[1] This definition immediately recalls Weber and indeed much twentieth-century sociology has followed him in focusing on the nature and dynamic of organizations. There is, however, a level of analysis intermediary between that of collective action as such and that of organizations. This concerns what I shall call *collectivities*. A collectivity exists where persons co-ordinate their actions because they believe themselves to have a common identity.

The difference between collectivity and mere collective action turns upon the consciousness which agents have of themselves. It may well be that persons co-ordinating their actions have much in common – perhaps they occupy the same class position and so have shared interests – and that it is what they have in common that leads them to co-ordinate their actions. But unless they believe themselves to have something in common and treat this as the basis of their collective action, they are not a collectivity.

The distinction is brought out by Anthony Giddens's discussion of the kinds of attitudes members of the same class may have. He differentiates class awareness from class-consciousness. Of the former he writes: 'in so far as class is a structurated phenomenon, there will tend to exist a common awareness and acceptance of similar attitudes and beliefs, linked to a common style of life, among members of the class.' But this class awareness does not involve the recognition by those having it that they belong to the same class and are different from members of other classes. Class awareness stems from a shared class position but does not acknowledge its existence. Class-consciousness, however, does. Giddens distinguishes between three levels of class-consciousness – class identity, involving the minimal recognition of shared class membership, conflict consciousness, in which oppositions of interest between different classes are also acknowledged, and revolutionary class-consciousness, the '*recognition of the possibility of an overall reorganization in the institutional mediation of power . . . and a belief that such a reorganization can be brought about through class action*'.[2]

So unless class-consciousness in one of these three forms exists a class is not a collectivity. This is not to make class-consciousness a condition of the existence of class *tout court*. The Marxist theory of class treats it, as we saw in section 2.2, as an objective social relationship: classes may exist and class struggle go on without class-consciousness necessarily being manifest. For class struggle to occur some degree of collective action is necessary: members of the same class must co-ordinate their efforts in order either to increase or to reduce the rate of exploitation. But this need not involve recognition of shared class identity.

It is unlikely, however, that persistent class struggle would not lead to the development of some degree of class-consciousness. Through much of the history of exploitive societies relationships have in all probability been what Michael Mann describes as asymmetrical – that is, the dominant class has had a far higher degree of consciousness and organization than the dominated. Thus he argues that in classical Greece the slave-owners were a collectivity, 'fully conscious of their common position and of their need to defend its political conditions', while the slaves, possessing no common language or culture and scattered among typically small economic units, 'lacked the capacity for extensive organization'.[3] Slaves did not have the structural capacities necessary to form a collectivity capable of defending their interests.

So classes may but need not be collectivities. One should not, however, generalize from this case and say that collectivities necessarily emerge from the recognition of pre-existing social relationships. The formation of a collectivity may *create* a social relationship. The most important example is that of nations. Benedict Anderson defines a nation as 'an imagined political community': 'the members of even the smallest nation will not know most of their fellow-members, meet them, or even hear of them, yet in the mind of each lives the image of their communion'.[4] It is a necessary condition of the existence of a nation that its members believe that it exists. There are no nations in themselves, only nations for themselves (see further section 4.4).

The most important cases of collectivities are indeed classes and nations. Organizations embrace state apparatuses, political parties, trade unions. The difference between organizations and collectivities is that the former have a structure while the latter need not. In particular, any organization has some procedure through which decisions binding on all its members are arrived at. Of course, the formally laid-down procedures may not identify the real site of decision-making, and in any case decisions are often sabotaged or at least altered in their implementation; such issues form the focus of the sociological analysis of organizations.[5] Nevertheless, no organization can exist without some mechanism for determining how its members should act as members of that organization. A sense of collective identity by contrast does not entail the existence of any such procedure. A worker may refuse to cross a picket line because she believes in class solidarity without there having been any collective decision by the proletariat as a whole to support the strike.

There is all the same a close relationship between organizations and collectivities. A belief in shared identity may give rise to a particular organization in the way in which colonial liberation movements tended to arise out of a growing sense of national consciousness among the subjects of the European empires. Again, the formation of an organization may strengthen a shared identity, in the way in which the spread of trade unions promotes class-consciousness (at least in the forms of class identity and conflict consciousness). The kind of effect may be quite unintended: that the expansion of the English state contributed to the emergence of English nationalism was in no sense anticipated by such great state-builders as Henry II or Edward I. At the limit, however, the interaction between organization and collectivity may involve the former claiming the represent, embody, or even be the latter, in the way in which Stalinist parties identify themselves with the working class, or some liberation movements with the nation.

Various issues are raised by the foregoing discussion. The first concerns the very rationality of collective action. This takes the form above all of the free-rider problem, that is, of whether it is rational for any individual to engage in collective action even if the goal of that action is one he or she desires. Secondly, collectivities exist if and only if their members co-ordinate their actions in the light of the identity they believe themselves to share. This raises the issue of the beliefs agents have about society, in other words, the question of ideology. Thirdly, is there any priority of importance among different kinds of collectivity? Or, put more generally, is historical materialism correct to treat the division of society into classes as the most fundamental kind of social conflict?

The rest of this chapter is devoted to a discussion, inevitably fragmentary and inconclusive, of the second and third issues. The first I shall defer until section 5.3 I prefer to consider the free-rider problem in the context in which it has been posed mainly within Marxism, namely that of whether it is rational to participate is socialist revolution, and more generally in relation to the question of social transformation, which forms the focus of chapter 5. In the meantime I shall first examine the classical Marxist theory of ideology and whether, as it is sometimes taken to imply, the stability of class societies depends on the masses' belief in the legitimacy of the existing order (section 4.2). Having established the falsehood of this 'dominant ideology thesis', I then argue that a weaker version, which abandons the claim that ideology is necessarily false consciousness and treats it instead, following Gramsci, as the articulation of interests, can be sustained (section 4.3) The fact that ideologies typically address ('interpellate') agents as the bearers of various identities, leads to an extended historical discussion of whether the palpable reality of national identities and conflicts undermines the primacy accorded by Marxism to class antagonisms (section 4.4). The conclusion, that it does not, casts some light on the hoary old question of base and superstructure (section 4.5).

4.2 FALSEHOOD AND IDEOLOGY, I

Consider the following definition of ideology: an ideology is:

(1) a set of widely held beliefs;
(2) whose acceptance is socially caused;
(3) which are false;
(4) whose acceptance is in the interests of the ruling class.

I do not in fact think this is a satisfactory definition: (3) and (4) in particular are introduced less because I believe them to be true (since I do not) but rather in order to help focus discussion of how people engage in collective action.

(1) may seem innocuous, but in fact is inconsistent with one very influential Marxist conception of class-consciousness. Erik Olin Wright writes:

> There are two quite different usages of the expression 'class-consciousness' in the Marxist tradition. For some theorists it is seen as a counterfactual or imputed characteristic of classes as collective entities, whereas for others it is understood as a concrete attribute of human individuals as members of classes.[6]

Ideology is understood here very much in the second sense. The main example of the first is, of course, Lukács's conception of imputed class-consciousness. In *History and Class Consciousness* he tends to treat the proletariat as a collective subject endowed with consciousness in essentially the same way as individual subjects have beliefs and desires. This is, quite simply, wrong: classes are not supraindividual persons but groups of agents with a shared position in the relations of production, which *may* form themselves into collectivities, although there is nothing inevitable about this and indeed some classes, such as ancient slaves, may find the obstacles to doing so too great. Treating class-consciousness as something which can be imputed to agents simply by virtue of their objective relationship to the means of production massively understates the difficulties involves in subordinate classes actually becoming collectivities. Moreover, it mistakes the role played by class-consciousness in the process: it isn't the 'objective' property of the class but rather a means by which the latter forms itself into a collectivity.[7]

Ideology, then, is 'a concrete attribute of human individuals'. 'Understood in this way', says Wright, 'to study "consciousness" is to study a particular aspects of the mental life of individuals, namely, those elements of a person's subjectivity which are *discursively accessible to the individual's own awareness*.'[8] Persons hold ideological beliefs, not classes. However, they do so because of social mechanisms. Such is the claim made by (2). As Jon Elster puts it, 'the study of ideology purports to explain why many similarly situated individuals come to accept the same views, or to produce them simultaneously.'[9] Explaining why an individual holds ideological beliefs is a matter of analysing social processes, not of diagnosing intellectual error or individual pathology. Ideology is *social* consciousness.

It is also, according to (3), *false* consciousness. The concept of ideology indeed has its origins in Bacon's theory of idols, which was taken up by such *philosophes* as Helvétius and Holbach in their critique of the *préjugés*, above all religion, preventing mankind from recognizing its interests. The main agency through which false beliefs were inculcated into the masses was provided by the clergy. Marx took over and radicalized this analysis by inserting it into his general theory of class struggle. As Jorge Larrain puts it, 'ideology for Marx, as a distorted consciousness has a particular negative connotation whose two specific and connected features are, firstly, that it conceals social contradictions and, secondly, that it does it in the interest of the ruling class.' There is thus an intimate relation between (3) and (4). To quote Larrain again, ideology serves the interests of the dominant class 'not because it has been produced by the ideologists of the class – which may or may not be the case – but because the concealment of contradictions objectively works in favour of the dominant class's interest'.[10] The acceptance of ideological beliefs is in the interests of the ruling class *because* they are false, mystifying the reality of exploitation and oppression.

One cannot, however, use (4), the claim that ideological beliefs are in the ruling class's interest, to explain (1), their widespread acceptance. To do so would be to commit the fallacy of functional explanation, to account for a social phenomenon in terms of the benefits it brings.[11] We require some mechanism by virtue of which to explain how the prevailing ideology is one that benefits the ruling class. Marx in different writings offers two such mechanisms.

The first is given in this famous passage in *The German Ideology:*

The ideas of the ruling class are in every epoch the ruling ideas: i.e. the class which is the ruling *material* force of society is at the same time its ruling *intellectual* force. The class which has the means of material production at its disposal consequently also controls the means of mental production, so that the ideas of those who lack the means of mental production are on the whole subject to it.[12]

This analysis is evidently a development of the Enlightenment critique of religion as a conspiracy of priests and rulers to keep the masses in the dark. It differs primarily in rooting the generation of mass illusions in broader class relations. But it is vulnerable to the kind of objection made to the *philosophes*, namely that it treats the subordinate classes as passive receptacles of ideas inculcated in them from above. The effect, as Marx himself put it in the third 'Thesis on Feuerbach' is to 'divide society into two parts, one of which is superior to society', whether it be the priests or indeed those who seek to liberate the masses from their illusions.[13]

The second mechanism is not vulnerable to the same objection. It is provided by the theory of commodity fetishism in *Capital*. According to this theory the fact that under capitalism social relationships between producers are mediated by the exchange of commodities means that 'the definite social relation between men themselves . . . assumes here, for them, the fantastic form of a relation between things.'[14] As a result the historically specific phenomenon of capitalism is universalized, naturalized. There is thus a material basis for bourgeois ideology: the operation of the market economy itself induces ideological beliefs in the agents of capitalist production. Far therefore from depending on some conspiracy by the ruling class the acceptance of ideological beliefs is spontaneously generated by capitalist relations of production themselves. The trouble with this theory lies in its very stength: how, given the existence of commodity fetishism, can workers ever break free? The theory, at least in the version given here, involves a fallacy. For capitalist relations themselves to bring about the acceptance of ideological beliefs their appearance must admit of only one interpretation, namely that they are relations between things rather than social relationships. But this is not so: *all* theories are underdetermined by the evidence for them. Even if capitalist relations do present themselves in the naturalized, fetishized manner which Marx with some reason claims they do, there is an indefinite number of different ways of interpreting these same appearances.[15]

There is, however, a deeper difficulty with the definition of ideology we have been discussing. The passage cited above from *The German Ideology* is the *locus classicus* of what has come to be known as the dominant ideology thesis, summarized as follows by Nicholas Abercrombie, Stephen Hill and Bryan Turner:

> Through its control of ideological production, the dominant class is able to supervise the construction of a set of coherent beliefs . . . The dominant ideology penetrates and infects the consciousness of the working class, because the working class comes to see and to experience reality through the conceptual categories of the dominant class. The dominant ideology functions to incorporate the working class within a system which is, in fact, operating against the material interests of labour. The incorporation in turn explains the coherence and integration of capitalist society.[16]

Versions of the dominant ideology thesis are very widely held. Indeed, it is a characteristic feature of Western Marxism that it focuses on mechanisms of ideological domination as the principal means through which capitalist social formations are reproduced. But the thesis's influence stretches much further. Elster, for example, asserts that 'it *is* a massive fact of history that the values and the beliefs of the subjects tend to support the rule of the dominant groups.'[17]

Is it really? Immanuel Wallerstein thinks not:

> It is doubtful if very many governments in human history have been considered 'legitimate' by the majority of those exploited, oppressed and mistreated by their governments. The masses may be resigned to their fate, or sullenly restive, or amazed at their temporary good fortune, or actively insubordinate. But governments tend to be endured, not appreciated or admired or loved or even supported.[18]

Abercrombie, Hill and Turner challenge the dominant ideology thesis not simply in its Marxist form, but also in the version offered by Talcott Parsons, namely the idea that it is the normative integration of actors into society which explains social stability. They argue that the the penetration of the dominant ideology into the subordinate classes has generally been slight. The principal mechanisms of social control have been provided by armed coercion or what Marx called the 'silent compulsion of economic relations'. The main role of the dominant ideology has been to secure the cohesion and reproduction of the *ruling* class, not to integrate the masses within the existing social order.

Taken as claims about the past Abercrombie, Hill and Turner's arguments are extremely difficult to appraise, given that we posses records mainly of what members of the dominant class thought and said. However, historians in recent years have begun to investigate the popular culture of early modern Europe, perhaps the first period of which such studies would be possible. The results are fascinating and tend in favour of the critics of the dominant ideology thesis.

Thus Keith Thomas argues in his monumental study of popular belief in sixteenth- and seventeenth-century England against the view, held by Durkheim among others, that the spread of irreligion was a consequence of the Industrial Revolution: 'not enough justice has been done to the volume of apathy, heterodoxy and agnosticism which existed long before the onset of industrialism'. He shows that

> the hold of orthodox religion upon the English people had never been complete. Indeed it is problematical as to whether certain sections of the population at this time had any religion at all. Although complete statistics will never be obtainable, it can be confidently said that not all Tudor or Stuart Englishmen went to some kind of church, that many of those who did went with considerable reluctance, and that a certain proportion remained throughout their lives utterly ignorant of the tenets of Christian dogma.[19]

Thomas's *Religion and the Decline of Magic* is a macrostudy drawing on a vast range of sources. A similar picture of popular irreligion has been painted by a number of microstudies, above all by Carlo Ginzburg's *The Cheese and the Worms*, which is based on the trials by the Inquisition of Domenico Scandella, nicknamed Menocchio, a miller from Montereale in Fruili. Menocchio was burned at the stake at the end of the sixteenth century. His crime was to have expressed heretical religious beliefs, preferring a naturalistic pantheism to Christian theology's transcendent God. Menocchio's importance, Ginzburg argues, was that he 'projected onto the written page, elements taken from popular tradition. It is this tradition, deeply rooted in the European countryside, that explains the tenacious persistence of a peasant religion, intolerant of dogma and ritual, tied to the cycle of nature, and fundamentally pre-Christian'.[20]

There is, then, growing evidence of the limited degree to which Christianity penetrated the rural masses of pre-industrial Europe. Abercrombie, Hill and Turner indeed claim that

> Catholicism was the *minority* religion of Europe in the Middle Ages ... the urban elite was a practising, orthodox Catholic social group, but the rural majority preserved their pre-Christian beliefs, festivals and practices. The urban dominant class had their priests; the rural poor of Languedoc, Brittany, Lancashire, Yorkshire and Norfolk had their sorcerers, witchcraft, pagan rites and folk culture.[21]

How is this phenomenon to be interpreted? Thomas in his discussion of such pre-Christian beliefs and practices as astrology and magic tends to invoke anthropological and sociological theory, explaining them in functional terms, pointing to the degree of predictability and control they offered over a natural and social environment which was dangerous and uncertain. Their decline is correlatively accounted for in terms of the way in which a variety of changes ranging from improvements in communications to the introduction of insurance made reliance on magic and the like redundant. In a perceptive review of *Religion and the Decline of Magic* Edward Thompson challenges Thomas's functionalism, arguing that the prevalence of pre-Christian beliefs and practices must be understood as evidence of resistance on the part of the peasants and artisans of early modern Europe to the dominant class and their ideology. Thus:

> In so far as the common people sensed that they were being 'got at' by the Church, to that degree the elements of an anti-culture will have formed, dissimulating these doctrines, rejecting those, knitting together Christian ritual with surviving pagan beliefs, translating doctrine into a symbolism more appropriate to their own life experience.[22]

Thompson's argument focuses attention on the extent to which the differences between popular and 'high' cultures became a *locus* of class struggle in what Peter Burke calls the 'Triumph of Lent', 'the systematic attempt made by some of the educated . . . to change the attitudes and values of the rest of the population' in the sixteenth and seventeenth centuries, an attempt common to both the Protestant Reformation and the Catholic Counter-Reformation.[23] Ginzburg argues that this attempt was fundamentally a response to the German Peasants' War and the Anabaptists' reign in Münster in the 1520s and 1530s, which brought home 'the necessity of reconquering, ideologically as well as physically, the masses threatening to break loose from every form of control from above':

> This renewed effort to achieve hegemony took various forms in different parts of Europe, but the evangelization of the countryside by the Jesuits and the capillary religious organization based on the family, achieved by the Protestant churches, can be traced to a single current. In terms of repression, the intensification of witchcraft trials ands the rigid control over the marginal groups such as vagabonds and gypsies corresponded to it. Menocchio's case should be seen against this background of repression and the effacement of popular culture.[24]

To talk of the 'effacement of popular culture' is almost certainly too strong: other historians such as Burke and Thompson point to survivals of pre-Christian beliefs and practices well into the twentieth century. Nevertheless, the very sources of Ginzburg's book (and of his earlier *The Night Battles*) indicate the extent to which we depend for our knowledge of popular beliefs on institutions such as the Inquisition and witchcraft trials whose purpose was precisely to regulate and alter these beliefs. Michel Foucault has focused attention on the emergence at the end of the eighteenth century of new forms of power which he calls the disciplines. He contrasts them with the spectacular and barbaric executions characteristic of absolutism, a form of power which 'in absence of continuous supervision . . . was recharged in the ritual display of its reality as "super-power".' The disciplines, represented by such typical institutions of modernity as the prison, the factory and the hospital, involve instead the regulated and systematic supervision of individual behaviour thereby penetrating 'down to the finest grain of the social body'.[25] It seems plausible to regard the efforts to 'reform' religious belief and social conduct in early modern Europe as precursors of this more intrusive and intensive exercise of social power.

Anthony Giddens has the disciplines in mind when he writes of 'surveillance . . . the accumulation of "information" – symbolic materials which can be stored by an agency or collectivity', and 'the supervision of the activities of subordinates by their superiors within a collectivity'. He argues that 'as an integral and pervasive element of social integration, surveillance in each sense only becomes of major importance with the advent of capitalism.' In pre-capitalist class societies, the extraction of surplus-labour depended on 'extra-economic coercion', the armed force of the state or of local landowners. 'The power of those who needed to extract coercively taxation, or other forms of tribute or services from populations subject to their rule, did not penetrate many aspects of daily life, which were nourished from other sources.' To put it in the terms provided by David Lockwood, system-integration depended on the military power of the ruling class. Social integration, involving the existence of shared beliefs and traditions, was sharply separate, operating chiefly at the level of local peasant communities and largely ignored by the dominant class. Capitalist exploitation, however, depends primarily on the economic pressures on workers to sell their labour-power and its rate is generally directly related to the level of labour productivity. The systematic supervision of the subordinate class both inside and outside the process of production therefore becomes of much greater importance to the exploiters. 'The "state" is a much more intrusive and comprehensive set of institutions in capitalist than in class-divided [i.e. pre-capitalist class] societies, so far as those subject to its administration internally are concerned.'[26]

Gidden's analysis is illuminating. It finds support from Michael Mann's discussion of the limitations of what he calls '*infrastructural power*', i.e. 'the capacity to actually penetrate society and to implement logistically political decisions' of that apparently most formidable of pre-capitalist states, the empire:

> The empire . . . was still a relatively fragile interaction network lacking intense control over its subjects. . . . Little was required of the masses besides regularly handing over payments in kind and in labour. Control over them, though savage, was erratic. More was required of the dispersed ruling group, but it was not uncongenial to them. The empire was not territorial, nor was it unitary. It was a system of *federal domination* by a king or emperor through provincial, marcher, and even 'foreign' rulers and elites. This was for fundamentally logistical reasons: I calculated that no conqueror, no matter how formidable, could organize, control and supply his troops and administrative officials on a routine basis over more than an eighty- to ninety-kilometer route march. The king or emperor used his professional army in reserve to dominate, to cow. But everyone knew that it would take a formidable logistical exercise to employ. As long as local elites handed over tax or tribute their local control would not be interfered with.[27]

In the light of these arguments we can see why what Mann calls '*intensive power* . . . the ability to organize tightly and command a high level of mobilization or commitment from the participants' is a feature primarily of capitalist societies.[28] It was only with the advent of modernity that the ruling class acquired both an interest and, increasingly, the means (thanks to a range of innovations ranging from printing through the railway to the modern mass media) to penetrate the daily life of the masses. We can see this happening in a variety of ways. For example, Edward Thompson has pointed to the replacement of the 'task-oriented' conception of time inseparable from the irregular patterns of work dependent ultimately on the cycles of nature by time thought of as linear and homogeneous, 'time-measurement as a means of labour-exploitation' or, more crudely, time as money.[29] But this growth in the surveillance of the subordinate classes might lead one to conclude that while the dominant ideology thesis may be false when applied to pre-capitalist societies it is true of the capitalist mode of production.

Such a conclusion would be mistaken. A number of studies of

working-class consciousness have been made in the past three decades
which provide little support for any belief in an all-pervading
dominant ideology. Mann summarizes the findings of a number of
British and American surveys dating from the height of the post-war
boom in the 1950s and 1960s as follows:

1 Value-consensus does not exist to any significant extent;
2 there is a greater degree of consensus among the middle class than
   among the working class;
3 the working class is more likely to support deviant values if those
   values relate to concrete everyday life or to vague populist
   concepts than if they relate to an abstract political philosophy;
4 working-class individuals also exhibit less internal *consistency* in
   their values than middle-class people.

He suggests that the relative quiescence of the Western working class
'might be more convincingly explained by their pragmatic acceptance
of specific roles than by any positive normative commitment to
society'.[30]

Elsewhere Mann argues that, 'forced to alienate his own productive
powers in return for economic rewards, the worker develops a
dualistic consciousness, in which control and money, work and non-
work, become separated.' The result is 'nothing more nor less than
the narrowing down of conflict to aggressive economism and
defensive control'. Class-consciousness never develops further than
what we called conflict consciousness following Giddens (see section
4.1 above). Lacking any conception of an alternative society to
capitalism, workers focus on the narrowly economic struggle over
wages. 'Surges of class-consciousness are continually undercut by
economism, and capitalism survives.'[31]

This general thesis has found support and been enriched by a
number of detailed analyses. Huw Beynon's celebrated study of shop
stewards at Ford Halewood at the end of the 1960s is concerned with
the most important form of conflict consciousness found in the
British working class, 'factory class-consciousness':

> It understands class relationships in terms of their direct manifestation
> in conflict between the bosses and the workers within the factory. It is
> rooted in the workplace where the struggles are fought out over the
> control of the job and the 'rights' of managers and workers. Inasmuch
> as it concerns itself with exploitation and power it contains definite
> political elements. But it is a politics of the factory. . . . In its least
> developed form it is revealed in sporadic bloody-mindedness and
> 'malingering' – the 'fuck 'em' attitude that most managers are familiar

with and find distasteful. The underlying structure of this view is not radically different from that which underpinned the consciousness of the stewards at Halewood.[32]

Halewood is well known as a militant car plant, and Beynon shows how the stewards were able to pursue quite sophisticated strategies in response to management initiatives. Their Achilles' heel lay in the fact that theirs was a *factory* class-consciousness, centred on the immediate conflict within the process of production and largely ignoring the wider structures of social power concentrated in the state. As Beynon puts it, their understanding of conflict within the factory 'did not extend to a developed form of political consciousness, rather it represented a very direct, common-sense reflection of workers' experience within the car plant.'[33] They thus lacked the essential constituent of revolutionary class-consciousness, a view of how collective action could transform society.

In this respect the Halewood stewards were in the same position as the much less militant workers employed by 'ChemCo' and studied by Theo Nichols and Peter Armstrong: 'The Chemco work-force, at least for most of the time, is characterized by the fatalism of men who do not control, nor see any way of controlling, the world in which they live.' But this fatalism did not spring from normative integration into capitalism. 'These workers can see imperfections, illogicalities, differences in living standards, can even think sometimes of better societies. What they lack is the faith or certainty that these better societies *are* possible.' Consequently, 'the real triumph of capitalist hegemony is seen in the fact that, for the most part, these workers do not affirm *or* deny its values. For them, capitalism is just part of an unalterable order of things (not necessarily a proper or just one).'[34] Thus, as Therborn puts it, 'resignation, deference, and accommodation . . . in many or most bourgeois-democratic countries, are probably more important components of consensus than is a sense of representation.'[35]

4.3 FALSEHOOD AND IDEOLOGY, II

The dominant ideology thesis must, then, be accounted false (although a weaker version, as we shall see, can be defended). Does the dominant ideology thesis in its demise take the theory of ideology with it? Abercrombie, Hill and Turner seem at times to imply as much.[36] This iconoclasm is a refreshing corrective to Western Marxism's obsession with ideology, but it could have misleading consequences. A main thrust of this book has been to insist that human beings must be seen as agents, conscious actors moved by beliefs and desires. Further, we suggested in section 4.1 that the formation of collectivities depends critically on the beliefs that agents have about their social identity.

The analysis of ideology is essential to social theory, provided that 'ideology' is understood as, in Marx's words, 'the legal, political, religious, artistic or philosophic – in short ideological forms in which men become conscious of this conflict [i.e. that between the forces and relations of production] and fight it out'.[37] Such an understanding of ideology implies rejecting conditions (3) and (4) of the definition given in section 4.2. Ideological beliefs need not be false, nor does this acceptance necessarily benefit the ruling class. Instead we should follow Therborn in using 'ideology' simply to 'refer to that aspect of the human condition under which human beings live their lives as conscious actors in a world that makes sense to them in different ways'.[38]

Conceiving ideology as false consciousness is implied by the claim involved in the dominant ideology thesis that class societies survive by virtue of the acceptance by the subordinate class of the false belief that their exploitation is just. Once we see that the claim itself is false there is no need to identify ideology with illusion. Ideological beliefs are, like all beliefs, either true or false, but the truth-value of a belief does not enter into the criteria to be used for distinguishing between the ideological and the non-ideological. The epistemological notion of ideology as false consciousness, deriving ultimately from the Enlightenment critique of religious *préjugé*, must finally be rejected.[39]

Such a move has the positive effect of allowing us to broaden the study of ideology by relating it to that of practical consciousness in general. Anthony Giddens has stressed what he calls the 'knowledge-ability' of human agents, the fact that the members of a society know far more about the nature of the world in which they live than most social scientists are prepared to give them credit for.[40] There are indeed deep philosophical reasons why this should be so, as Graham Macdonald and Philip Pettit bring out when discussing Donald Davidson's Principle of Charity:

> The actions which the beliefs [i.e. those which inform practical activity] are invoked to explain are people's everyday, more or less successful exchanges with one another and with their environment; actions such as those of finding food, making deals, building huts, and so on. The success of these exchanges cannot be generally put down to coincidence and fortune. But if we are to make the success intelligible without invoking the forces of accident, we must suppose that the beliefs underlying the actions are true: were they false, success would be the

product of accident. Thus we find in the beliefs informing practical activity a set of beliefs in which the interpreter may safely assume a preponderance of truth.[41]

Macdonald and Pettit's examples of practical activity imply a consensual view of social practice as the co-operative pursuit of shared goals. What happens once we drop this picture, and focus instead on the salience in social life of conflicts of interest deriving from agents' different positions within exploitive relations of production? We do not therefore enter the world of false consciousness. Agents on both sides of the class divide are likely to have many true beliefs concerning the conflictual relationship they find themselves in. We have seen, for example, the evidence that many British workers have a lively sense of the antagonisms between them and management. But if anything the ruling class is likely to be *more* aware than the subordinate classes of the existence of social contradictions.

Foucault has written of the 'rationality of power' as that of 'tactics which are often perfectly explicit at the limited level where they are inscribed – local cynicism of power', of 'talkative tactics whose "inventors" . . . are often without hypocrisy'.[42] Historians have been able to uncover documents in which policy-makers discuss the alternative strategies available to them with astonishing lucidity. I shall take just one example, from the crucial period betwen the end of the Boer War and the beginning of the First World War during which many of the institutions of modern South Africa were established. Liberal commentators and Weberian social scientists tend to see the system of racial domination in that country as a consequence of ethnic divisions, i.e. those between black and white, Afrikaner and English-speaking whites, Zulu, Xhosa and other African 'tribal' groupings. Yet in the period between 1901 and 1914 leading ruling-class figures, particularly those around the British High Commissioner, Lord Milner, and in the great mining houses, were ready to discuss the case for a set of institutional arrangements broadly similar to what later came to be known as 'separate development', in remarkably utilitarian terms.

Thus a leading white 'liberal', Howard Pim, proposed a rationale for keeping Africans in tribal Reserves (the forerunners of the modern 'Homelands') rather than in urban townships ('locations') in a manner strongly reminiscent of more recent Marxist analyses:

In a Reserve . . . the native lives under natural conditions which he understands and has created for himself. Look forward a few years. For a time the location consists of able-bodied people, but they grow older, they become ill, they become disabled – who is to support them?

They commit offences – who is to control them? The Reserve is a sanatorium where they can recruit; if they are disabled they remain there. Their own tribal system keeps them under discipline, and if they become criminals there is not the slightest difficulty in bringing them to justice. All this absolutely without expense to the white community . . . As time goes on these location burdens will increase, and the proportion of persons in the location really able to work will still further diminish. The number of actual workers, taking the less healthy location conditions into account, will therefore be absolutely less than in a population of equal numbers in a Reserve, and this difference in the number of workers will in itself also go some distance to make up for the smaller accessibility of the Reserve native . . . it is a fair assumption that at the outside one-fifth of the location population (I take it that the location consists of families) is able to work. This means that the wages paid by the employers will have to be sufficient to support four other persons besides the workman. Can it be supposed that this will lead to a reduction in native wages?[43]

There is little evidence of false consciousness there. But do not such considerations lead one towards a conspiracy theory of history? No. In the first place, no person or collectivity has unlimited powers. Agents may indeed conspire, but they may not be able to achieve their common objective. Secondly, even if they do succeed, their action may have unintended consequences which undermine their achievement. Conspiracies exist: the mistake lies in believing that they always (or even usually) succeed. This doesn't mean that one should fall into the implicit functionalism espoused by Foucault, who seems to have believed that conscious actions were necessarily self-defeating, weaving through their interaction a pattern quite different from that sought after by individual agents but nevertheless possessing a rationality and logic of its own.[44] Conspiracies sometimes succeed: the state and capital did remould South African society in the early years of this century along the lines broadly envisaged by Pim. At the same time, there are no mechanisms which guarantee that unintended consequences will necessarily serve to perpetuate prevailing power-relations. There is much evidence that the creation of the Reserves itself led rapidly to the proletarianization of the African population and therefore to the emergence of the black urban working class which today threatens the existence of both apartheid and capitalism in South Africa.[45]

Does not the claim that agents generally have many true beliefs about social contradictions undermine condition (2) of the definition of ideology given at the beginning of section 4.2, namely that ideological beliefs are socially caused? To see why this is not so, let us consider Elster's discussion of ideology. He defends a fairly traditional account of ideology: not only, as we saw in section 4.2, does he accept the dominant ideology thesis but he also identifies ideology with false consciousness. The argument goes like this. 'A belief is rationally caused if (i) the causes of the belief are reasons for holding it and (ii) the reasons cause the beliefs *qua* reasons, not in some accidental manner.' The social causes of beliefs do not generally cause them in this way and so one must assume that 'a socially caused belief will not be rationally grounded.' Furthermore, 'there is a presumption that true beliefs are rationally grounded', which, in conjunction with the preceding steps, 'creates a case for the falsity of socially caused beliefs'.[46]

Elster distinguishes between two kinds of social causation of beliefs, interest-explanation and position-explanation, that is, respectively:

> explanations that refer to the *interests* of the believer (or some other agent) and those that refer to his economic or social position ... All position explanations are causal, but interest-explanations may be causal as well as functional. A belief, that is, may be explained by the fact that it is *shaped* by interests as well as by the fact that it *serves* certain interests.[47]

Let us ignore functional interest-explanations, i.e. those which account for ideological beliefs in terms of the interests they serve. Elster's presumption that socially caused beliefs are not rationally grounded, combined with his search for 'microfoundations', leads him to draw on work on cognitive psychology and explain such beliefs as the result either of the interference of psychic drives in the process of belief-formation or of distortions in that process itself.[48] There is no reason to join Elster in this collapse into psychologism.

In the first place, the opposition between position- and interest-explanations seems overstated. If interests are related to agents' position in the relations of production (and even if the account given in section 3.5 is wrong any Marxist theory of interests must assert as much), then it does not seem that any sharp distinction between position and interests can be made out. The concept of interests, as I have suggested, concerns the interaction between agents' beliefs and desires and their objective social positions. In his discussion of ideology, however, Elster identifies interests with agents' subjective wants, or indeed with the drives underlying these wants.

Secondly, the 'presumption that true beliefs are rationally grounded' is quite untenable. As William Shaw puts it, 'it is an elementary truth of logical analysis that the origin of a belief is not relevant to its evaluation as true or false.'[49] Thirdly, and more positively, why should one presume that socially caused beliefs are not rationally grounded? Agents seeking to pursue their interests may form many beliefs concerning the nature of society and their position within it. They may do so quite reflectively, but the resulting beliefs are socially caused in the sense that their formulation reflects the position, needs and purposes of the agents concerned. Elster might object that to describe such beliefs as socially caused is to deprive the notion of causation of any meaning. But he would be wrong: the beliefs concerned are socially caused in the sense that, were those who hold them not in a certain position in the relations of production, they would probably not have come to accept them. Nevertheless, there is no reason to assume that the acceptance of these beliefs necessarily involved some interference with processes of rational reflection. To suppose otherwise implies, surely falsely, that knowledge can never be perspectival, formulated within a framework shaped by specific interests and purposes.[50]

The primary sense in which ideologies are socially caused is that they are articulations of interests. They are attempts to give conscious expression to the needs of agents occupying particular positions within the relations of production. Since interests differ and conflict, so too will ideologies. Does this mean that all ideologies are true, in a reversal of the false consciousness thesis? No, for at least three reasons. First, a particular ideology may not succeed in its attempt to articulate the interests of a given class. Precisely because they depend on the objective structure of class relations, interests are by no means easy to ascertain. The class struggle, I suggested in section 3.5, is, among other things, the process through which agents seek to establish what their interests are. The formulation of ideologies is itself part of this process.

Secondly, viewing society from a particular class position involves having a certain perspective on the world, which may set limits to what one sees or does not see. This need not involve any interference with the cognitive processes of belief-formation. Indeed, the most interesting Marxist position-explanations, those by Marx himself of political economy in *Capital* and *Theories of Surplus-Value*, and by Lukács of the 'antinomies of bourgeois thought' in *History and Class Consciousness*, focus the way in which the most theoretically sophisticated articulations of capitalist class-interests, precisely because of their sophistication, are likely to involve characteristic blindnesses. These centre on the mistaken treatment of capitalist rationality as the ultimate form of rationality, with which what Giddens identifies as the 'principal ideological forms', '*the represen-*

tation of sectional interests as universal ones ... the denial or transmutation of contradictions ... [and] ... the naturalization of the present', are closely associated.[51] Such forms are likely to be found in articulations of the interests of a class whose domination is of necessity historically limited and transitory.

Thirdly, 'ideologies actually operate in a state of *disorder*', as Therborn puts it.[52] The fundamental reason for this is that it is through the class struggle that agents come to articulate their interests. The most important discussion of these questions remains that by Gramsci. His pragmatist epistemology led him to reject the problematic of false consciousness. Discourse generally is for Gramsci the articulation of interests: 'Our knowledge of things is nothing more than ourselves, our needs and interests.' This preoccupation with practical consciousness led him to argue that there is to be found in the consciousness of subordinate classes in general and the proletariat in particular 'the co-existence of two conceptions of the world, one affirmed in words and the other displayed in effective action', by which Gramsci meant especially class struggle.[53]

This state of affairs

> signifies that the social group in question may indeed have its own
> conception of the world, even if only embryonic; a conception which
> manifests itself in action, but occasionally and in flashes – when, that
> is, the group is acting as an organic totality. But this same group has,
> for reasons of submission and intellectual subordination, adopted a
> conception which is not its own but is borrowed from another group;
> and it affirms this conception verbally and believes itself to be
> following it, because this is the conception which it follows in 'normal
> times' – that is when its conduct is not independent and autonomous,
> but submissive and subordinate.[54]

The result is that

> the active man-in-the-mass [i.e. the worker] has a practical activity, but
> has no theoretical consciousness of his practical activity, which
> nonetheless involves understanding the world in so far as it transforms
> it. One might almost say that he has two theoretical consciousnesses
> (or one contradictory consciousness): one which is implicit in his
> activity and which in reality unites him with all his fellow-workers in the
> practical transformation of the real world; and one, superficially
> explicit or verbal, which he has inherited from the past and uncritically
> absorbed. But this verbal conception is not without consequences. It
> holds together a specific social group, it influences moral conduct and
> the direction of will, with varying efficacity but often powerfully
> enough to produce a situation in which the contradictory state of

consciousness does not permit any action, any decision or any choice, and produces a condition of moral and political passivity.[55]

It is not clear how a conception of the world can be said to be implicit in the practice of a given class. I prefer to say that, in this case, workers form beliefs which seek to articulate their interests as an exploited class. Thus amended, Gramsci's concept of contradictory consciousness is of fundamental importance, since it provides a theoretical interpretation of the phenomenon of dual consciousness discussed in section 4.2. The inconsistencies in working-class attitudes noted by Michael Mann are a reflection of class struggle. The 'means of mental production' – the education system, the mass media etc. – do not so much induce in workers a systematically false consciousness as prevent the formation of a coherent revolutionary class-consciousness, in particular by impeding the kind of theoretical reflection which would be necessary to remove inconsistencies and to arrive at a coherent analysis of existing society.

A weaker version of the dominant ideology thesis can therefore be sustained. The dominant ideology is dominant in the sense that the ruling class will seek to prevent subordinate classes from developing an ideology which systematically challenges its right to rule. Chris Harman puts it very well:

> Of course, all sorts of *subordinate* ideologies exist, which express direct experiences of subordinate classes. But *any* ruling class takes action the moment these begin to generalize into an alternative world-view that challenges its hegemony. For example, look at the attitude of the mediaeval Catholic Church towards 'heretical' movements – seeking to absorb some elements in them (the Franciscans etc.) but to persecute others.[56]

Gramsci himself suggests that 'the contradictory state of consciousness' among workers will itself create 'a condition of moral and political passivity'. While this may be so, one should not ignore various devices through which contradictions may apparently be eliminated. Of these the most important is the concept of the nation. The idea that different classes share a common interest as members of the same nation has the particular virtue that it is consistent with a limited degree of social conflict. Nationalist ideology need not deny the existence of class antagonisms. It merely insists that these are secondary compared with the shared identity of all citizens, whatever their class position. Nationalism thus accommodates a degree of social criticism: indeed, one of the oldest themes of English radicalism is that the ruling class are an alien breed, an idea which still survives in the notion that Thatcherism is the instrument of American capital and/or the City.[57]

These remarks on nationalism are, as they stand, pretty functionalist, since they concentrate on its effects, i.e. the containment of class antagonisms. To go beyond such a form of explanation requires a shift in theoretical focus. So far I have treated ideologies purely from a cognitive point of view, that is, as bodies of assertoric sentences whose acceptance or rejection agents justify on the grounds of their truth or falsehood. But the concept of interpellation requires us to view them as a different kind of speech-act, which subsumes the individual under a particular form of identity depending on the manner in which it addresses him or her.

Althusser introduces the concept of interpellation in his celebrated essay on ideology:

> Ideology 'acts' or 'functions' in such a way that it 'recruits' subjects among the individuals (it recruits them all), 'or 'transforms' the individuals into subjects (it transforms them all) by the very precise operation which I have called *interpellation* or hailing, and which can be imagined along the lines of the most commonplace everyday police (or other) hailing: 'Hey, you there!'

> Assuming that the theoretical scene I have imagined takes place on the street, the hailed individual will turn round. By this mere one-hundred-and-eighty degree physical conversion, he becomes a *subject*. Why? Because he has recognized that the hail was 'really' addressed to him, and that 'it was *really him* who was hailed' (and not someone else).[58]

Althusser's thesis that interpellation transforms individuals into subjects is closely bound up with the claim that the form of subjectivity is itself essential to the functioning of ideology, where the latter is conceived as individuals' imaginary relation to their real conditions of existence. To accept this would be to reduce agency, as it is understood in this book, to an ideological illusion. Therborn tends towards a similar approach, as when he writes that 'to conceive a text or an utterance as ideology is to focus on the way it operates in the formation and tranformation of human subjectivity.'[59] Such formulations are redolent of the oversocialized conception of human nature which, as we saw in section 3.5, Therborn shares with Parsons and, indeed with Althusser, in which individuals are not agents but rather raw material which ideology transforms into subjects ready to submit to their predestined role in the relations of production. That such a view predominates in Althusser's extremely functionalist account of interpellation is evident from passages such as the following: 'the individual *is interpellated as a (free) subject in order that he shall submit freely to the commandments of the Subject, i.e. in order that he shall (freely) accept his subjection.*'[60]

A different and much more helpful version of interpellation is sometimes offered by Therborn:

> The ideological interpellations unceasingly constitute and reconstitute who we are. A single human being may act as an almost unlimited number of subjects, and in the course of a single human life a large number of subjectivities are in fact acted out. In any situation, particularly in a complex modern society, a given human being usually has several subjectivites, although as a rule only one at a time. Ideologies differ, compete, and clash not only in what they say about the world, but also in telling us who we are, in the kind of subject they interpellate . . . For example, when a strike is called, a worker may be addressed as a member of the working class, as a union member, as a mate of his fellow workers, as the long-faithful employee of a good employer, as a father or mother, as an honest worker, as a good citizen, as a Communist or an anti-Communist, as a Catholic, and so on. The kind of address accepted – 'Yes, that's how I am, that's me!' – has important implications for how one acts in response to the strike call.[61]

Ideologies do not here interpellate us as subjects or even the bearers of Parsonian social roles. Rather, a particular ideology invites us to accept a particular kind of social identity. Moreover, since 'ideologies differ, compete, and clash' the individual has some choice as to *which* identity he or she will accept – worker, citizen, Catholic etc. No longer, as in Althusser's account of interpellation, does the naked individual confront a super-Subject (for example, the policeman as representative of social order). Nor does acceptance of the address necessarily imply subjection. It can, indeed, be a liberation: consider, for example, the difference between the interpellations 'black' and 'Negro' in the US of the 1960s. Those who accepted the first form of address participated implicitly in a reversal of values ('Black is Beautiful') and endorsed the need for a political struggle against the racist power-structure of American society.

The kind of ideological struggle which leads to the contradictory consciousness discussed by Gramsci involves then not simply a confrontation of different views of the world but also a conflict of interpellations, in which people are invited to accept different social identities. Dual consciousness within the Western working class is characterized by the acceptance of two identities – as worker and as citizen, as member of a class and as member of a nation-state. These identities imply an involvement in different kinds of social conflicts, the class struggle between capital and labour and the power struggle between nation-states. We must now consider the relationship between these two forms of conflict.

4.4 NATION, STATE AND MILITARY POWER

One of modernity's bigger surprises – and not only for Marxists – has been the endurance and depth of pervasive national, racial and tribal divisions. The history of capitalism since 1848 has not borne out Marx's and Engels's confident assertion in the *Communist Manifesto* that 'national differences and antagonisms between peoples are daily more and more vanishing, owing to the development of the bourgeoisie, to freedom of commerce, to the world market, to uniformity in the mode of production and in the conditions of life corresponding thereunto.'[62] It has consequently become commonplace to the point of tedium to say that historical materialism ignores, or at least is incapable of explaining national conflict.

An interesting version of this criticism is made by G. A. Cohen, in a way which connects with the question of social identity broached in our discussion of interpellation in section 4.3. Cohen objects to Marx's philosophical anthropology because it treats human beings as essentially producers who realize themselves by the full use of their capacities:

> In his anti-Hegelian, Feuerbachian affirmation of the radical objectivity of matter, Marx focused on the relation of the subject to an object that is no way subject, and, as time went on, he came to neglect the subject's relation to itself, and that aspect of the subject's relation to others which is mediated (that is, indirect) form of relation to itself. He rightly reacted against Hegel's extravagant representation of all reality as ultimately an expression of self, but he overreacted, and he failed to do justice to the self's irreducible interest in a definition of itself, and to the social manifestations of that interest.[63]

As it stands, Cohen's criticism of Marx's conception of human nature amounts to an acknowledgement of the dimension stressed by the hermeneutic tradition, of the need human beings have for an identity involving membership of a community typically constituted by enduring tradition. He goes on, however, to connect this need to national and racial identities:

> I claim, then, that there is a human need to which Marxist observation is commonly blind, one different from and as deep as the need to

cultivate one's talents. It is the need to be able to say not what I can do
but who I am, satisfaction of which has historically been found in
identification with others in a shared culture based on nationality, or
race, or some slice or amalgam thereof.[64]

Cohen is probably right in claiming that such a need exists. He may
also be right to suggest that nationalism is one way of fulfilling this
need, a need bound up with enduring features of human existence, the
unavoidable contingencies of birth, suffering, bereavement and
death.[65] If, however, he is suggesting that what we might call the need
for identity *explains* the existence of national divisions, then he is
quite wrong. Such a view (it is not clear whether Cohen holds it) lends
itself to the belief that nations are pregiven natural entities.

Ernest Gellner, no friend of Marxism, rightly repudiates this myth,
arguing that 'nations are not inscribed into the nature of things', nor
are nation-states 'the manifest ultimate destiny of ethnic or cultural
groups', but rather 'the crystallization of new units, suitable for the
conditions now prevailing, though admittedly using as their raw
material the cultural, historical and other inheritances from the
prenationalist world'. The formation of a nation consists in 'the
general imposition of a high culture on society, where previously low
cultures had taken up the lives of the majority'. This involves 'the
establishment of an anonymous, impersonal society' consisting of
'mutually substitutable, atomized individuals' bound together by 'a
school-mediated, academy-supervised idiom, codified for the requirements of reasonably precise bureaucratic and technical communication'.[66]

Gellner thus emphasizes the historical novelty, indeed the modernity
of national identities, rather than their primordial character. Their
formation is, he argues, a consequence of 'the imperative of exo-
socialization', by which he means 'the production and reproduction
of men outside the local intimate unit' which formed the core of pre-
modern societies. And 'exo-socialization' itself springs from the needs
of industrial society for a homogeneous, socially mobile and educated
population, in comparison with the stable hierarchies and fixed
identities of agrarian societies.[67]

There are two obvious difficulties with Gellner's analysis. The first
lies in the concept of 'industrial society'. Here he follows a
sociological tradition founded by Saint-Simon in characterizing
modernity by the kind of technology used rather than the social
relations prevailing within it. This leads Gellner to discover an
immutable logic of industrialization governing all societies such that
'in the long run . . . we shall be all affluent.'[68] Secondly, to explain

nationalism by the 'imperative of exo-socialization' is to commit the functionalist fallacy. This is far from denying any merit to Gellner's discussion of nationalism. Indeed, its defects can partly be remedied by developing the distinction drawn by Giddens between 'class-divided societies' where surplus-extraction does not require the penetration of the everyday lives of the masses and capitalism where it does (see section 4.2) above). But this modification does not meet the change of functionalism. A satisfactory explanation of nationalism must involve an account of the historical processes through which national identities replaced the old local unities.

And here we run into an additional problem for Marxism. The formation of nationality typically involves the incorporation of existing political and cultural units into the territory of a centralized and bureaucratic state and their forced assimilation to the culture usually of the class which dominates that state. In other words, nationalism is about the formation of *nation-states*. We now live in a world of such states. It is a fundamental theme of contemporary historical sociology that the relations between states, and in particular their military rivalries, are irreducible to class divisions and therefore cannot be explained by Marxism.[69]

For example, Theda Skocpol writes that 'the state . . . is fundamentally Janus-faced, with an intrinsically dual anchorage in class-divided socio-economic structures and an international system of states.' Thus 'the international state system as a transnational structure of military competition was not originally created by capitalism. Throughout modern world history, it represents an analytically autonomous level of transnational reality – *interdependent* in its structure and dynamics with world capitalism, but not reducible to it.'[70]

Giddens makes a similar point and generalizes from it to the effect that 'Marxism has no tradition of theorizing violence either as an integral and chronic feature of repression, or as the "world violence" of the contemporary system of power blocs and nation-states.' This criticism is plainly connected with the claim that the extraction of surplus-labour is not the only, or even the primary form of exploitation:

Certain fundamental forms of exploitation do not originate with capitalism, or even with class divisions more generally. . . . There are three main axes of exploitation of this sort, in my opinion. These are exploitative relations between states, particularly in respect of control of the means of violence; exploitative relations between ethnic groups; and exploitative relations between the sexes.[71]

The most substantial attempt to make out this kind of argument is likely to be Michael Mann's major three-volume study, *The Sources of Social Power*. In the first volume, published in 1986, Mann identifies four sources of social power, conceived as organizational means for achieving human objectives. These are ideological, economical, political and military relationships. One of Mann's chief contentions is that social theory should not concern itself with treating one of these sources as primary, explaining the others in terms of it, but rather with analysing the concrete ways in which the four kinds of social relationship interact within particular power-organizations.[72]

Perhaps the most distinctive aspect of Mann's first volume is its stress on the importance of military power: I have already cited one such analysis, of the logistically limited reach of pre-modern states, in section 4.2. Mann criticizes Marx because 'his general theory insisted on regarding militarism as parasitic and unproductive.' Mann offers a number of examples which show that this is not so: in the ancient monarchies of the Near East, the classical Greek *poleis* and the Roman Empire military power stimulated economic growth: 'But if militarism and states can be productive, their resulting forms may themselves causally determine further economic development, and so economic forms will also have military and political preconditions'.[73]

These themes – the specificity of military power and of competition between nation-states, the plurality of power-relations and their irreducibility to class antagonisms – have a distinct intellectual lineage, originating as they do in Weber's writings. The stress laid by the 'bourgeois Marx' on the *Machtstaat* seems at times to violate his own methodological canons by according primacy to military competition between nation-states, as in Weber's 1895 Freiburg address: 'Processes of economic development are in the final analysis also *power-struggles*, and the ultimate and decisive interests at whose service economic policy must place itself are the interests of national *power*.'[74] Underlying such assertions is the ultimately Nietzschean claim that social relations are fundamentally relations of power: 'The structure of dominancy and its unfolding is decisive in determining the form of social action and its orientation toward a "goal".'[75] Some of those who criticize historical materialism in the terms we have been discussing make their Weberian theoretical allegiances explicit.[76]

At one level the claim that Marxism ignores the military rivalries of nation-states seems simply inept. The period during which Weber developed his social theory, roughly between 1890 and 1920, was precisely that during which a highly gifted generation of Marxists focused their attention on this very phenomenon. Two examples must suffice. Trotsky sought to capture the historical peculiarities of the Russian social formation by analysing processes of uneven and combined development within both the capitalist world economy and the European state-system.[77] Bukharin argued that the epoch of what Hilferding called finance capital and Lenin imperialism is characterized, internally, by a tendency towards state capitalism and, externally, by the propensity of economic competition between capitals to assume the form of military rivalries among states.[78] This theoretical tradition has been further developed by the theory of state capitalism pioneered by Tony Cliff, according to which military competition between East and West enforces the dynamic of capital accumulation on the 'socialist' countries, and the theory of the permanent arms economy elaborated notably by Michael Kidron and Chris Harman, which analyses the mechanisms through which high levels of military expenditure made possible the long boom of Western capitalism in the 1950s and 1960s.[79] Some attempts have been made to generalize from these results, for example by Colin Barker and myself, notably by arguing that there can be no Marxist theory of 'the' state, but only of a plurality of states interacting within a world system characterized by economic and military competition between capitals.[80]

It certainly seems difficult to treat this body of Marxist writing as ignoring military power or treating it simply as 'parasitic and unproductive'. Neo-Weberian social theorists might still object that such work focuses on military rivalries *under capitalism*, whereas, as Skocpol and Giddens observe, the international state-stystem ante-dated the rise of capitalism. Surely this fact indicates that such rivalries represent an enduring form of social power which cannot be reduced to class antagonism? I obviously cannot give an adequate reply to this objection, especially since its more powerful statement, by Mann, consists in a rich and extended history of social power from hunter-gatherer societies to the emergence of the modern capitalist nation-state *circa* 1760. I shall confine myself to making one theoretical point and giving one example.

Let me say first that I do not find Mann's distinction between military and political power convincing. His main reason for rejecting the classic Marxist and Weberian view of the state as 'the repository of physical force in society' is the following:

> Most historic states have not possessed a monopoly of organized military force and many have not even claimed it. The feudal state in some European countries in the Middle Ages depended on the feudal military levy controlled by decentralized lords. Islamic states generally lacked monopoly powers – for example, they did not see themselves as having power to intervene in tribal feuding. We can distinguish the

political from the military powers of both states and other groups. *Political powers are those of centralized, institutionalized, territorial regulation; military powers are those of organized physical force wherever they are organized.*[81]

This seems more a difference in degree than in kind. Centralized territorial control is unlikely to get very far without the ability to back up state decisions with force; equally, warfare among local notables is likely to be endemic unless some carve-up of territory is recognized. Territorial regulation and military force go together, even if their conjunction does not entail the classic Weberian definition of the state as 'a human community that (successfully) claims the *monopoly of the legitimate use of physical force* within a given territory'.[82] I shall therefore not distinguish between military and political power in what follows.

Both the theoretical argument I wish to give and its historical illustration are drawn largely from the work of Robert Brenner. He contends, as we saw in section 2.3, that pre-capitalist relations of production – and in particular the direct producers' access to the means of production and the consequent reliance of the exploiting class on extra-economic coercion – made 'modern economic growth', the development of the productive forces based on labour-saving investments, extremely difficult. Brenner argues that this situation had one very important consequence:

> In view of, the difficulty, in the presence of pre-capitalist property relations, of raising returns from investment in the means of production (via increases in productive efficiency), the lords found that if they wished to increase their income, they had little more choice but to do so by *redistributing* wealth and income away from their peasants or from other members of the exploiting class. This meant they had to deploy their resources toward building up their *means of coercion* – by investment in military men and equipment. Speaking broadly, they were obliged to invest in their politico-military apparatuses. To the extent that they had to do this effectively enough to compete with other lords who were doing the same thing, they would have to maximize both their military investments and the efficiency of these investments. They would have had, in fact, continually and systematically, to improve their methods of war. Indeed, we can say the drive to *political accumulation*, to *state-building*, is the *pre-capitalist* analogue to the capitalist drive to *accumulate capital*.[83]

This is an argument of the most far-reaching implications. It explains the military conflicts of pre-capitalist social formations in terms of the relations of production prevailing within them and therefore provides a rebuttal of the claim that Marxism cannot account for such conflicts. The premisses of Brenner's argument involve three crucial elements. First, there is his analysis of the limitation which features common to *all* pre-capitalist class societies place on the development of the productive forces (direct producers' access to the means of production, exploiters' reliance on extra-economic coercion). Secondly, there is the assumption that exploiters (and indeed exploited) are disposed, other things being equal, to improve their material well-being. This is a weak and plausible assumption. Theorists in the Nietzsche-Weber tradition have, by contrast, tended to invoke, if not the will to power, then at least the pretty strong and highly disputable claim that the struggle for domination is an inherent feature of human existence. Indeed, it is difficult to see how one can explain forms of power and conflict supposedly irreducible to class antagonisms except by some such assertion as that made by Weber in 1896: 'Anyone who wants to pursue an earthly policy must be free of illusions and be acquainted with the fundamental fact of the eternal struggle of men with one another.'[84]

Thirdly, Brenner assumes that the exploiting class is itself fragmented. Such a situation is the precondition of the military competition involved in 'political accumulation', as the following remark about feudal landowners makes clear: 'The very prerogatives (force/jurisdiction) required by every individual lord to ensure his reproduction (as a lord) *vis-à-vis* the peasants constituted a threat to other lords, and made for a generalized tendency to intra-lordly competition and conflict *which made "political accumulation" necessary*.'[85]

I argued in section 2.2 that the nature of the exploiting class is an element of the relations of production. Thus, competition between capitals is a necessary condition of capitalist relations of production. Brenner's argument underlines the importance of so conceiving production relations, since it suggests that much of the dynamic of pre-capitalist social formations arose from military conflicts among the exploiters.

These conflicts can take a variety of different forms, depending on whether they involve individual exploiters, an empire and its semi-barbarous marches, or autonomous states. Mark Elvin argues that 'competition among equals, whether the Southern Sung and the Mongols, or the contestants in the Japanese civil wars, or the states of early modern Europe, is an indispensable precondition of progress in military technology.'[86]

Mann indeed can be said to generalize this argument, emphasizing the dynamism of what he calls '*multi-power-actor civilizations*', in which 'decentralized actors competed with each other within an overall framework of normative regulation.' The chief examples he gives of such civilizations are ancient Phoenicia and Greece, and mediaeval and early modern Europe. Drawing especially on a study of English state finances betweeen 1130 and 1815 Mann argues that the

> states and the multistate civilization [of early modern Europe] developed primarily in response to pressures emanating from the geopolitical and military spheres. Thus theories that assign the state's main function as the regulation of its internal 'civil society' – whether this is seen in functional or Marxist class-struggle terms – seem simplistic. All states do possess such functions, but over this particular geographical and historical terrain, they appear from the perspective of financial costs to have been largely derivative of their geopolitical role.[87]

Mann further argues that the decentralized character of Europe's 'multi-power-actor civilization' underlies the process of economic growth which culminated in the Industrial Revolution. This explanation of the 'European dynamic' runs the risk of degenerating into a mere celebration of the market, of the competitive struggle between economic actors. In the hands of Mann's co-thinker John Hall it at times becomes mere tautology: 'it is the depth of market penetration throughout European society that ensured the ultimate success of the market principles.'[88] Such explanations of European growth are not uncommon: quasi-Marxist versions exist in the work of Paul Sweezy and Immanuel Wallerstein, who treat the expansion of world trade as the principal cause of the development of capitalism. Brenner describes such explanations as 'Smithian', since they follow Adam Smith in believing that the very existence of market relationships will induce economic actors to make productivity-enhancing investments. Thus, 'capitalism is assumed to explain the onset of modern economic growth, while pre-capitalist property relations somehow magically disappear.'[89]

Mann and Hall argue that the processes of economic and military competition inherent in the character of European civilization from the Dark Ages onwards were responsible for 'sustained economic growth' based on technological innovation which began *circa* AD 1000 and has continued to the present day.[90] This benign picture of what Hall (following Hugh Trevor-Roper) calls the 'rise of Christian Europe' leaves out of account the terrible crisis which afflicted the continent in the later Middle Ages. In his major study of late mediaeval Normandy Guy Bois has described in meticuluous detail the hellish cycle which set in during the second half of the thirteenth century, in which growth of population and output would be succeeded by ecological collapse and mass starvation. Bois estimates that half the population of eastern Normandy died in the generation of the Black Death (1348 to 1380); recovery was followed by two further crises. Between 1415 and 1422 'the conjunction of military events [invasion by the English], a terrible food crisis and plague' caused another catastrophe, in which half the population perished. A period of uneasy peace and rapid population growth formed only a prelude to what Bois calls 'Hiroshima in Normandy (1436 to 1450)', in which peasant insurrection, war and famine wiped out another third of the population in the five years after 1436.[91]

Late-mediaeval Normandy suffered particularly acutely, but the crisis of feudalism was a generalized phenomenon of fourteenth-century Europe. Thus M. M. Postan argues that perhaps as much as 50 per cent of the population of England perished in the Black Death. Like Bois he sees this catastrophe as a consequence of long-term economic trends which the plague intensified but did not cause. In particular, Postan identifies an overall 'decline in the area and the output of agriculture in the later Middle Ages'. Moreover, he presents considerable evidence of a *lack* of technological dynamism in feudal England. Thus:

> The inertia of mediaeval agricultural technology is unmistakable. Some progress there was, but it was, so to speak 'bunched' into certain periods at the beginning and the end of the era. Over the Middle Ages as a whole it was slow and uneven, and far greater in the management and arrangement on fields than in the implements employed in cultivation, or in the actual processes of planting, manuring, weeding and reaping.[92]

The work of mediaeval economic historians such as Postan and Bois suggests that the fourteenth-century crisis cannot be simply dismissed, as it is by Hall, as a 'temporary setback' to a process of 'long-term improvement'.[93] It is difficult to have much respect for a historical sociology which so brushes aside a catastrophe in which such an enormous proportion of the European population perished. Nor did the later Middle Ages experience the last such generalized crisis to have afflicted the continent prior to the Industrial Revolution. What historians call the 'general crisis of the seventeenth century' set in around 1620 and reached its most acute phase between 1640 and 1670. Population stagnated or declined. Some countries, notably Italy, experienced deindustrialization. The two main areas of international trade, the Mediterranean and the Baltic, declined. The Spanish and Portuguése empires contracted. Even Dutch overseas expansion slowed down. The Thirty Years War devastated central Europe. The continent was shaken by an enormous wave of social revolt, whose climax was the English Revolution of 1640 to 1660.[94]

Postan offers a Malthusian explanation of the late-medieval crisis. Diminishing returns in agriculture meant that the land could not support a growing population: the fourteenth-century catastrophe was the brutal process through which some sort of equilibrium was established between population and land. Mediaeval Europe's relative lack of technological dynamism plays a crucial role in this account:

> If we accept that Ricardo's irreversible trend of diminishing returns operated only so long and so far as it remained unchecked by investment and innovation, then the absence of innovation and paucity of investment would go a long way to explain why the late-mediaeval recovery was so slow and tardy.[95]

But why this absence of innovation? Brenner, in his widely discussed critique of 'neo-Malthusian' economic historians such as Postan and Emmanuel Le Roy Ladurie, argues that it is only comprehensible in the context of feudal relations of production:

> The inability of the serf-based economy to innovate in agriculture even under extreme market pressures to do so is understandable in view of the interrelated facts, first, of heavy surplus-extraction by the lord from the peasant and, secondly, the barriers to mobility of men and land which were themselves part and parcel of the unfree surplus-extraction relationship. . . . Given these property or surplus-extraction relationships, productivity crisis leading to demographic crisis was more or less to be expected sooner or later.[96]

The crisis of late-mediaeval Europe was thus a crisis of the feudal mode of production, arising from the manner in which the direct producers' access to the means of production and the lords' reliance on extra-economic coercion deprived both classes of the incentive to develop the productive forces intensively through labour-saving investment. It is only against this background that the rise of 'organic states' is intelligible. Brenner argues that:

> The long-term tendency, prevalent throughout the feudal epoch (from *circa* 1000–1100), to 'political accumulation' – that is, the build-up of larger, more efficient military organization and/or the construction of

stronger surplus-extracting machinery – may be viewed as conditioned by the system's limited potential for long-term economic growth, and, to a certain extent, as an alternative to extending or improving cultivation.[97]

Brenner contends further that the differential strengths of lord and peasant help to explain the variable forms taken by the states of early modern Europe. Bois detects a long-term tendency for the rate of levy (i.e. the rate of surplus-extraction) to fall in medieval Normandy from the thirteenth century onwards.[98] Brenner argues that this trend reflected the relative strength of French peasant communities, which were increasingly able to establish full property rights over the land they worked. This led to a growing centralization of coercive power in the monarchy, in other words, the emergence of the absolutist state in France:

> It was precisely the esconced position of the [French] peasantry which *compelled* the lords to turn to the state for revenues. Many of them had only small demesnes. And they could not, locally and individually, successfully raise levies on customary tenures. To extract a surplus from the customary peasantry, the lords had to turn to the concentrated power of the state apparatus (tax/office).

Surplus-extraction increasingly took the form of royal taxation, from which the lords benefitted through their establishment of property rights over state office: 'In sum, the absolutist state was no more guarantor of the old forms of property based on decentralized feudal reaction. Rather, it came to express a *transformed* version of the old system.'[99]

By contrast, the English lords' greater power over their peasants could be seen in the emergence in the eleventh and twelfth centuries of 'an unusually strong monarchy [which] reflected an unusually strong aristocracy hierarchically organized in the most highly developed feudal state in Europe'. Seigneurial powers were actually increased in the late twelfth and thirteenth centuries and the rate of levy only came under pressure in England well into the fourteenth century. The peasants were able, thanks to the scarcity of labour which followed the Black Death, to prevent their re-enserfment, but not powerful enough to establish the secure possession of the land which their French counterparts won: 'With the peasants' failure to establish essentially freehold control over the land, the landlords were able to engross, consolidate and enclose, to create large-scale farms and to lease them to capitalist tenants who could afford to make capitalist investments.' The result was a rapid growth of agricultural productivity sufficient to release 40 per cent of the population into industrial pursuits by the end of the seventeenth century:

> England remained largely exempt from the 'general economic crisis of the seventeenth century' which sooner or later struck much of the continent. This crisis, much like the previous 'general economic crisis of the fourteenth century', was in the last analysis a crisis of agrarian productivity, resulting as had its predecessor from the maintenance of relationships of property or surplus-extraction which prevented any advance in productivity.[100]

Brenner's analysis thus provides a powerful counter-argument to those such as Skocpol, Giddens and Mann who argue that the emergence of the 'organic states' of early modern Europe reflected a dynamic autonomous of class relations. It does so by showing that the tendency towards state-building was a consequence of feudal relations of production, and in particular of the lords' inability to increase the rate of exploitation by productivity-enhancing investments. Brenner's account thereby supports Perry Anderson's claim that Absolutism was '*a redeployed and recharged apparatus of feudal domination*, designed to clamp the peasant masses back into their traditional social position', involving 'a *displacement* of politico-legal coercion towards a centralized, militarized summit'. The intense military competition between the early modern monarchies – Anderson calls them 'machines built overwhelmingly for the battlefield' – was a concentrated and centralized form of the struggle between lords and their retainers which Brenner traces back to the end of the first millenium AD.[101]

Once in place, the international state system and the military and diplomatic rivalries inherent in it led to what Charles Tilly calls 'a ruthless competition in which most contenders lost. The Europe of 1500 included some five hundred more or less independent political units, the Europe of 1900 about twenty five'. The chief mechanism of natural selection in this Darwinian world was military competition. 'Preparation for war', Tilly observes, 'has been the great state-building activity. The process has been going on more or less continuously for at least five hundred years.'[102]

Nevertheless, internal class-relations are crucial in explaining which states were victors and losers in this process. The eighteenth century was dominated by the struggle between Britain and France for European and increasingly world supremacy, a contest whose outcome was finally sealed at Waterloo. But the state which triumphed was significantly different from its continental counterparts. As Christopher Hill observes, the seventeenth-century English Revolutions produced

> a state in which the administrative organs that most impeded capitalist development had been abolished, Star Chamber, High Commission, Court of Wards, and feudal tenures; in which the executive was subordinated to the men of property, deprived of control over the judiciary, and yet strengthened in external relations by a powerful navy and the Navigation Act; in which local government was safely and cheaply in the hands of the natural rulers, and discipline was imposed on the lower orders by a Church safely subordinated to Parliament.[103]

This state was no weakling on the world stage. Anderson describes the Hanoverian state as 'an *ascendant colonial power*, rapidly rising towards international hegemony across five continents.'[104] This hegemony was underpinned by a rising level of military expenditure: the real spending of the British state rose fifteenfold between 1700 and 1815, with civil expenses never rising above 23 per cent of total outlays.[105] The capacity of the British state to finance such an expansion of its military activities reflected the explosive growth of the productive forces released by the emergence of capitalist production relations, first in agriculture, then in industry.

Gabriel Ardant observes of eighteenth-century Europe:

> In spite of having much less territory and a much smaller population than the Austrian and French monarchies, England was undeniably the dominant power . . . It seems hardly questionable that England derived her power in a great degree from her financial resources. Great Britain's economic structure provided the foundation for her fiscal capacity by allowing her to give the most important role to the taxation of commercial activities.

The continental monarchies, by contrast, were faced with endemic difficulties in financing their military activities. The interpenetration of lords and absolutist state meant that the nobility were exempt from taxation. The main burden consequently fell on the peasantry, still implicated in feudal production relations which condemned agriculture to stagnation or slow growth. The relatively unmonetized nature of economic relations encouraged the state to rely on tax-farmers. This, combined with the sale of offices, another source of royal revenue, made corruption and state dependence on tax-exempt nobles endemic. From time to time the burden of taxation, sapping the rural economy, provoked the peasants to rebel; taxation was the main cause of rebellion in early modern Europe. It is little wonder that it was the fiscal crises of the Stuart and Bourbon monarchies which ushered in the Revolutions of 1640 and 1789 respectively.[106]

The war-making capacity of early modern states came to depend increasingly on whether or not they were able to draw on the intensive development of the productive forces made possible by capitalist production relations. The essence of imperialism, as Lenin and Bukharin analysed it during the First World War, lay in the generalization of the pattern which had allowed Britain to emerge as the dominant power. In the course of the nineteenth century two competitive logics – the military struggle between the great powers and the economic interaction of accumulating capitals – fused. Access to the military technologies necessary to survive in what A. J. P. Taylor called the struggle for mastery in Europe now depended on the prevalence internally of industrial capitalism. The rise of Germany demonstrated the quantum-leap in power which the interpenetration of capitalism and militarism could achieve. Even much feebler and more backward actors on the European stage such as Tsarist Russia were forced into an alliance with foreign capital in order to acquire the necessary industrial base. The scene was set for the emergence of the militarized state capitalisms analysed by Bukharin. Their competitive struggle, at once military and economic, ushered in, with the outbreak of hostilities in August 1914, what the early Communist International called an 'epoch of wars and revolutions', an epoch which reached a provisional conclusion only with the nuclear destruction of Hiroshima and Nagasaki in August 1945. But this outcome only transposed the same kind of competition onto a global scale, with the partition of Europe between two superpowers whose conflict has perpetuated unprecedentedly high levels of peace-time arms expenditure, and the extension, with decolonization, of the European state system and the economic and military competition endemic to it to the rest of the world. The consequence is that the old story of forcible assimilation into new 'national' cultures and bloody territorial disputes is repeated in every corner of the planet, often in extremely savage form, thanks to the benefits of advanced military technology.[107]

The history of the past 150 years is thus that of the subordination of the process of 'political accumulation' – warfare and state-building – which emerged within feudal relations of production to the competitive accumulation of capital, a transformation which has involved the increasing interpenetration of the state and capital and the inclusion of the whole of humanity within such arrangements. It is in this context that we can understand another phenomenon of modernity – the interpellation of almost every member of the human race as the bearer of a national identity. As Gellner puts it, 'having a nation is not an inherent attribute of humanity, but it has now come to appear as such.'[108]

The process through which this came to be so had a number of different phases, closely bound up with the development of European capitalism and its colonial expansion, which are carefully analysed by Benedict Anderson in his book *Imagined Communities*. However, it is arguable that perhaps the most decisive phase in the development of nationalism came in the second half of the nineteenth century, for it was then that the subjects of most European states came to be treated as citizens, enjoying both political rights and membership of a community defined by shared nationality. The way in which this occurred is an important instance of what a recent collection of brilliant historical essays call the 'invention of tradition'. Eric Hobsbawm defines an 'invented tradition' as 'a set of practices, normally governed by overtly or tacitly accepted rules, and of a ritual or symbolic nature, which seek to inculcate certain values and norms of behaviour by repetition, which automatically implies continuity with the past'. Hobsbawm observes that 'modern nations generally claim to be the opposite of novel, namely rooted in the remotest antiquity, and the opposite of constructed, namely rooted human communities so "natural" as to require no definition other than self-assertion.' However, national consciousness involves 'a constructed or "invented" component . . . [and] . . . is associated with appropriate and, in general, fairly recent symbols or suitably tailored discourse (such as "national history")' and therefore is an important instance of the 'invention of tradition'.[109]

Hobsbawm suggests that the period between 1870 and 1914 was one in which traditions were mass-produced throughout Europe. This reflected a situation in which 'the state increasingly defined the largest stage on which the crucial activities determining human lives as subjects and citizens were played out.' The rulers of Europe, presiding over rapidly industrializing and urbanizing societies and increasingly engaged in the arms race which precipitated the Great War, were faced with 'unprecedented problems of how [the state could] . . . maintain or even establish the obedience, loyalty and co-operation of its subjects or members, or its own legitimacy in their eyes.'[110] Traditional mechanisms for securing consent, the local loyalties and stable hierarchies of pre-industrial Europe, were being undermined by economic and social change and by the spread of the suffrage and the doctrines of political equality associated with it.

The solution to these problems consisted in part in the construction of inclusive national communities in which members of all classes would see themselves as sharing the same identity. This required a drive to remedy a situation in which, even in Europe's most nationally conscious major state, French peasant school children in the Lozère were unable to say in 1864 to which state they belonged.[111] A variety of devices were used under the Third Republic to construct a sense of national identity – lay state schools providing universal primary education, the invention of public ceremonies (Bastille Day dates from 1880) and the mass construction of public monuments involving the creation of an entire republican iconography.[112] It was in this same period at the end of the nineteenth century that much of the elaborate public ritual now regarded as time-honoured features of the British monarchy was invented as part of an effort by the rulers of the United Kingdom, faced with a growing challenge from new industrial powers such as Germany and the US, to project the state as an institution meaningful to all its subjects.[113] Such examples suggest that the formation of national identities must be understood in the context of historical processes, about which Marxism – far from being silent – is indispensable to making intelligible.

I conclude that the existence of national divisions and of military conflicts does not constitute the decisive theoretical rebuttal to Marxism which many contemporary social theorists believe it to be. This does not prevent it from being an enormous political problem for revolutionary socialism. Elster ascribes to Marx the view that 'non-class collective actors tend to become increasingly marginal over time', and argues that the persistence of national, ethnic and racial conflicts is a counter-example to this claim.[114] If, as I have argued in this section, the explanation of these conflicts requires resort to the concepts of historical materialism, then the scientific validity of Marxism is not undermined by the phenomenon of national divisions. However, it may be that such conflicts are sufficient to prevent the working class acquiring revolutionary consciousness in the sense given in section 4.1 and thereby becoming an autonomous collective actor. We shall return to this question in chapter 5.

4.5 A NOTE ON BASE AND SUPERSTRUCTURE

The case of military conflicts between nation-states discussed in the previous section provides an instructive example of a common misunderstanding of the methodology of historical materialism. No serious student of European history can deny the salience of warfare and state-building over the past millenium. Social theorists such as Skocpol, Giddens and Mann conclude that the importance of organizations such as states and armies, which are not directly structures of econonomic power, undermines the explanatory primacy claimed by Marxism for the forces and relations of production. Put more generally, the thought is that where the form of articulation of a social formation, its visible organization into social hierarchies and institutions, does not directly correspond to the structure of class relations defined by agents' position within the relations of production, this primacy cannot hold. This often leads to a distinction between capitalism, where such a correspondence does seem to hold, and pre-capitalist societies, where it does not. Giddens writes: 'Whereas Marx gave primacy to allocative resources in his materialist theory of history, I argue that in non-capitalist societies co-ordination of authoritative resources [roughly speaking, those which facilitate politico-ideological domination] forms the determining axis of societal integration and change.' Thus, 'non-capitalist societies *are not* modes of production, even though like all societies they obviously *involve* modes of production.'[115]

Similar kinds of consideration appear to be involved in M. I. Finley's choice of 'the word "status", an admirably vague word with a considerable psychological element' in order to characterize social stratification in classical antiquity. To attempt to identify classes distinguished by their relation to the means of production, Finley suggests, is to project onto ancient society a form of economic rationality unique to the market systems of our own day. The differentiation of society into such distinct and identifiable instances as economy and polity is a feature of modernity, whereas, writes Lukács in a passage quoted approvingly by Finley, 'the structuring of [pre-capitalist] society into castes and estates means that economic elements are *inextricably* joined to political and religious factors.'[116]

Like most objections to Marxism, this argument isn't especially new. Marx himself responded to a similar criticism of his summary of historical materialism in the 1859 Preface that

> this is all very true for our own times, in which material interests are preponderant, but not for the Middle Ages, dominated by Catholicism, nor Athens and Rome, dominated by politics.... One thing is clear: the Middle Ages could not live on Catholicism, nor could the ancient world on politics. On the contrary, it is the manner in which they gained their livelihood which explains why in one case politics, in the other case Catholicism, played the chief part.[117]

To take the example of 'political accumulation' (warfare and state-building) discussed in section 4.4 far from its salience contradicting the explanatory primacy of the forces and relations of production, the entire point of historical materialism is to account for such phenomena. To grasp this point requires distinguishing sharply between the vocabulary used to characterize a social formation's form of articulation, its institutional organization, and the theoretical concepts of historical materialism. Too often even Marxists fail to do so. Thus Althusser sought to develop Marx's *obiter dictum* cited above into a general theory, starting from the idea that every social formation is a plurality of instances, of which the chief are the economic, political and ideological. Modes of production are differentiated, Althusser claimed, according to which instance is dominant: thus feudalism is distinguished by the dominant role played by the political. The economic exercises a determining role only indirectly, by selecting a particular instance as dominant. Apart from the elaborate machinery of instances which Althusser established and the considerable conceptual and political problems involved in the notion of determination in the last instance, his schema suffered from the fundamental fault that it projected onto all social formations the form of articulation characteristic of the capitalist mode of production, where such a differentiation, particularly between economy and polity, indeed occurs.[118]

The form of articulation represents a different (and lower) level of abstraction from that represented by the basic concepts of historical materialism. Consider two of these concepts, those of base and superstructure. Cohen defines the latter as 'those non-economic institutions whose character is explained by the nature of the economic structure.'[119] While this definition is basically correct, three qualifications should be made. First, as Elster rightly observes, there is no reason to follow Cohen in excluding ideologies from the superstructure thus defined: we should say instead that 'any non-economic phenomenon is part of the superstructure if that can be explained in terms of the economic structure.' Secondly, and again following Elster, 'explain' here should not carry the restrictive functionalist meaning given it by Cohen, who confines the superstructure to 'non-economic phenomena that can be explained by their *stabilizing influence* on the relations of production'.[120]

Chris Harman defends a view of the superstructure similar to Cohen's, arguing that ' "non-economic" institutions' in class society 'are concerned with *controlling* the base, with *fixing* existing relations of exploitation, and therefore in putting a limit on changes in the relations of production, even if this also involves stopping further development of the productive forces.'[121] This view of the superstructure as a necessarily conservative element is, in part, a consequence of Harman's view of production relations as constantly changing in response to the development of the productive forces; the superstructure then arises from the ruling class's interest in preserving the existing social structure (see section 2.2 above). But unless we share this view, why so restrict the superstructure to a stabilizing role, especially since the effect is to reduce subversive non-economic phenomena – for example, revolutionary ideologies and movements – to the status of an anomaly?

Thirdly, 'economic' here has a technical meaning derived from Marxist theory. Cohen identifies the 'economic structure' (again in my view too narrowly) with production relations alone; I prefer to treat the base as comprising both forces and relations of production, a usage which corresponds, for example, to Marx's requirement that 'consciousness must be explained from the contradictions of material life, from the conflict between the social forces of production and the relations of production.'[122]

The distinction between base and superstructure is, then, an analytical one, since the base in terms of which the superstructure is explained is constituted by that key theoretical couplet, the forces and relations of production. Now it is a typical property of such explanatory concepts that their content does not coincide with that of descriptive concepts, which seek primarily to summarize the findings of observation. Theoretical concepts could not fulfil their role unless this were so, since explanation typically proceeds by identifying underlying relationships not directly accessible to observation. As Marx puts it, 'all science would be superfluous if the outward appearance and the essence of things co-incided.'[123] Ste Croix's rebuttal of Finley can be seen as a forceful elaboration of this point: class is a theoretical concept essential to the analysis of classical antiquity even though exploitive relationships rarely found expression in class-consciousness or overt political conflict.[124]

The same point can be applied to the distinction between base and superstructure. There is no reason to suppose that the analytical distinction between the forces and relations of production and those social phenomena which they explain should necessarily correspond to a distinction between separate sets of economic and non-economic institutions. As Harman puts it:

> The distinction between base and superstructure is not a distinction between one set of institutions and another, with economic institutions on one side and political, judicial, ideological etc. institutions on the other. It is a distinction between *relations* that are directly connected with production and those that are not. Many particular institutions include both.[125]

Indeed, such a differentiation of economic and non-economic institutions is a historical rarity. Thus Brenner contends that 'a "fusion" (to put it imprecisely) between "the economic" and "the political" was a distinguishing and constitutive feature of the *feudal class structure and system of production*.'[126] This fusion, Marx argues, is a general feature of pre-capitalist modes of production:

> In all forms in which the direct labourer remains the 'possessor' of the means of production and labour conditions necessary for the production of his own means of subsistence, the property relationship must simultaneously appear as a direct relation of lordship and servitude, so that the direct producer is not free; a lack of freedom which may be reduced from serfdom with enforced labour to a mere tributary relationship. The direct producer . . . is found here in possession of his own means of production, the necessary material labour conditions required for the realization of his labour and the production of his means of subsistence. He conducts his agricultural activity and the rural home industries connected with it independently . . . Under such conditions the surplus-labour for the nominal owner of the land can only be extorted by other than economic means.[127]

The fusion of economy and polity in pre-capitalist modes of production is thus a consequence of the specific form of surplus-extraction, of the dependence of the exploiting class on extra-economic coercion. It therefore in no way contradicts the explanatory primacy of the forces and relations of production. It follows that the dynamic of pre-capitalist modes should differ in form from that of capitalism. Bois criticized Brenner's 'political Marxism', arguing that it ignored the fact that 'in the feudal system the rate of seigneurial levies shows a tendency to fall which originates in the structural contradiction of small-scale production and large-scale property.'[128] This tendency is clearly constructed on an analogy with Marx's law of the tendency of the rate of profit to fall and seems to involve an illicit generalization of the autonomous economic dynamic characteristic of the capitalist mode. Brenner argues:

> Just as the feudal system of class-relations was 'politically' constituted, it tended to impose an 'extra-economic' dynamic on the course of feudal economic evolution . . . as a function, in particular, of the lords' growing needs for *politically motivated consumption*, arising from their needs both to maintain a dominant position *vis-à-vis* the peasantry and to protect themselves *vis-à-vis* one another.[129]

The tendency to 'political accumulation' and not some spurious falling rate of levy was thus the feudal equivalent of the falling rate of profit. The very concept of an autonomous and self-regulating economy could only be formulated in the *Wealth of Nations* subsquent to the wide-spread penetration of capitalist production relations. Maurice Dobb observes:

> What principally distinguished economic writers prior to the eighteenth century from those who followed after was their belief in economic regulation as the essential condition for the emergence of any profit from trade ... so long as surplus-value was conceived as reliant on conscious regulation to produce it, the notion of *economic objectivity* – of an economy operating according to laws of its own, independent of men's conscious will – which was the essence of classical political economy could scarcely develop.[130]

The differentiation of economy and polity is thus a feature of capitalist production relations, in which the extraction of surplus-labour depends primarily on economic pressures arising from the direct producers' lack of access to the means of production. Far from hypostatizing this form of articulation by extending it to pre-capitalist social formations, historical materialism provides a general explanation of why the analytical distinction between base and superstructure should not correspond to distinct sets of economic and non-economic institutions in these societies. Whether the distinction is a useful one depends on its explanatory power. I hope that I have at least indicated in section 4.4 some of the ways in which Marxism can account for a range of phenomena which are apparently irreducible to class relations. There are, of course, many other such phenomena, of which the most important are those of race and gender. The considerations adduced in this section are relevant to the issues raised by these as well. Feminists and black nationalists often complain that the concepts of Marxist class theory are 'gender-blind' and 'race-blind'. This is indeed true. Agents' class position derives from their place in production relations, not their gender or supposed race. But of itself this does not provide grounds for rejecting Marxism, since its chief theoretical claim is precisely to explain power-relations and forms of conflict such as those denoted by the terms 'nation', 'gender' and 'race' in terms of the forces and relations of production. The mere existence of national, sexual and racial oppression does not refute historical materialism, but rather constitutes its *explanandum*. The only interesting question is whether or not Marxism can actually explain these phenomena.[131]

CHAPTER 5

TRADITION AND REVOLUTION

5.1 REVOLUTION AS REDEMPTION: BENJAMIN AND SARTRE

One of the most suggestive intellectual encounters in the history of Marxism was the exchange of correspondence in the 1930s between Theodor Adorno and Walter Benjamin that has come to be known as the 'Adorno–Benjamin debate'. Their different assessments of 'mass' culture – Benjamin stressing the revolutionary possibilities inherent in new methods of production and reproduction such as film, Adorno denying subversive potential to any but the most esoteric high art – continue to set the parameters of Marxist cultural theory, including current discussions of post-modernism. Their arguments also highlighted the tensions between Hegelian and anti-Hegelian Marxism, Adorno following Lukács at least in this respect, that he investigated the mediations which integrate every phenomenon into the social totality, Benjamin fascinated instead by the direct correspondences he sought to establish between cultural products and their material contexts.[1]

It is, however, the political implications of the debate which concern me here. One does not have to assent to the accusations made of Adorno by the German far left in the 1960s, namely that his editing of Benjamin's writings concealed the latter's commitment to orthodox Marxism, to see already adumbrated in Adorno's letters to Benjamin the pessimistic view of a social world pervaded by commodity fetishism, which is developed much more fully in post-war works such as *Minima Moralia*, *Negative Dialectics* and *Aesthetic Theory*. Thus he warns Benjamin against

> any appeal . . . to the actual consciousness of actual workers who have absolutely no advantage over the bourgeois except in their interest in the revolution, but otherwise bear all the marks of mutilation of the

typical bourgeois character. . . . It is not bourgeois idealism if, in full knowledge and without mental prohibitions, we maintain our solidarity with the proletariat instead of making of our own necessity a virtue of the proletariat, as we are always tempted to do – the proletariat which itself experiences the same necessity and needs us for knowledge as much as we need the proletariat to make the revolution.[2]

Thus already in 1936 Adorno believed there to be a structural separation of theory and practice, represented by Marxist intellectuals and the working class respectively. This analysis was radicalized in Horkheimer's and Adorno's *Dialectic of Enlightenment* (1944), in which the class is thought to be systematically incorporated into capitalism, transformed into passive, isolated consumers through the operations of commodity fetishism. That Benjamin was committed to a more revolutionary perspective is clear from his intellectual testament, the extraordinary 'Theses on the Philosophy of History', written between Benjamin's final disillusionment with Stalinism after the Hitler–Stalin pact of August 1939 and his suicide in June 1940, when he believed that he could not escape the Nazi armies invading France.

The 'Theses' therefore date from that moment – 'midnight in the century' – when the hopes created first by the October Revolution and then by the struggles of the 1930s were finally snuffed out, when all projects for collective emancipation had run aground, shattered on the rocks of fascism and Stalinism. Read against this background, the 'Theses' have been interpreted as Benjamin's abandonment of the 'Bolshevism' which he had espoused in the 1930s.[3] They are, in my view, better understood as an intransigent and, given the context in which they were written, moving affirmation of the revolutionary potential of the working class. Michael Löwy indeed describes the 'Theses' as 'one of the most radical, path-breaking and seminal documents of revolutionary thought since Marx's "Theses on Feuerbach" '.[4]

The importance of the 'Theses' lies in Benjamin's argument that the triumph of fascism and the complicity of both Stalinism and social democracy in that triumph require, in Richard Wolin's words, 'an acknowledgement of the fact that in its reliance on the Enlightenment myth of historical progress, historical materialism has remained a prisoner of the same logic which it wanted to transcend'.[5] Benjamin wrote: 'Nothing has corrupted the German working class so much as the notion that it was moving with the current. It regarded technological developments as the fall of the stream with which it thought it was moving.' In a famous image he conjured up the angel of history facing the past, 'a single catastrophe which keeps piling up wreckage upon wreckage', but propelled by 'a storm ... blowing from Paradise', 'what we call progress', into the future. Instead of recognizing that history brought with it no guarantees, vulgar Marxism viewed it as an inevitable progress motored by the development of the productive forces. Avoidance of future disasters, Benjamin argued, would presuppose a critique not just of 'the historical progress of mankind' but also 'the concept of its progression through a homogeneous, empty time'.[6]

That Benjamin advocated the rethinking of Marxist categories rather than their abandonment is made absolutely clear by this passage from the preparatory materials for the 'Theses'. 'Three moments must be made to penetrate the foundations of the materialist view of history: the discontinuity of historical time; the destructive power of the working class; the tradition of the oppressed.'[7] Revolution does not swell inevitably from the process of social evolution. It is an irruption into the chain of everyday happenings, 'a tiger's leap into the past'. Revolution has a fundamental relation to the past, not to the future, because it draws its strength from and activates the oppressed's memories of exploitation and struggle: workers' 'hatred and ... spirit of sacrifice ... are nourished by the image of enslaved ancestors.'[8]

Revolution thus conceived involves a particular view of historical time. Benjamin repudiates the common-sense notion of the historian as 'establishing a causal connection between various moments in history'. To this he counterposes the concept of 'now-time' (*Jetztzeit*), of 'a present which is not a transition, but in which time stands still and has come to a stop'. To be open to such 'a Messianic cessation of happening' is essential to the Marxist. Through doing so 'he remains in control of his powers, man enough to blast open the continuum of history.' Revolutionary socialism must conduct itself in the same way as did those Jews for whom 'every second of time was the strait gate through which the Messiah might pass.'[9]

The religious language in which Benjamin asserts that revolution is not the inevitable consequence of historical progress but rather 'blast[s] open the continuum of history' is not simply metaphorical. It reflects the persistent influence on what Benjamin himself described as his 'Janus-faced' thought, even at its most Marxist, of certain classical themes of Jewish Messianism. At the beginning of Thesis XIV he cites Karl Kraus's aphorism 'Origin is the goal.' Wolin observes:

> for the Kabbalistic idea of redemption, *origin is goal*; that is, the return
> to the condition of universal harmony represented by the [prelapsarian]

Tree of Life, usually envisioned in terms of a return to paradise or a restoration of the Davidic kingdom. Though the idea can at times take the form of a static, purely restorative conception of redemption, quite often it is infused with radical and Utopian elements.[10]

Benjamin's Messianism is of the latter kind, radical and Utopian. It nevertheless involves an 'antithetical relation [between] . . . the realm of redemption [and] . . . the historical world, such that in the latter we are provided only with the most fleeting and ephemeral traces of the path to salvation'. Thes are the 'now-times', 'the few unique visions of transcendence that grace the continuum of history'. The relationship between 'now-time' and the normal course of events is one of absolute discontinuity: 'The Messianic age is not the *culmination* of history, but rather its *termination*, a qualitative leap into a realm beyond history. As such, direct organic movement from the one stage to the another is impossible.'[11]

The relationship between Benjamin's Messianism and his Marxism is complex. Löwy suggests that it involves

active interpenetration and combination of both elements. There exists an intimate link, a *correspondance* in the Baudelairian sense, between each term of the profane revolutionary Utopia and of the sacred Messianic sphere, between the history of redemption and the history of class struggle: to the Lost Paradise corresponds the pre-historic classless communist society, egalitarian and non-authoritarian, living in edenic harmony with nature; to the expulsion from the Garden of Eden, or to the Tempest blowing men away from Paradise, towards Hell, correspond 'progress', industrial civilization, capitalist-commodity society, the modern catastrophe and its pile of wreckage; to the Coming of the Messiah, the proletarian-revolutionary interruption of history; and to the Messianic Age, the re-establishment of Paradise with its edenic adamite language, corresponds the new libertarian-communist classless society and its universal language.[12]

The difficulty with what Löwy calls Benjamin's 'romantic anarchism' is that it makes revolution so discontinuous with the ordinary sequence of events as to be unthinkable. Revolution belongs to *Jetztzeit*, the time of redemption, qualitatively distinct from the historical world in which men and women live and work and struggle. It is so starkly counterposed with the 'continuum of history', the Hell of commodity fetishism, which Benjamin sought to uncover in his great unfinished study of Baudelaire, that the emergence of the one from the other appears unthinkable. Conceiving revolution as a Messianic irruption into history is a decisive break with the evolutionism of vulgar Marxism. But in the absence of any analysis of the processes by virtue of which the working class is likely 'to brush history against the grain', then the obvious terminus of Benjamin's critique of the concept of historical progress is the pessimism of Adorno.[13] Indeed the latter did follow Benjamin to the extent of advocating 'the attempt to contemplate all things as they would present themselves from the standpoint of redemption', seeking to 'displace and estrange the world, reveal it to be, with its rifts and crevices, as indigent and distorted as it will appear one day in the Messianic light.'[14] But this perspective allowed Adorno to maintain a critical distance from the world of late capitalism; it did not enable him to identify any social force capable of overcoming the universal fragmentation of experience induced by commodity fetishism and of transforming that world.

The same antinomy between the passive and isolated existence to which capitalism condemns us and revolution as absolutely discontinuous with this normality that runs through Benjamin's 'Theses' is present in the work of another highly idiosyncratic thinker who also sought to pursue his own distinctive preoccupations within a Marxist framework – Sartre. The most important instance of this antinomy in his discussion of the series and the fused group in the first volume of the *Critique of Dialectical Reason*. The series, Sartre says, is 'the being of the most ordinary, everyday gatherings'. He gives the example of a bus queue. It is a social relationship, but one where individuals are connected to one another via their common dependence on the bus. '*The series* represents the use of alterity as a bond among men under the passive action of an object.' A radio broadcast is another such relationship: the listeners are bound together by their common relationship to a speaker whom they do not control, 'impotence as a real bond between members of a series.' Most important of all:

> In bourgeois democracies, elections are passive, serial processes. Each elected, of course, decides to vote as Other and through Others; but instead of deciding in common and as a united *praxis* with the Others, he allows it to be defined inertly and in seriality by opinion. Thus an elected assembly represents the gathering *as long as* it has not met, as long as its members are the inert product of an inert alterity and as long as crude multiplicity, as a numerical relation between the parts, expresses the relations of impotence amongst collectives and power-relations in so far as these forces are forces of inertia.[15]

But human beings are not irredeemably condemned to seriality. History is full of cases of 'what [André] Malraux, in *Days of Hope*, called the Apocalypse – that is to say, the dissolution of the series into a fused group'. The main example which Satre gives is of the storming of the Bastille. The members of a fused group consciously act together. They do so in response to some urgent threat which requires 'the common unity of a *praxis* which is everyone's'. The existence of such a threat is a necessary condition of the Apocalypse:

> The essential characteristic of the fused group is the sudden resurrection of freedom. . . . The explosion of revolt, as the liquidation of the collective, does not have its *direct* sources either in alienation revealed by freedom, or in freedom suffered as impotence; there has to be a conjunction of historical circumstances, a definite change in the situation, the danger of death, violence.[16]

The very urgency of the danger is the source of the fused group's fragility. It is 'a mere means to common security'.

> But if circumstances demand the persistence of the group (as an organ of defence, of vigilance, etc.), while people's hearts are untouched by an urgency or hostile violence, which might occasion common *praxis*; if its *praxis*, turning back upon itself, in the form of organization and differentiation, demands the unity of its members as the pre-existing foundation of all its transformations, then this unity can exist only as an inert synthesis within freedom itself.[17]

The emergence of a fused group is therefore the commencement of a process in which the practico-inert, the anti-dialectical opposite of free *praxis*, reasserts itself, for example in the form of bureaucratized institutions. The relevance of this analysis to the fate of the Russian Revolution should be obvious.

The fused group, 'the sudden resurrection of freedom', is thus an essentially temporary phenomenon which soon gives way to the power of the practico-inert. The fundamental antithesis in Sartre's thought between purposive individual action and its objective context (see section 2.4 above) shapes his discussion of seriality and the fused group. Any social relationship transcending an immediate collective response to the present threat of death represents the triumph of the practico-inert. Sartre does, unlike Benjamin, seek to specify the kind of historical situation which produces fused groups. But the very term which he uses to denote 'the dissolution of the series into a fused group' is surely significant. The Apocalypse is God revealing himself to his creatures. It is, in a sense, the equivalent in Christian theology of Benjamin's *Jetztzeit*, the 'Messianic cessation of happening'. Both Benjamin and Sartre thus mystify revolution by conceiving it as absolutely discontinous with the normal course of events. Using the

'Theses on the Philosophy of History' as a leitmotif, I shall argue in the rest of this chapter that Marx's analysis of the proletariat is essential to any tenable theory of socialist revolution. Claims that the working class is in the process of disappearing or is irredeemably fragmented are considered and dismissed (section 5.2), as is that argument that it would be irrational for proletarians to participate in a revolution (section 5.3). I then examine the idea, put forward by Benjamin among others, that revolutions necessarily conceive themselves as the restoration of some past state of affairs (section 5.4). This theory ignores the specific character of socialist revolutions, but, as I finally argue, one tradition, Marxism itself, is a necessary condition of the success of such revolutions (section 5.5).

5.2 MARXISM AND THE PROLETARIAT

The origin of the antinomy of routine fragmentation and redemptive irruption may be traced in Sartre's case to his metaphysical individualism, his insistence that 'the only practical dialectical reality, the motive force of everything, is *individual action*.'[18] On such a view structures can be conceived only as negative, the practico-inert sedimentation of past acts, which act as a limit and constraint on individual *praxis*. The kind of collective action involved in the fused group consists in the transcendence of structure, the temporary liquefaction of the practico-inert. Once we see, as I argued (following Giddens) in chapters 1 and 2, that structures *enable* as well as constrain, then we cannot treat individual action as 'the motive force of everything'. Structural capacities, the powers agents possess by virtue of their position in the relations of production, typically cannot be exercised by individual persons. Their exercise requires the construction of collectivities through which agents co-ordinate their actions on the basis of a recognized common identity. The relationship which structures have to such a collectivity is more than that of providing the immediate stimulus to common action which gives rise according to Sartre to the fused group, 'the danger of death, violence'. Their position within production relations provides class actors with the means to realize their objectives and consequently with an interest in acting collectively (see section 3.5). Structures are thus continuously present in such collective action, rather than dissolved by it.

The same general view of the relationship between structure and action is present in the classical Marxist theory of the working class. This theory has been recently caricatured by André Gorz, according to whom Marx conceived the proletariat as a secular equivalent of

Hegel's Absolute Spirit, the protagonist of an eschatological philosophy of history whose culmination is the revolution. Gorz calls thus 'a *truthful* reading' of Marx, though he prudently concedes that it involves 'no attempt to recover the *historical* itinerary of Marx's own thought which complete fidelity'.[19] The closest Marx comes to conceiving the proletariat as a philosophical category is in the 1843 Introduction to *A Contribution to a Critique of Hegel's Philosophy of Right*, where he regards workers as passive matter awaiting the activating spark of philosophy, though Lukács does of course treat the proletariat as the Hegelian absolute subject-object in *History and Class Consciousness*, a book which Benjamin admired and which may have influenced his conception of revolution as a Messianic intervention in the mundane world.[20]

Marx's rejection of his earlier view of the working class as the passive opposite of philosophy was a critical element in the formation of historical materialism in such works of the mid- and late 1840s as the *Economic and Philosophic Manuscripts*, *The German Ideology* and *The Poverty of Philosophy*. In these writings the proletariat is increasingly conceived as the class, formed within capitalist relations of production, which has the capacity to replace these with a classless communist society. This reconceptualization of the working class involves a shift from suffering and oppression to exploitation and power. The proletariat. Marx writes in the 1843 Introduction, 'is the *complete loss* of man and hence can win itself only through the *complete rewinning of man*'.[21] It is the depth of workers' misery which will drive them to revolt. In the *Communist Manifesto*, by contrast, Marx's focus is on the way in which 'the advance of industry, whose involuntary promoter is the bourgeoisie, replaces the isolation of the labourers, due to competition, by their revolutionary combination, due to association.'[22] Workers' position within capitalist production relations gives them the power collectively to challenge these relations.

Marx's reasons for regarding the proletariat as, in Hal Draper's words, 'the special class', were succinctly restated recently by Francis Mulhern:

> The working class is revolutionary, Marxists have maintained, because of its historically constituted nature as the exploited collective producer within the capitalist mode of production. As the *exploited* class, it is caught in a systematic clash with capital, which cannot generally and permanently satisfy its needs. As the main *producing* class, it has the power to halt – and within limits redirect – the economic apparatus of capitalism, in pursuit of its goals. And as the *collective* producer it has the objective capacity to found a new, non-

exploitative mode of production. This combination of interest, power and creative capacity distinguishes the working class from every other social or political force in capitalist society, and qualifies it as the indispensable agency of socialism.[23]

The different aspects of the workers' situation distinguished by Mulhern are closely related. Capitalism, Marx argues, tends towards the 'real subsumption of labour under capital', in which exploitation assumes the form of the extraction of relative surplus-value, thanks to increases in labour productivity themselves made possible by the transformation of the production process, initially in the form of the replacement of manufacture by machinofacture. This process involves the creation of the 'collective worker', the integration of individual wage-labourers into a co-ordinated and socialized production process.[24] Workers are thus exploited collectively; any resistance to their exploitation, if it is to go beyond relatively undeveloped forms such as absenteeism and sabotage, must therefore itself be collective. The interconnected character of production gives strategically placed groups of workers the power to paralyse often a wide range of economic processes. Workers' structural capacity collectively to organize against their exploitation derives from the form this exploitation takes.

A power may exist without being exercised. Sartre's analysis of seriality does reveal with considerable acuity a central feature of capitalist social formations, namely that those living within them tend to conduct themselves as passive and isolated consumers dependent on the initiatives of others.[25] Revolution certainly is a qualitative leap from such a situation. Marx's theory of commodity fetishism shows him to be aware of the fragmented character of people's experience of capitalism. Draper imagines him confronted with the working class as it actually is:

> Mentally crippled by the ruling ideas they absorb . . . cramped by tradition and habit into patterns of acquiescence. *You expect these wretches to make a revolution?*

> Marx's answer is: no. These people as they are cannot make a revolution or build a new world. They will have to be changed and transformed before they are fit to take power or wield it. But they will not be changed by preachments, books, leaders, or commands. They will become fit to rule only through their own struggle – a course of struggles against intolerable conditions, to change the conditions and thus change themselves.[26]

It is the class struggle under capitalism which, for Marx, provides the bridge between the 'continuum of history' and the *Jetztzeit* of revolution. It is able to fulfill this role because every strike is simultaneously a struggle *within and against* capitalism. Workers engaging in strikes and other forms of industrial conflict are typically concerned with such issues as higher wages or better conditions, i.e. they are pursuing the improvement of their condition within the framework of capitalist production relations. At the same time they are compelled in order to achieve this objective to organize collectively against their employer. In other words, the methods which they use are those of class struggle, rooted in the antagonistic interests of labour and capital. The duality of trade-union struggle helps to explain the duality of working-class consciousness discussed in section 4.2. The pursuit of what Daniel de Leon dismissed contemptuously as 'palliatives' is therefore part of what Marx described as the 'protracted and more or less concealed civil war between the capitalist class and the working class'. It was in this respect that with the growth of capitalism, Marx believed, 'there also grows the revolt of the working class, a class constantly increasing in numbers, and trained, united and organized by the very mechanism of the capitalist process of production.'[27] Marx distinguished himself by his insistence that the trade-union struggle was indispensable as a means of transforming the working class into a political force with the capacity to overturn capital and build communism. His insistence that the proletariat can only change society by changing itself through a protracted process of molecular economic battles with its exploiters comes out clearly in his declaration in 1850 that 'we say to the workers: You have 15, 20, 50 years of civil war to go through in order to alter the situation and to train yourselves for the exercise of power.'[28]

If one were to name that aspect of Marx's thought which is currently regarded with most scepticism even by those generally sympathetic to his ideas, it would probably be this belief that the struggle of the working class within capitalism will generate a collective actor capable of installing socialism. At its most vulgar this scepticism takes the form of the claim, made most forcefully by Gorz in his book *Farewell to the Working Class*, that the proletariat is in the process of being abolished by technological change. Empirically this assertion does not hold water. If we take the case of the most important economy, the US, we find that in 1982, at the height of the last major recession, while the number of manufacturing employees, (18,853,000), was lower than its peak four years previously (20,505,000), it was still higher than the figure for 1960 (16,796,000).

What had fallen was the proportion of manufacturing employees in the work-force, from 31 per cent in 1960, to 23.7 per cent in 1978 and 21 per cent in 1982.[29] What is misleadingly called 'deindustrialization' typically takes the form of a fall in the share of output and employment taken by manufacturing rather than an absolute fall. (Though even in Britain, which has suffered real deindustrialization since the late 1970s, manufacturing employees still numbered 5,399,600 in September 1985, over a quarter of all employees.)[30]

Marx indeed noted: 'the extraordinary increase in the productivity of large-scale industry, accompanied as it is by both a more intensive and a more extensive exploitation of labour-power in all other spheres of production, permits a larger and larger part of the working class to be employed unproductively.' Thus in 1861 the largest single group of employees was domestic servants, who numbered 1,202,648, compared with 642,607 textile workers, 565,835 miners and 396,998 metal-workers.[31]

This passage from *Capital* is instructive, since it suggests that Marx did not identify the working class with any particular set of occupations, for example, those in manufacturing industry: domestic servants are 'part of the working class', albeit an unproductive portion in the sense of not creating surplus-value. In line with Marx's general relational understanding of class, the proletariat is best defined as all wage-labourers

(1) compelled by lack of access to the means of production to sell their labour-power; and
(2) the use of whose labour-power within the process of production is subject to the supervision and control of capital and its agents.

By these criteria, the working class has grown considerably in the present century with the enormous expansion of routine white-collar positions whose occupants are, by the above definition, as proletarian as any miner or car-worker. The changes in recent years which have led Gorz and his like to speak of the tendential disappearance of the working class, and of which the contraction of manufacturing's share of output and employment in the Western economies is the most widely noted symptom, are best seen as an instance of a process which has occured throughout the history of industrial capitalism, namely the recomposition of the proletariat in response to an altering structure of capital accumulation. Another such symptom, the growth of manufacturing industry in new centres of capital accumulation outside the advanced economies, the newly industrializing countries concentrated especially in Latin America and East Asia, indicates that the working class has, on a global scale, expanded substantially.[32]

There are, of course, far more sophisticated criticisms of Marx than Gorz's pop sociology. Thus, Erik Olin Wright's recent book *Classes* represents an attempt to show that class structure is far more fragmented than Marx claimed. Wright had earlier developed the well-known theory of contradictory class locations. This was a relatively orthodox attempt to fit what is sometimes called the 'service class' of professional, managerial and administrative employees into Marxist class theory. Wright argued that in modern capitalism there are quite a large number of contradictory class locations, that is, positions which share some of the properties of both labour and capital: thus managers and supervisors must sell their labour-power in order to live, but perform various functions of capital, for example, directing the work of other wage-labourers on behalf of their common employer.

Various anomalies in the theory, however, led Wright to abandon it and to offer a new account of class which is a refinement of John Roemer's work on exploitation. Wright's main innovation is to distinguish between four kinds of productive asset whose unequal distribution generates exploitation – labour-power, means of production, organization and skills. A mode of production corresponds to each such asset: feudalism is based on unequal distribution of labour-power, capitalism of means of production, 'statism' of organization and socialism of skills.[34]

Wright argues:

> Since concrete societies are rarely, if ever, characterized by a single mode of production, the actual class structure of given societies will be characterized by complex patterns of intersecting exploitation relations. There will therefore tend to be some positions which are exploiting along one dimension of exploitation relations, while on another are exploited. Highly skilled wage-earners (e.g. professionals) in capitalism are a good example: they are capitalistically exploited because they lack assets in capital and yet are skill exploiters. Such positions are what are typically referred to as the 'new middle class' of a given class system.

The 'new middle class' of capitalism consists mainly in managers and bureaucrats who exploit thanks to their control over 'organizational assets'. Since they could establish themselves as the chief exploiting class in a 'statist' class system, 'it is no longer axiomatic that the proletariat is the unique, or perhaps even universally the central, rival to the capitalist class for class power in capitalist society . . . there are other class forces within capitalism that have the potential to pose an alternative to capitalism.'[35]

Wright's account of 'skill exploitation' is drawn from Roemer's work, and indeed he is (wisely) reluctant to treat it as the basis of a full-blown class structure: furthermore, Wright's attempt to provide empirical support for his reconceptualization of class is least successful in the case of those workers who are exploiters supposedly because of their possession of skills or credentials.[36] He is more firmly committed, however, to the notion of 'organization-asset exploitation'. But this concept involves a number of difficulties. In the first place, it does not seem plausible to make the kind of sharp differentiation of various productive assets attempted by Roemer and Wright. Feudal exploitation, for example, cannot consist simply in control over labour-power: Barry Hindess and Paul Hirst argue persuasively that a degree of control over the means of production secured through feudal landed property and the various forms of rent is essential to the extraction of surplus-labour in this mode of production (note also that G. A. Cohen's table of modes, reproduced in section 2.2, ascribes to the lords some control over the means of production as well as over labour-power).[37] The point can surely be generalized: since production involves particular combinations of both labour-power and the means of production, an exploiting class can only reliably extract surplus-labour if it has at least some control over both. The differences among modes of production depend on the various ways in which this control can be secured. Thus in the case of capitalism a ruling-class monopoly of the means of production enables the exploiters also to control labour-power.

It seems equally difficult to separate out 'organization', at least in the sense in which it is understood by Wright, as the 'conditions of co-ordinated co-operation among producers in a complex division of labour'.[38] Control over such assets will be of more than academic relevance to an exploiting class interested in controlling, to varying degrees, labour-power and the means of production. Wright doesn't have much to say about the nature of 'organizational assets'. Some studies of managerial power distinguish between 'allocative' or 'strategic' control and 'operational' control. The former consists in 'the power to employ resources or to withdraw them, in line with one's own interests and preferences', the latter in 'control over the day-to-day use of resources already allocated'. It seems plausible to treat those professional managers who are involved in the exercise of strategic control, for example participating in investment decisions, as the part of the capitalist class, even though they may have no significant shareholding in the corporation concerned.[39] What reason is there to regard those in positions which involve them only in operational control as involved in exploitation by virtue of their control over rather meagre 'organizational assets'?

Wright gives two main reasons for doing so. First, he argues that his earlier theory of contradictory class locations 'rested almost exclusively on relations of domination'.[40] In deed, as we saw in section 2.4, Wright's identification of class with domination was a critical element in his abandonment of the labour theory of value for a Roemerian account of exploitation. Nevertheless, Wright had offered an analysis of managers in positions of operational control based upon Marx's own theory of exploitation:

> The delegation of power to managers poses certain problems to capital, in particular, the problem of ensuring that this power be used in responsible and creative ways. . . . Income, as a graded structure of bribes, is a crucial element in creating the motivational inducements to such behaviour. And this implies . . . that managers' incomes will contain an element above and beyond the cost of reproducing the value of labour-power (i.e. reimbursing them for the costs of the production and reproduction of their skills), an element which reflects their position as a contradictory location within class relations.[41]

The idea is that managers are paid a portion of the surplus-value extracted from the workers whose labour they supervise and control in order to ensure that they perform this role in a reliable and effective manner. Not only is this a plausible claim to make, but Wright's own research provided evidence that 'managers receive an income which is systematically above the value of their labour-power.'[42] However, he now rejects this earlier proposal to treat managerial positions as an instance of 'strategic jobs', i.e. 'jobs which are difficult to monitor but are highly sensitive to differences in conscientiousness' because 'we cannot derive any clear class relations from the analysis of strategic jobs as such.'[43] But why should we expect that managerial positions involve 'clear class relations'? The only answer can be that Wright has some other reason for seeking to treat 'organizational assets' as a distinct productive resource.

And indeed he does:

> The formal operational criteria used [by Wright on the basis of his theory of contradictory class locations] in much of the empirical analysis of classes could be applied to either capitalist or 'actually existing socialist societies' almost without modification. There were no elements within the analysis of class relations which could give any real specificity to the class structures of post-capitalist societies or point the direction for the analysis of post-capitalist classes within capitalism.[44]

Wright's analysis of 'organizational assets' as a distinct basis of exploitation cannot be separated from his belief that there exists a post-capitalist mode of production other than socialism and communism, namely 'statism', in which the main exploiting class consists of bureaucrats and managers. 'Actually existing socialist societies' are in fact 'state bureaucratic socialist', combing the 'statist' and socialist modes of production.[45]

Wright's mode of reasoning here is typical of a very wide-spread response by contemporary social theorists. No moderately honest and intelligent observer of the USSR and societies like it can deny that they display the features which make capitalism obnoxious – social inequality, sexual, national and racial oppression, political repression, widespread poverty and (in cases such as Poland, Yugoslavia and China) unemployment. Since Marx claimed that such features are characteristic of class societies and will gradually disappear subsequent to the abolition of capitalism, social theorists conclude that their persistence under socialism has proven Marx wrong. Historical materialism, with its focus on the development of the productive forces and the class struggle, cannot account for all forms of social oppression and domination. The Nietzschean and neo-Weberian preoccupation with power characteristic of much contemporary social theory springs from this source: since forms of domination such as that of men over women do not disappear with the abolition of class exploitation then we must treat such forms as autonomous sources of social power. Roemer's and Wright's reconceptualization of exploitation and class is a variant of this kind of response, which seeks to remain within the framework of Marxism by discovering new kinds of exploitation – 'skill-exploitation' and 'organization-asset exploitation' – which persist after the abolition of capitalism.

There is another, more economical way of coming to terms with 'actually existing socialism'. This is to say that if inequality and oppression of a kind which Marx associated with capitalism are to be found in social formations which call themselves socialist, this is *prima facie* evidence for denying them such a title and indeed for describing them as capitalist instead. The main reason for treating the USSR and its ilk as 'post-capitalist' is that the state owns the means of production, but the kind of ownership which counted for Marx was effective possession of the means of production, not legal property relations (see section 2.2). Tony Cliff and others have indeed developed a theoretical account of the 'socialist societies' which treats them as instances of bureaucratic state capitalism, a variant of the capitalist mode in which the means of production are collectively controlled by a central political bureaucracy on whom the dynamic of accumulation is enforced through the competitive pressure, both military and economic, of other states.[46]

If we accept this analysis – and the case for doing so seems to me overwhelming – then Wright's case for the concept of 'organizational-asset exploitation' collapses. As we have seen, there is an alternative account of groups such as managers, based on his earlier theory of contradictory class locations, which gives due weight to the concept of exploitation, albeit treated in classical Marxist and not Roemerian terms. It is a strength and not a weakness of that account that it may be applied to state-capitalist social formations. It is ironic that Wright should give as one reason for rejecting this theory that it opens the door to 'domination-centred concepts of class [which] tend to slide into what can be termed the "multiple oppressions" approach to society'.[47] For the alternative he provides could be called the 'multiple exploitation' approach, in which society consists in complexes of intersecting and cross-cutting exploitation-interests generated by access to a variety of different resources – skills, organizational assets, means of production, labour-power. It is not clear what prevents this list of productive assets from being extended to include the kinds of sources of social power on which theorists of domination focus, for example, the military power on which Michael Mann lays such stress. If this is so, the difference between Wright's conception of exploitation and Nietzschean and neo-Weberian notions of power and domination seems only verbal.

5.3 THE RATIONALITY OF REVOLUTION

The objections we have so far considered to the classical Marxist theory of the working class have been empirical, in the sense that they have involved the claim, for example, that the class structure of contemporary capitalism is far more fragmented than Marx had thought. But there is another kind of criticism, which is primarily conceptual, bringing into question the very possibility of collective action. This is what has come to be known as the free-rider problem. It is one of the most important findings of rational-choice theory and arises from the nature of a public good. Mancur Olson, in his classic formulation of the problem, defines a public good as

'any good such that, if any person X_i in a group $X_1, \ldots X_i, \ldots, X_n$ consumes it, it cannot feasibly be withheld from the others in that group.'

Crucially, while not all members of the group need contribute to producing the good, the good is available to all, and excluding non-contributors is either impossible or too costly to be feasible. Given these latter two properties of public goods, jointness of supply and non-excludability, why should any individual member of the group contribute to producing them? Provided the group is sufficiently large, his or her own contribution will be too small to make any perceptible difference to the production of a public good. Since he or she cannot be prevented from consuming it, it is rational for him or her to free-ride rather than incur the cost of contributing. Therefore, 'large organizations [cannot] support themselves without providing same sanction, or some attraction distinct from the public good itself, that will lead individuals to help bear the burden of maintaining the organization.'[48]

It is important to appreciate that the public good benefits the free rider. It is in his or her interest that it is produced. The problem is whether it is rational to do what is in one's interests, provided that one's interests are shared by a sufficiently large group for one's contribution to make no appreciable difference to the outcome and that one will benefit from the outcome whatever one does. Public goods have been classically thought of as the services produced by the state, for example the activities known these days by the Orwellian term 'defence'. But Olson, and, following him, Allen Buchanan, also explore the implications of treating solidarity as a public good. Thus Olson argues that 'compulsory membership and picket lines are of . . . the essence of trade unionism' since its benefits 'could offer the rational worker no incentive to join; his individual efforts would not have a noticeable effect on the outcome, and whether he supported the union or not he would still get the benefits of its achievements'. The argument cuts, Olson argues, to the heart of Marxism. Marx had relied on individual workers pursuing their interests to generate class action. But: '*class-oriented action will not occur if the individuals that make up a class act rationally.*' This is as true of socialist revolution as it is of strikes:

> A worker who thought he would benefit from a 'proletarian' government would not find it rational to risk his life and resources to start a revolution against the bourgeois government. It would be just as reasonable to suppose that all of the workers in the country would voluntarily restrict their hours of work in order to raise the wages of labour in relation to the rewards of labour. For in both cases the individual would find that he would get the benefits of the class action whether he participated or not.[49]

William Shaw comments:

> The situation of the proletariat as depicted by Olson and Buchanan is
> an instance of what A. K. Sen . . . calls the 'isolation paradox', which is
> characterized by two features. First, regardless of what other persons
> do, each is better off doing A than B. Second, each prefers everyone
> doing B to everyone doing A. The outcome in this situation is that
> individual strategy dominates, with each doing A, and a Pareto-inferior
> outcome results. Sen's paradox is just the generalization to *n*-person of
> the notorious Prisoner's Dilemma.[50]

The Prisoner's Dilemma takes the following form. Two prisoners,
held in isolation from one another, are confronted with the following
set of choices (table 5.1):

TABLE 5.1   THE PRISONER'S DILEMMA

	Prisoner 2	
Prisoner 1	Not Confess	Confess
Not Confess	1 year each	10 years for Prisoner 1; 3 months for Prisoner 2
Confess	3 months for Prisoner 1; 10 years for Prisoner 2	8 years each

The optimal solution would be for both not to confess, since then
they would each get a year in gaol. However, if one confesses and the
other doesn't, the silent prisoner will end up with a ten-year term,
while the stool-pigeon will get off very lightly. So the rational strategy
is for each to confess, even though the outcome is the suboptimal
situation of both getting eight years. Nevertheless, the alternative
strategy of co-operation required to achieve the optimal outcome, i.e.
both remaining silent, is not a stable solution to the game, since each
has an incentive to defect.

The Prisoner's Dilemma and its extensions, of which the free-rider
problem is one, exert a peculiar fascination for many social theorists.
They suggest that collective action is an inherently problematic
project, that the atomized situation of individuals, which Sartre
analysed under the concept of seriality, indeed condemns the working
class to impotence. Buchanan, following Olson, argues that the
alternative is to force workers to be free: 'if . . . there is a public goods
problem for the proletariat, coercion of the proletarians by a
dedicated elite may be needed even where the entire proletariat is

convinced that its own interests dicate the overthrow of the system.'[51] Such a solution to the free-rider problem would have been repellent to Marx, for whom 'the proletarian movement is the self-conscious, independent movement of the immense majority, in the interest of the immense majority.'[52]

There are two ways of responding to the free-rider problem consistent with the classical Marxist conception of socialism as the self-emancipation of the working class rather than the gift of a revolutionary elite. The first remains within the framework of rational-choice theory. It has long been recognized in the case of the Prisoner's Dilemma that both prisoners confessing ceases to be the dominant strategy once the game is iterated indefinitely. R. Duncan Luce and Howard Raiffa argue in their classic study of game theory that when the Prisoner's Dilemma is repeated,

> in most cases an unarticulated collusion between the players will develop, much in the same way as a mature economic market often exhibits a marked degree of collusion without any communication among the participants. This arises from the knowledge that the situation will be repeated and that reprisals are possible.[53]

So if the game is iterated n times, then in every game short of the nth both prisoners will have an incentive to co-operate, for if one defects, then he knows that he can be punished by the other prisoner in the next game. (The nth game itself will revert to the simple Prisoner's Dilemma, since the possibility of reprisal no longer exists, but this restriction is not relevant here.)

Shaw applies this finding to the case of the proletariat:

> Olson and Buchanan claim to have shown that collective action by the workers is irrational, but the logic of their argument presupposes, incorrectly, that the simple Prisoner's Dilemma captures fully the circumstances and preferences of the working class. When this presupposition is amended, however, the possibility of rational collective action by the proletariat in defence of its interests cannot be ruled out ... once the original dilemma is modified to mirror the proletariat's situation more accurately, then even totally self-regarding proletarians may find a way to realize their common interests. Enlightened egoists can be brought into collusion because of their knowledge that the situation will be repeated and that reprisals are possible; they can have self-interested reasons to stand by their agreements.

Shaw argues further that the Prisoner's Dilemma assumes too extreme a form of self-interest on the part of individuals: 'Conditional altruism is a plausible motivational assumption that envisions the workers as neither self-sacrificing nor moralistic on the one hand, nor egoistic on the other hand: One is willing (and would like) to co-operate but only if others join in.[54]

It is not clear that the possibility of reprisal enforcing a cooperative strategy when the Prisoner's Dilemma is repeated is a satisfactory solution to the free-rider problem, since Olson and Buchanan both stress the importance of coercion in achieving solidarity among workers. Shaw's suggestion that the isolation paradox is at fault in representing motivations as narrowly self-interested seems more promising. A response along these lines has being developed recently, albeit in a still somewhat tentative form, by G. A. Cohen:

> Each worker finds himself in a particular objective situation, with a particular set of interests and values, and consequently, a particular optimally rational course of action . . . in virtue of the mix of situations in which they are placed, and a predictable distribution of psychological variations, there are bound to be enough proletarians whose motiv-ations are such that each, being rational, they are bound to act in a revolutionary way.[55]

Cohen makes this claim as part of his argument that 'when capitalism is decline and socialism is possible, there are bound to be so many workers who have good reasons for joining the fight against capitalism that a successful socialist revolution will inevitably ensure' (see section 2.3 above). What concerns us here, however, is the nature of these 'good reasons'. Cohen imagines a number of different considerations which might motivate a revolutionary worker:

> One would be his desire to share the burden of bringing socialism about, which would otherwise fall heavier on each of the rest, or on each of some subset of them. Another would be his commitment to a more purely Kantian idea of fairness. A third would be the exhilaration induced in him by participation. And a fourth would be that he would be ashamed not to participate, when so much is at stake, and when others, perhaps more zealous than he, are risking so much. Even if he would not be very ashamed to contemplate his own inactivity, he might be moved by the prospect of how his fellow workers would contemplate it.[56]

What these kinds of revolutionary motivation have in common (and Cohen suggests that there could be others) is that none involves giving the inevitability of socialism as a reason for participating in the revolutionary movement. None is therefore vulnerable to the free-rider problem; indeed, they are all reasons for not free-riding. The first two clearly involve the agent's appeal to more or less articulated moral principles. Buchanan states a fairly obvious objection to 'appealing to moral principles as a *Marxian* response to the public goods problem', namely that 'it requires a wholesale rejection of Marx's fundamental claim that the proletarian's motive is self-interest or the interests of his class.'[57] Cohen's argument may not be vulnerable to this objection. He seems to treat an agent's motivation as a particular set of preferences ('interests and values') which entail, given the optimizing principle (see section 1.2), 'a particular optimally rational course of action'. A commitment, for example, to fairness would simply be one preference among others, not analytically distinguishable from, let us say, the desire to maximize income. An agent's moral commitments would thus simply serve to constitute her interests along with other preferences more directly concerned with her material welfare. Cohen's claim simply is that capitalism will produce workers with preference-sets which lead them to participate in revolution. These preference-sets may include acceptance of moral principles such as fairness, or they may not, as in the case of the worker who is exhilarated by participation in struggle; what is crucial about them is something else – that they all give workers reasons to participate irrespective of the fact that their participation will make no difference to the eventual outcome.

Another way of putting this is to say that Cohen, like Shaw, seeks a solution to the free-rider problem within the framework of rational-choice theory and in particular of the utilitarian theory of action. This theory, let us recall, treats the ends of action as random and concentrates on the ways in which optimizing agents will seek the most efficient means of realizing their preferences. The second kind of response to the free-rider problem consists, quite simply, in shaking off the bonds of the utilitarian theory of action. I have already argued, in section 3.4, that we should think of agents, in the terminology provided by Charles Taylor, not as the simple weighers of rational-choice theory, for whom the main problem is one of giving a consistent ordering to their preferences but as strong evaluators, who can shape and alter their desires.

Once we make this shift the Prisoner's Dilemma and its extensions become less pressing. Amartya Sen observes: 'Central to this problem is the assumption that when asked a question, the individual gives the answer which will maximize his personal gain. How good is this assumption? I doubt if it is very good.' Sen's reason for taking this stance has centrally to do with the concept, already mentioned in section 3.4, of commitment, which 'involve[s], in a very real sense, counter-preferential choice, destroying the crucial assumption that a chosen alternative must be better than (or at least as good as) the others for the person choosing it.'[58]

Consider a political prisoner under interrogation. If she confesses, many of her comrades will be caught, themselves tortured, and probably executed. Yet the pain of her own torture is unbearable. She would prefer to confess. By doing so she would be maximizing her own welfare. The pain involved in the thought of what her comrades would suffer if she confessed does not outweigh the relief which an end to her own torture would bring. Yet the prisoner does not confess, because her commitment to the movement of which she is part overrides her own preferences. One might describe her choice as irrational, but this seems a damagingly restricted conception of rationality, since the prisoner's counter-preferential commitment may arise from a political engagement that is both reflectively held and deeply felt. One of the few redeeming features of the twentieth century's proliferation of torture chambers is that there have been many cases like the one imagined. It is the assumption that the behaviour involved is irrational which in the end makes the Prisoner's Dilemma, despite its analytical subtleties and undoubted importance, so irredeemably crass.

Buchanan might object that commitment is nothing but a Kantian notion of moral obligation, whose recognition involves austerely overriding our desires in accordance with the universal dictates of reason. But Sen specifically rejects 'viewing behaviour in terms of the traditional dichotomy between egoism and universalized moral systems. . . . Groups intermediate between oneself and all, such as class and community, provide the focus of many actions involving commitment.'[59] Commitment involves evaluation, but the agent who chooses to override his or her preferences is not so much the abstract moral self of deontological ethics as the bearer of much more concrete social identities. The point can be made more sharply when we recall something Taylor says about strong evaluation: 'Motivations or desires don't only count in virtue of the attraction of the consummations but also in virtue of the kind of life and kind of subject that these desires properly belong to.'[60]

Now important decisions by workers over whether to engage in class action often involve reflection on the 'kind of subject' they wish to be. The great miners' strike of 1984–5 in Britain is a case in point. The bitter debates over participation in the strike typically involved a choice between two kinds of identities. The strikers were encouraged to see themselves as acting for their communities, their union, their industry, their class. The scabs, especially in Nottinghamshire, were invited to regard themselves as trade unionists of a different kind,

committed to a high-wage, high-productivity, strike-free industry and
taking their decisions through procedures such as the use of postal
ballots which mirror the serial structures of bourgeois democracy.
The identifications involved in being a striker were complex and
evolving. Early in the strike miners were encouraged to see themselves
as workers very much of a traditional sort – for example, in Arthur
Scargill's appeals to 'stand up like men and fight.' As the strike went
on, the sense of class identity of many strikers widened: as a result of
the active role played by the women of the mining communities, they
began to see their class as broader than traditional male stereotypes,
as consisting in both women and men; as a result of the repression
they experienced and the solidarity they received, miners began to
draw connections between their own situation and, for example, the
oppression of blacks and gays. The shame which many strikers
showed when they returned to work in the dying days of the strike is
illustrative of the degree to which moral considerations entered into
their motivations. They recognized, like those who did stay out, that
it was better to stick it out to the end, even if the end were
increasingly certain defeat.

Drawing attention to the phenomenon of commitment is not
intended simply to dismiss out of hand the free-rider problem. Shaw
rightly observes that 'the Prisoner's Dilemma and related puzzles
highlight actual obstructions in the social world. . . . The collective
action and group solidarity necessary for achieving socialism have to
be forged from the individualistic behaviour of unco-ordinated
monads, from the atomism of the present systems'.[61] Rational-choice
theory captures fundamental features of our social world. Furthermore, any student of strikes and revolutions know that that workers
frequently engage in the careful calculation of costs and benefits
before engaging in collective action. Free-riding is always a real
option. But it is frequently rejected. To explain why this happens we
must recognize that the utilitarian theory of action does not provide
an exhaustive or adequate account of agency.

Moreover, the idea that acting in accordance with one's interests
and acting in the light of moral considerations involve two quite
different orders of choice is fallacious. Typically the entities in the
light of commitments to which persons act are social collectivities –
family, nation, class. It is often out of a sense of commitment that
someone acts in what he or she perceives as his or her class interest
rather than free-ride. As Sen puts it:

> Moral considerations involving the question 'if I do not do it, how can
> I morally want others to do it?', do affect the behaviour of people. The

'others' involved may be members of narrowly defined groups or classes, or widely defined societies, but such considerations do have a role in influencing choice.[62]

There are many Marxists who would greet with scorn the idea that moral considerations of this kind often inform class action. But their objection, if theoretically articulated, is likely to stem from a Kantian conception of morality as a set of universal rules. But once we acknowledge, as I urged in section 1.4, that the best way of making sense of Marx's evaluative commitments is to ascribe to him an Aristotelian, virtue-based morality which is concerned with the empirically identifiable, historically specific conditions of human well-being (*eudaimonia*), this objection seems much less powerful. Let us recall that for Aristotle the virtues are dispositions to behave in ways that both help to achieve *eudaimonia* and are themselves partially constitutive of it. Does not Marx's account of how the class struggle itself develops and transforms workers to the point where they can overthrow capitalism and build communism contain echoes of Aristotle's theory of the virtues?

The foregoing discussion of the free-rider problem has proceeded on the assumption that socialist revolution is in the interests of the proletariat. Adam Przeworski has recently suggested that this assumption is questionable, since even if socialism is an improvement on capitalism, the costs of the transition from one mode of production to the other are too great for it to be worth undertaking. Przeworski writes: 'All that is needed for workers to rationally opt for socialism out of their material interests are two conditions: that socialism be more efficient in satisfying material needs than capitalism and that moving toward socialism would immediately and continually improve workers' material conditions.'[63]

The trouble comes with the second condition:

> Suppose . . . that socialism is superior to capitalism. The crux of the problem is whether this superiority is sufficient for workers to opt for socialism. If it can be shown that conditions exist under which a move in the socialist direction would be inferior to a move along the path of capitalism, then one could no longer deduce workers' socialist orientation from their material interests.

Przeworski believes the antecedent of the sentence last cited is true. Capitalists will respond to their threatened expropriation by disinvestment and even by armed resistance. This response so raises the cost of the transition to socialism that it is rational for workers instead to pursue class compromise, involving an economic strategy whose aim is to increase both wages and profits on the basis of the partial socialization of investment along Keynesian lines.[64]

'That moving toward socialism would *immediately and continually* improve workers' material conditions' is an extremely strong condition, although Przeworski shows that social democrats have frequently been willing to endorse it.[65] Revolutionary socialists have been much less sanguine. Bukharin wrote in 1920, generalizing from the experience of the Great French Revolution and the American Civil War as well as October 1917:

> The experience of all revolutions, which from the very point of view of the development of productive powers had a powerful, positive influence, shows that this development was bought at the price of an enormous plundering and destruction of these powers. It is not possible any other way, in so far as we speak of revolution. For in the revolution, the shell of production relations, i.e. the personal apparatus of labour, is exploded, and this means, and *must* mean, a disturbance of the process of reproduction and consequently also a destruction of productive powers.

> If that is so – and it is absolutely so – then it must be a priori evident that the proletarian revolution is inevitably accompanied by a strong decline of productive powers, for no revolution experiences such a broad and deep *break* in old relationships and their *rebuilding* in a new way. And nevertheless, the proletarian revolution constitutes from the very point of view of the *development* of productive powers an objective necessity. This objective necessity is provided by the fact that the economic shell has become *inconsistent* with the development of productive powers. *World productive powers are not compatible with the state-national structure of society, and the contradiction is 'solved' by war. War itself becomes incompatible with the existence of the basic productive power – the working class – and the contradiction can only be solved – really solved – by revolution.*[66]

The revolutionary view of the transition to socialism is, then, that it is a case of *réculer pour mieux sauter*: the temporary retrogression of the productive forces involved in overthrowing capitalism is a necessary condition of their further development under socialism. But why should workers suffer material sacrifices now for the sake of some future improvement? The answer which Bukharin gives is that the material situation of workers under capitalism is liable to deteriorate because of this mode of production's tendencies towards crises and wars. Przeworski considers this argument, albeit in a rather confused and dismissive fashion. A situation in which

> compromise is impossible, workers make economic demands, provoke a political crisis, and in this crisis the only choice may come to be that

between socialism and authoritarian capitalism, is the one typically envisaged by Marxists as the road to socialism. This is a scenario that leads to the *politique de pire*: in this view, the worse the economic situation under capitalism, the more likely socialism becomes. I am persuaded that this strategy of crisis-mongering is unfeasible and irresponsible.[67]

Quite aside from the pomposity of the last sentence, this won't do as an argument at all. Przeworski ends up by accusing revolutionaries of actively seeking to provoke economic crisies. But even third-period Stalinists weren't silly enough to think that they had, or should have caused the Great Depression of the 1930s. The *politique de pire* of which they were the main practitioners consisted rather in acting on the belief that a Nazi conquest of power would so heighten the contradictions of German society as to be merely the prelude to proletarian revolution. Forgetting the follies of the Stalinized Comintern, if we consider the classical Marxist tradition, the central tenet of its theory of crises is that they spring from structural features of the capitalist mode of production. The tendency of the rate of profit to fall is a consequence of the competitive activities of individual capitals, not of the collective acts or omissions of either bourgeoisie or proletariat. Przeworski by contrast seems to accept a neo-Ricardian theory of crises, according to which they are caused by distributional struggles by labour and capital over the relative shares of wages and profits in national income.[68] The political implications of analytical Marxism's rejection of Marxist economic theory (see section 2.4) here become evident.

The nub of the difference is this. For classical Marxism, the economic situation under capitalism is liable to deterioriate independently of the improvements which workers or capitalists consciously seek. If this is true, then what Przeworski describes as a principal condition of class compromise, namely that 'workers have a reasonable certainty that future wages will increases as a function of current profits', cannot be met.[69] On the contrary capitalists will in time of crisis seek reductions in existing wages without there being any secure prospect of living standards rising in the future. Przeworski, however, appears to believe that economic crises are in principle avoidable, that suitably organized state intervention can prevent them: thus, he regards 'a comprehensive, consistent system of public control over investment and income distribution' as both feasible and desirable.[70] Which of these views is correct depends on a variety of theoretical and empirical issues which cannot be explored, let alone settled here. Two points are worth making, though.

First, the classical Marxist is *not* required to accept the doctrine of immiseration, i.e. the view that there is a built-in tendency for real wages to fall. Marx, of course, rejected this theory as part of his more general break with Ricardian economics.[71] The classical Marxist is committed to two rather different claims, first, that capitalism is prone to regular economic crises, which, unless certain offsetting mechanisms are in operation, give rise to periods of endemic economic stagnation, political conflict, military rivalries and, in some parts of the world, famine, and, secondly, that the action of nation-states is insufficient to prevent such crises. The history of the twentieth century, with what now seems to have been the interlude of the 1950s and 1960s, looks like a pretty good confirmation of these claims.[72]

Secondly, what do socialists do in the situation Przeworski describes, where 'compromise is impossible'? He clearly believes that it would be wrong for workers to 'make economic demands' since this might 'provoke a political crisis' in which the choice is 'between socialism and authoritarian capitalism'. But consider the alternative. If workers do not defend their economic interests for fear of driving capital into the arms of reaction they are likely to be compelled to accept worse wages and conditions – the kinds of 'concessions' which have become such a feature of labour relations in the US since the late 1970s. The justification for their doing so is presumably that once capitalism is restored to profitability then a compromise from which both bourgeoisie and proletariat benefit can be struck. The dilemma was long ago stated by the German trade-union leader Fritz Tarnow, addressing the German Social Democratic Party (SPD) congress in 1931:

> Are we sitting at the sick-bed of capitalism, not only as doctors who want to cure the patient, but as prospective heirs who cannot wait for the end or would like to hasten it by administering poison? We are condemned, I think, to be doctors who seriously wish a cure, and yet we have to retain the feeling that we are heirs who wish to receive the entire legacy of the capitalist system today rather than tomorrow. This double role, doctor and heir, is a damned difficult task.[73]

The reward the German SPD received for acting as 'responsible' doctors of capitalism was, of course, Hitler. The outcome has not usually been as bad. But workers' leaders who have played a similar part, for example, the British Trade Union Congress, which struck a Social Contract with the Labour government in the 1970s, and the American labour leaders who in the early 1980s willingly negotiated 'concessions' to the employers, have generally received in exchange little but the weakening of their organizations and the demoralization of their rank and file. In the case of *Solidarność* in Poland, the pursuit by its leaders of a 'self-limiting revolution', which required 'responsible' behaviour on its members' part, helped to disarm one of the most powerful workers' movements ever seen in the face of the military power of the state.[74] Defenders of social democracy such as Przeworski tend to argue that terrible things will ensue unless workers act as doctors of capitalism in crisis. Frequently the terrible things happen anyway because the severity of the crisis means that capitalists demand more from workers than they are prepared to give except under compulsion. It is not 'crisis-mongering', but a sober reflection of historical experience to point this out. During the First World War Lenin quoted Schiller in support of his advocacy of revolution to end the bloodshed: 'Better a horrible end than a horror without end.' Perhaps today we should emend this to: Better a horrible end that saves humanity than one which destroys it.

5.4 REVOLUTION AND REPETITION

These reflections on the rationality of revolution ought to underline the indispensable role played by ideologies in forging collective actors. Thus the phenomenon of commitment is centrally concerned with the identifications a person makes, the collectivities of which she believes herself part. Frequently, as in the case of the miners' strike, engaging in collective action turns on a choice of social identities. At the same time, each identity is constituted by beliefs about the place in the social world that it involves, the relationships into which it is woven, the historical processes from which it has emerged.

In this context, let us consider one of Benjamin's darkest sayings in the 'Theses on the Philosophy of History', namely that revolution is 'a tiger's leap into the past'. This is perhaps the most extreme of a number of formulations which present revolution as based on tradition, having an orientation to the past rather than the future. Such a view seems bizarre in the extreme, since revolution is conceived by Marxists as a social and political transformation, a break with the past, and since the concept of tradition has been used since Burke by the proponents of counter-revolution to designate the organic social continuities which those who seek global change threaten to disrupt and destroy.

The lien between historical tradition and political reaction is well presented by the Tory philosopher Roger Scruton when he writes: 'When a man acts from tradition he sees what he *now* does as belonging to a pattern that transcends the focus of his present interest, binding it to what has previously been done and done successfully.' Tradition embraces 'all those practices which serve to define the individual's "being in society". It constitutes his image of himself as a fragment of the greater social organism, and at the same time as the whole of that organism implicit in this individual part'. Scruton gives the family as an example of such a practice. The justification of this institution is simply that it exists and that it does so because it has existed in the past. Herein lies the political content of the concept of tradition, that it rules out, indeed is incompatible with the reflective examination of the purpose and effects of established social practices. 'Tradition restores the individual to the present act: it shows the reason *in* the act, and stills the desire for a justifying aim.'[75]

A social practice is, then, traditional if it is at least partially constitutive of a person's social identity and if the reason for engaging in it is that things have been done this way in the past. The recent work of historians studying the 'invention of tradition', which we touched on in section 4.4, has shown that often such practices are comparatively recent constructs. Hallowed traditions turn out not to be naturally given from the past, but to have been formed in a context of often bitter social and political struggle. I shall give two examples, both from southern Africa. They suggest that the ethnic identities which are so often the bases of overt political action in the region are comparatively recent historical formations.

The first is that of Afrikaner nationalism. Much political commentary on South Africa consists in little more than a parade of clichés which treat all Afrikaans-speaking whites as members of a nation whose common interest above all in preserving white power overrides other conflicts, and whose political and social conduct has changed little since the Great Trek of the 1830s and the Boer republics to which it gave rise. In an important study Dan O'Meara shows that this view, held by many bitter opponents of apartheid, merely mirrors nationalist ideology. This ideology was itself formulated in the 1920s and 1930s by a comparatively small group of intellectuals, mainly around the Afrikaner Broederbond, as a response both to South Africa's subordinate status within the British Empire and the large-scale urbanization and proletarianization of the hitherto rural Afrikaans-speaking population. Central to the ideology was the concept of a divinely created, organically integrated Afrikaner *volk* whose course could be traced through a largely mythological history of the past three centuries and whose unity transcended class antagonism. The nationalist intelligentsia, through a variety of initiatives ranging from an organized intervention into the white trade unions to the ritual re-enactment of the Great Trek in its centenary year of 1938, sought, O'Meara argues, to interpellate Afrikaans-speaking whites as members of this *volk*. By doing so they hoped to win mass support for a political project which centred on gaining control of the state, and then using its power to achieve both political independence of Britain and the growth of Afrikaner capital, hitherto much weaker than its English-speaking counterparts. They succeeded, partly thanks to their own efforts, partly as a result of the shock waves which the emergence of a powerful urban black working class during the wartime economic boom sent through South African society. The National Party came into office in 1948, and mobilized the resources of state power ruthlessly to entrench its position and to destroy its enemies.[76]

Afrikaner nationalism is a case of the fairly conscious use of pre-existing cultural and political divisions to construct a national identity. The formation of tribal identities in southern Africa seems to have been an unintended consequence of broader historical processes. Terence Ranger has recently focused attention on the 'invention of tribalism'. His immediate concern is with Zimbabwe, but the thesis he develops is of more general application. The African population of Zimbabwe is thought of by both outside observers and its own members as divided into the Shona majority and Ndebele minority; there are also various Shona sub-groups – 'Manyika', 'Zezuru', 'Karanga', 'Kalanga' etc. Ranger argues, however, that the pre-colonial peoples of the Zimbabwean plateau defined themselves, not ethnically, but politically, as subjects of a particular chief or of the Ndebele state. Tribal identities, far from being 'deeply-rooted, immemorial, natural', are a product of colonial times. Ranger identifies a variety of factors as at work in the process through which these identities were formed: the racist assumptions of colonial administrators who expected to find tribes, who thought of the Ndebele as a 'warrior race' like the Zulu and who imposed on them various supposedly Zulu 'tribal laws'; the interest in a distinct Ndebele identity of the chiefly class, whose authority over commoners was thereby enhanced; the emergence of urban job hierarchies which associated people assumed to come from a certain tribal background with particular categories of work – Ndebele-speakers with over-seeing, 'Manyika' with domestic service, etc.; the effective invention of regional Shona dialects by various missions, which turned particular vernaculars into written languages and then through their control over African schooling transmitted their version of Shona to the black elite in much larger areas than the locality from which the original dialect sprang. Ranger stresses that 'the process . . . was certainly not just a matter of colonialist manipulation. It involved all sorts of African initiatives and creativities.' Nevertheless, 'identity has come to be thought of as a matter of language, culture, and ethnicity and even though the supposed linguistic, cultural and ethnic divisions are all spurious, such identity is regarded as something deeply-seated and "natural".'[77]

To identify the contingent and constructed character of national and ethnic identities such as those of Afrikaner or Ndebele is not to seek to explain them away. The fact that people act in the light of such identities is of enormous importance to the politics of both South Africa and Zimbabwe. Ranger sometimes writes as if the invented character of Zimbabwean tribalism makes it a mere epiphenomenon of deeper processes, irrelevant, say, to the coercion of Ndebele-speaking peasants by the Mugabe government.[78] Observation of contemporary South African politics underlines why this attitude is mistaken: the virulent 'tribal' divisions among black people in South Africa are, like those in Zimbabwe, largely of recent invention, but they are one factor in explaining the survival of white rule and could play a bloody part in that country's future.[79] The significance of studies such as O'Meara's and Ranger's is somewhat different. First, they challenge the essentialism so common in social theory which treats the existence of national, ethnic, tribal and racial identities as self-explanatory and which is closely associated with the Nietzschean and Weberian thesis that conflicts arising from such identities are inherent in the human condition. Secondly, they undermine the relation to the past which, according to Scruton, is all the reason traditions need to continue to exist. The historical continuities which traditions invoke turn out, only too often, to be fictions.

What the studies we have been discussing do not do is challenge the association between tradition and reaction which Scruton, in line with conservative thought from Burke to Oakshott, sought to establish. But there can be revolutionary inventions of traditions, or so Marx thought. His reflections on the relation between tradition and revolution at the beginning of *The Eighteenth Brumaire of Louis Bonaparte* form the context of his most famous saying on human agency:

> Men make their own history, but they do not make it just as they please; they do not make it under circumstances chosen by themselves, but under circumstances directly encountered, given and transmitted from the past. The tradition of all the dead generations weighs like a nightmare on the brain of the living. And just when they seem engaged in revolutionizing themselves and things, in creating something that

has never yet existed, precisely in such periods of revolutionary crisis they anxiously conjure up the spirits of the past to their service and borrow from them names, battle-cries and costumes in order to present the new scene of world history in this time-honoured disguise and this borrowed language. Thus Luther donned the mask of the Apostle Paul, the revolution of 1789 to 1814 draped itself alternately as the Roman Republic and the Roman Empire, and the revolution of 1848 knew nothing better to do than to parody, now 1789, now the revolutionary tradition of 1793 to 1795.[80]

These revolutions conceived of themselves not as transformations, but as repetitions, as representing continuity, not discontinuity. The examples which Marx gives could be multiplied. Thus the seventeenth-century English Revolution not only constantly appealed to biblical episodes to interpret itself, but, in line with a tradition which was to continue into the nineteenth century, tended to describe the court and its allies as alien usurpers, Norman predators who had illegitimately seized the land.[81] Such cases encouraged Gilles Deleuze to argue:

There aren't instances of repetition in history, rather repetition is the historical condition under which something new is actually produced. It isn't to the reflection of the historian that a resemblance between Luther and Paul, the revolution of 1789 and the Roman Republic etc., presents itself, rather it's first for themselves that the revolutionaries decide to conduct themselves as 'resurrected Romans', before becoming capable of action which they began by repeating in the manner of an appropriate past, thus in conditions such that they necessarily identify with a figure of the historical past. *Repetition is a condition of action before being a concept of reflection.*[82]

Marx, however, believed that that the self-image of repetition is peculiar to bourgeois revolutions, rather than a universal feature of all social transformations. French capitalism, he noted, dispensed with the paraphernalia of 'resurrected Romanity' after 1815:

Wholly absorbed in the production of wealth and its peaceful competitive struggle, it no longer comprehended that ghosts from the days of Rome had watched over its cradle. But unheroic as bourgeois society is, it nevertheless took heroism, sacrifice, terror, civil wars, and battles of peoples to bring it into being. And in the classically austere traditions of the Roman republics its gladiators found the ideals and the art-forms, the self-deceptions that they needed in order to conceal from themselves the bourgeois limitations of the content of their struggles and to maintain their passion on the high plane of great historical tragedy. Similarly, at another stage of development, a century earlier, Cromwell and the English people had borrowed speech, passions and illusions from the Old Testament for their bourgeois revolution. When the real aim had been achieved, when the bourgeois transformation of society had been accomplished, Locke supplanted Habbakuk.[83]

The thought is, then, that since bourgeois revolutions seek the emancipation not of humanity but of capitalism, they must of necessity take a mystified form, those engaged in them finding models of and reasons for their actions from a usually mythologized past. Socialist revolutions, in which the proletariat in overthrowing capitalist exploitation also provides the preconditions of what Marx called 'human emancipation', do not need so to conceal their real character:

> The social revolution of the nineteenth century cannot draw its poetry from the past, but only from the future. It cannot begin with itself before it has stripped off all superstitions about the past. Earlier revolutions required recollections of past world history in order to dull themselves to their own content. In order to arrive at its own content, the revolution of the nineteenth century must let the dead bury their dead. There the words went beyond the content; here the content goes beyond the words.[84]

The actors in proletarian revolutions do not therefore need to present what they are doing as repetitions of a mythical past, as do those making bourgeois revolutions. This is one of a number of contrasts Marx draws depicting the structural difference between bourgeois and socialist revolutions. This difference arises from the fact that the latter involve, while the former do not, 'the self-conscious, independent movement of the immense majority, in the interest of the immense majority'. There have been many revolutions since 1848. How well do they conform to the pattern Marx identifies?

There have been many more cases of what Göran Therborn calls *'mobilization by revival'*, revolutions as repetitions.[85] One of the most fascinating examples is provided by the guerilla war of 1972 to 1979 in Zimbabwe. Like many such struggles it involved guerillas spreading through the countryside to secure the support of the peasants who make up the bulk of the population. The guerillas were mainly members of the Zimbabwe African National Union (ZANU), whose political allegiance was to 'Marxism-Leninism-Mao-Tsetung-thought'. In 'conscientizing' the *povo* (people) they focused on economic and political issues, above all the control of half the land by less than six thousand white farmers. However, a symbiotic relationship developed in Shona-speaking areas between the ZANU guerillas and highly traditional figures, the mediums of the *mhondoro*, the spirits of the chiefs of the past. This relationship had a number of aspects. It was made possible by the fact that peasant religion, oriented on the *midzimu* (ancestors), vested ownership of the land in the *mhondoro*, thus providing grounds for the African claim to the land seized by white settlers with the establishment of the colonial state in the 1890s. It allowed the guerillas to establish a continuity between their struggle and the *chimurenga* of 1896 to 1897, the great rising of Shona chiefs against white rule, in which mediums such as that of Ambuya Nehanda played some part. Black nationalists (and sympathetic historians such as Ranger) had presented a somewhat idealized version of the *chimurenga* in which mediums such as Nehanda's were thought to have performed a central role. The current Nehanda medium was drawn into the early stages of the guerilla war of the 1970s, to provide a talisman for the second *chimurenga*. Spirit mediums in many areas were often crucial to integrating the guerillas into peasant society. Moreover, they did not simply act passively as bridges between present and past but participated actively in a shift in political power, in which secular authority was transferred first from the chiefs to the guerillas and then, with the coming of independence in 1980, to the village committees of ZANU-PF, the ruling party.[86]

This example of 'mobilization by revival' does not necessarily refute Marx's claim that it is bourgeois revolutions which must present themselves as repetitions of the past. For the outcome of the peasant war in Zimbabwe, contrary to the professed ideology of its leaders, has been the extension of class privilege to a black elite rather than the inauguration of socialism. The 'invention of tradition' involved in the alliance between guerillas and spirit mediums is best seen as the construction of a new national identity, of an 'imagined community' stretching beyond the local chiefdoms to whom political allegiance was owed in the past to embrace the whole territory of the state created by white settlers in the 1890s and now called 'Zimbabwe'. As David Lan observes,

> all nationalisms make use of metaphors of the land, of soil and earth, of territory and boundary, of monuments and graves, of the heroes of the past who are ancestors of the nation. The symbolism of the *mhondoro* gains its extraordinary effectiveness as an expression of the struggle for Zimbabwe from its ability to combine the economic and political aspects of the struggle in a single unforgettable image: the chiefs of the past, independent and prosperous, benign and generous to their followers, in sole possession and control of their bountiful fertile

lands. It is an image that has proved attractive to ministers of state and senior members of ZANU-PF.[87]

This fusion of Shona custom and Zimbabwean national identity helps to make intelligible the repression practised by the Zimbabwean state against Ndebele-speaking peasants in the two western provinces of Matabeleland. Lan notes that 'only the religious and political institutions of the Shona have contributed to the symbolism of the new state.'[88] Ndebele-speakers have thereby been excluded from this imagined community and have remained loyal to the minority nationalist party, the Zimbabwe African People's Union (ZAPU). The repression they have consequently suffered can be seen, in part, as part of the process of forcible assimilation of 'deviant' cultures characteristic of the formation of national identities. Similar episodes were essential to the creation of European nation-states, but are so long in the past that they can be forgotten, thrown into the shade by the progress of the nation along its predestined path. The extension of the nation-state form to the rest of the world since 1945 at least has this benefit, that it throws into relief the bloody struggles through which nations are formed. The proliferation of nationalisms, each imagining itself in direct continuity with the heroic past of a people which usually only acquires any identity through the very struggle for an independent state, is a sign that the history of bourgeois revolutions did not come to an end in 1848 and indeed has opened a major new chapter in the past generation.[89]

Bourgeois revolutions have tended to take a particular form in the twentieth century – that of a predominantly peasant movement led by an intelligentsia created usually to serve the colonial state but seeking to win control of that state and use it as a lever of locally directed capital accumulation.[90] From Ireland in 1916 to Zimbabwe in 1979 the same pattern has been repeated. But it is not solely in this context that revolutionary inventions of tradition have taken place. The two most important political upheavals of the past decade – the Iranian Revolution of 1978 to 1979 and the rise and fall of *Solidarność* in Poland in 1980 to 1981 – can plausibly be described as cases of 'mobilization by revival'. Yet they do not otherwise conform to this pattern. Fred Halliday observes:

The novelty of the Iranian Revolution resides in a central contradictory paradox: on the one hand, its leadership and ideology were resolutely retrogressive, the first ones in the history of modern revolution to be unequivocally religious, and so deeply hostile to the idea of progress; on the other hand, the social context in which the Iranian Revolution took place, and the manner of its success, were far more 'modern' than that of any other comparable upheavals. Most importantly, this revolution took place exclusively in the cities, the first Third World revolution to do so. Its means of struggle, the mass demonstration and political general strike, were those normally associated with conflict in the developed capitalist countries. The country in which it occurred, over 50 per cent urbanized and with a per capita income of more than £2,000, was in socio-economic terms far more 'developed' than Russia in 1917, or China in 1949. It was in the combination of these two characteristics, 'reactionary' and 'modern', that the originality of the Iranian Revolution lay.[91]

Solidarność also displayed, though in less extreme form, the same paradox, a highly democratic mass workers' movement organizing at its height nearly 80 per cent of the Polish work-force, in which the dominant ideology was traditional Polish nationalism, and whose daily practices were impregnated with the ritual and iconology of the Catholic Church. Let us consider this instance of the paradoxical combination of a working-class struggle with traditional beliefs. For many commentators, even those as as sensitive and thoughtful as Tim Garton Ash in his book *The Polish Revolution*, the explanation is simple, since *Solidarność* was a quintessentially Polish movement, displaying the uniqueness of the national character; the paradox exists only in the eyes of the Western beholder seeking to impose crude categories such as class onto the recalcitrant reality of Polish society. Such an analysis, involving an essentialism which treats national identity as somehow self-explanatory, will no more stand up to historical examination than any other instances of its kind.

Those who accept the idea of Poland as a quintessentially Catholic nation for the past millenium must come to terms with the fact that only 43 per cent of the inhabitants of the Polish lands in 1770 were Roman Catholics. Norman Davies argues in his major history of modern Poland that talk of Polish national identity before the nineteenth century is anachronistic:

> In the old Republic, prior to [the final partition of] 1795, Polish nationality could indeed be defined in terms of loyalty to the state. The 'Polish nation' was usually reserved as an appellation for those inhabitants who enjoyed full civil and political rights, and thus for the nobility alone. It did not refer to a man's native language, his religion, or ethnic origin. Hence, in this context, there were many 'Poles' who might not be so described now; and there were masses of Polish-speaking inhabitants, in the peasantry or bourgeoisie, who did not regard themselves as Poles.

Davies's conclusion should not come as a surprise after the discussions of nationality earlier in this section and in section 4.4.

'The fact is: the modern Polish nation is the end-product of modern Polish nationalism' and was forged in the struggle against foreign rule in the nineteenth century. Its preponderance is dated variously, from the insurrection of 1864, from 1918, or even from 1945, since Polish-speakers were only some two-thirds of the population of the pre-war republic.[92]

The intense attachments binding the Polish working class to Catholicism must be dated even more recently, to the clergy's involvement in the resistance to Nazi occupation and to the history of post-war Poland, and in particular the manner in which the church became the main embodiment of national identity and framework for organized opposition under 'Communist' rule. Colin Barker writes: 'what distinguishes the church since 1945 is the complex combination of *opposition and accommodation* it has achieved with the party regime, and the mutual benefits that church and regime derive from each other.' The church hierarchy was able to negotiate a constant strengthening of its institutional position within Polish society, in exchange for consistently preaching restraint in moments of political crisis such as 1956, 1970 and 1980 to 1981. Barker observes:

> If there is an analogy for the church's role in modern Poland, it is to be found in an institution such as the British Labour Party: it offers a kind of symbolic legitimation of grievances and aspirations, while at the same time it discourages workers' militant self-activity in support of their demands. Time and again, faced with workers' revolts, the church hierarchy's response has been to call for tranquillity and demobilization.[93]

Barker argues that Polish workers' relationship to Catholicism was in any case complex. In the first place, they 'possess a "subconscious Protestantism". Quite pragmatically, they reject aspects of Catholic dogma that do not suit them, while seeing no reason for abandoning religious faith'. This was especially so in the realm of sexual morality. Secondly, Polish workers used the ambiguities of Christian theology to justify their actions, often in defiance of the church hierarchy. (The analogies between such behaviour and the liberation theology of Latin America should be obvious.) Barker quotes the remarkable memoir of the strikes in the Polish coastal cities which gave birth to *Solidarność* in August 1980 by a port worker in Gdynia:

> One year earlier the Pope prayed in Victory Square, that the Holy Spirit might come down to Earth, but when the Word became Flesh, the Vicar of Christ failed to recognize the Messiah under the overalls of the people of the coastal region, the Messiah that sacrificed himself for the

thirty-five millions. Contemporary Pharisees and Sadducees found it difficult to grasp that He who had been painted by Michelangelo and presented in the form of gilded Baroque statues deigned to put on a coarse overall, sweaty, dirty, and often stinking with alcohol.[94]

Here is the voice of an authentic proletarian Messianism to which Benjamin might have responded. The overall effect, however, of the prevailing ideology among Polish workers was that they imagined themselves members of a community constituted by language, religion and the memory of national oppression. This community included the army, under General Jaruzelski, seen to some extent as the heir to the military traditions of the pre-war Republic. An opinion poll taken in December 1981, days before the military coup, found that 95 per cent of respondents placed 'some trust' in *Solidarność*, 93 per cent in the church, 68 per cent in the army and only 7 per cent in the party.[95] This faith in the military was fatal: it encouraged the belief that the army could be trusted not to fire on Poles, an illusion soon shattered after the military moved against *Solidarność* on 13 December. This attitude was closely bound up with the broader belief that Poland could undergo a 'self-limiting revolution', part of whose justification was the idea that 'Pole can speak to Pole', that a shared national interest would permit social reconciliation to take place, a *modus vivendi* between the state and the workers' movement to be achieved. General Jaruzelski was clearer-headed, understanding that the antagonism of interests between *Solidarność* and the ruling bureaucracy admitted of no other solution than one destroying the other. The tragedy was that no such clarity existed on the workers' side.

The case of *Solidarność* suggests that Marx was right to argue that the proletariat could not seek to justify its actions by appealing to supposed continuities with the past. The reason lies in the organic connection which seems to exist between the invention of tradition and the construction of the imagined communities characteristic of nationalism. In the case of the characteristic bourgeois revolutions of the twentieth century, a real congruence existed between the social character of movements for national liberation, involving the genuinely common interest of workers, peasants, intellectuals and local capitalists (the 'four-class bloc' beloved of revolutionary nationalism from China in the 1920s to South Africa today) in ending colonial rule and the idea of national community embracing these various classes, however fictional the identity and history of that community might actually be. In such circumstances drawing the struggle's 'speech, passions and illusions' from an imagined past as well as from present oppression could strengthen the movement for an independent state and give it coherence and cohesion, in the manner, for example, in which the alliance of nationalist guerillas and *mhondoro* spirit mediums made a vital contribution to the peasant war in Zimbabwe.

The case of the working class is a different one. To constitute itself fully as a collectivity, that is, to achieve revolutionary class-consciousness, requires a lucid understanding of its position within capitalist society and of the power and interest which this position gives it to build communism. To say that the proletariat needs above all to comprehend the *present*, the interconnections of the capitalist world-system and the struggles which take place within it, is an exaggeration, but nevertheless one that makes a point. To imagine itself part of a nation is disabling, and sometimes fatally so. Benedict Anderson defines the nation as 'an imagined political community – and imagined as both inherently limited and sovereign'. Two consequences of this definition are especially relevant here. First 'the nation is imagined as *limited* because even the largest of them . . . has finite, if elastic boundaries, beyond which lie other nations. No nation imagines itself coterminous with mankind.' Workers who accept their national identification thereby see workers outside this community as alien; the common interest of the proletariat as an *international* class faced with a capitalist system which is increasingly globally integrated is denied expression. Secondly, the nation 'is imagined as a *community*, because, regardless of the actual inequality and exploitation that may prevail within each, the nation is always conceived as a deep, horizontal comradeship'.[96] To accept this comradeship is, for workers, to bind them to their exploiters. This attitude need not take the form of denying the existence of class conflict; it is more likely to involve the kind of dual consciousness discussed in chapter 4; the antagonism between labour and capital is not denied but it is treated as secondary to that between nation-states. A contemporary example is the tendency of trade unionists to respond to higher unemployment by demanding import controls and other forms of protectionism: the main fault-lines in the world today are thought be those between nations rather than classes.

These points are, from the standpoint of classical Marxism, elementary ones. That they need stressing is a reflection of the extent to which the left today believes that socialism and nationalism are consistent with one another. This widespread atitude was expressed by Eric Hobsbawm after the Falklands War, when he wrote: 'It is dangerous to leave patriotism exclusively to the right.'[97] Ernesto Laclau provided the most sophisticated defence of this view, arguing that *'ideological "elements" taken in isolation have no necessary*

connotation. . . this connotation is only the result of the articulation
of these elements in a concrete ideological discourse.' The concept of
the nation is one such 'element', in the abstract neutral with respect to
class interests. Proletarian hegemony can only consist. Laclau argued,
'in absorbing all national traditions and in presenting the anti-
capitalist struggle as the culmination of democratic struggles and
socialism as the common denominator in a total offensive against the
dominant bloc'. The failure of the German workers' parties to
understand this was, according to Laclau, a principal reason for the
Nazi victory:

> The working class should have presented itself as the force which
> would lead the historic struggles of the German people to their
> conclusion, and to socialism as their consummation; it should have
> pointed to the limits of Prussianism, whose ambiguities and com-
> promises with the old dominant classes had led to the national
> catastrophe, and it should have made an appeal to all popular sectors
> to fight for a national renaissance which could be condensed into
> common ideological symbols: Nationalism, Socialism and Democracy.[98]

In fact, the German Communist Party (KPD) did, in the late 1920s
and early 1930s, espouse this kind of 'National Bolshevism'. That the
outcome was the triumph of fascism, not socialism, had much to do
with the fact that the KPD was thereby allowing the Nazis to dictate
the terms of political debate. Stuart Hall justifies Laclau's claim that
'particular ideas and concepts [do not] "belong" exclusively to one
particular class' thus:

> Ideas and concepts do not occur, in language or thought, in that single,
> isolated way with their content and reference irremovably fixed.
> Language in its widest sense is the vehicle of practical reasoning,
> calculation, and consciousness, because of the ways by which certain
> meanings and references have been historically secured. But its cogency
> depends on the 'logics' which connect one proposition to another in a
> chain of connected meanings; where the social connotations and
> historical meanings are condensed and reverberate off one another.
> Moreover, these chains are never permanently secured, either in their
> internal systems of meanings, or in terms of the social classes and
> groups to which they belong.[99]

Now it is true that how a sentence is taken depends heavily on the
circumstances in which it is uttered and the other sentences to which
it is conjoined. It is also true that many of the more abstract terms of
ideological discourse are sufficiently general or even ambiguous to

admit of differing meanings: the case given above of the Gdynia striker who identified Christ with the Polish working class is a good example. It follows from neither of these propositions that such terms have *no* definite meaning. Yet it is this last claim to which an exponent of the thesis that ideological elements are class-neutral is committed. It is therefore not surprising that Laclau should, subsequent to advancing this thesis, have abandoned 'classism' completely for a post-structuralist philosophy of language in which the meanings of terms are indeed constantly changing by virtue of the shifting relations of difference which constitute them.[100] Hall gives the example of the term 'democracy', which indeed admits of different applications. Yet there is surely a limit to the extent of these applications, given the core-meaning of 'democracy', namely rule by the people. Furthermore, the different ways in which 'democracy' is understood by the liberal defenders and Marxist critics of Western capitalist polities – as respectively serial structures based on the passivity and fragmentation of the electorate and forms of decision-making involving the active participation of masses organized around their places of work rather than geographical constitutencies – suggest that the term expresses distinct and mutually incompatible concepts.

Similarly with respect to the concept of the nation, there are left variants of nationalism: we referred above, for example, to the English radical myth of the Norman Yoke. However, the term 'nation' preserves a core sense in all its usages, referring to a community bound or aspiring to its own state and transcending class antagonisms. For socialists to seek take over 'all national traditions' is to court disaster. As Hobsbawm put it, in a wiser mood, quoting Lenin, 'do not paint nationalism red.'[101] Socialists who present their case from the perspective of the imagined communities of nationalism merely help perpetuate a situation in which 'the tradition of all the dead generations weighs like a nightmare on the brain of the living.'

5.5 THE TRADITION OF THE OPPRESSED

Benjamin did not entertain the dangerous fantasy that socialism and nationalism can be married. The focus of his reflections on the relationship between tradition and revolution is elsewhere. The respects in which he believes revolution to bear an essential relation to the past are twofold. The first appears in the drafts of the *Passagenarbeit*, Benjamin's great unfinished study of Baudelaire and the Paris of the Second Empire:

To the form of the means of production, which to begin with is still dominated by the old (Marx), there correspond images in the collective consciousness in which the new and the old are intermingled. These images are ideals, and in them the collective seeks not only to transfigure, but also to transcend, the immaturity of the social product and the deficiencies of the social order of production. In these ideals there also emerges a vigorous aspiration to break with what is outdated – which means, however, with the most recent past. These tendencies turn the fantasy, which gains its initial stimulus from the new, back upon the primal past. In the dream in which every epoch sees in images the epoch which is to succeed it, the latter appears coupled with elements of prehistory – that is to say of a classless society. The experiences of this society, which have their store-place in the collective unconscious, interact with the new to give birth to the Utopias which leave their traces in a thousand configurations, from permanent buildings to ephemeral fashions.[102]

Benjamin elsewhere links the notion of a collective memory of primitive communism to Baudelaire's concept of the *correspondances*, which, he says, 'record a concept of experience which includes ritual elements . . . The *correspondances* are the data of remembrance – not historical data, but data of prehistory. What makes festive days great and significant is the encounter with an earlier life.'[103] Löwy argues that Benjamin must be understood from this perspective: 'instead of "progress", revolution is "a tiger's leap into the past", searching for the lost paradise, the archaic golden age of edenic harmony between human beings, as well as between humanity and nature.' Benjamin's conception of the classless past is shaped, Löwy suggests, not only by Jewish Messianism, but also by Bachofen's studies of 'gynocratic' and egalitarian primitive communist societies.[104] Consequently, as Wolin puts it, 'the tendency for the modern to have recourse to elements of prehistory is no longer perceived [by Benjamin] simply as a regression, but rather as a *prefiguration of Utopia*: as the awakening in the collective unconscious of the memory of a "pre-historic classless society".'[105]

The 'relationship between the oldest and the newest' rightly attracted some of Adorno's most stringent criticisms of the *Passagenarbeit*. He argued that 'the image of classlessness is put back into mythology' and that the notion of a 'collective unconscious', of Jungian provenance, could not be fruitfully used by Marxism: 'it should be a clear and sufficient warning that in a dreaming collective no differences remain between classes.'[106] Indeed, by rooting class-consciousness in the remembrance of prehistory Benjamin occludes the possibility of the proletariat attaining such consciousness. This can be seen in two ways. First, Mikhail Bakhtin, that other great original of Marxist cultural theory, develops an analysis of 'folkloric culture' which has many similarities to Benjamin's discussion of remembrance. Folkloric culture, which has a variety of manifestations but particularly the carnivals of early modern Europe and the discourse of the novel, commencing with Rabelais, involves a particular form of consciousness and 'can be traced back to a pre-class agricultural stage in the development of human society'. These origins explain various of its features, notably an emphasis on the collective experience of work and nature. The rhythms of agricultural labour also account for a 'negative feature' of 'folkloric time': 'The mark of cyclicity, and consequently of cyclical repetitiveness, is imprinted on all events occurring in this type of time. Time's forward impulse is limited by the cycle. For this reason even growth does not achieve an authentic becoming.'[107] The tendency for peasants to perceive time as cyclical has been noted by other writers.[108]

It is not clear how the working class, formed from the dynamic development of the productive forces by capitalism, can draw strength from a form of consciousness reflecting the seasonal rhythms of pre-industrial labour. That Benjamin does see it as a source of strength is clear from the fifteenth 'Thesis on the Philosophy of History', where he approvingly describes the revolutionaries of 1830 firing on the clock-towers of Paris, rejecting the linear, homogeneous time of bourgeois society for the cyclical time of 'a historical consciousness of which not the slightest trace has been apparent in Europe in the past hundred years', but whose 'monuments' are 'holidays, which are days of remembrance', fragmentary recollections of the pre-industrial carnival re-enactments of a classless past.[109] Benjamin's hostility to the vulgar-Marxist faith in the growth of the productive forces as the motor of inevitable socialist revolution here leads him to ignore the aspect of capitalism on which Marx places such stress in the *Communist Manifesto*, its dynamic, restless, revolutionizing character, throwing society into a flux from which the proletariat can draw the power and the desire to seize power.[110]

Benjamin's tendency to deny to capitalism any progressive aspects (quite in contradiction with his overestimation elsewhere of the revolutionary potential of new means of cultural production such as the cinema)[111] is associated with a second difficulty. He often laments the manner in which bourgeois society is systematically destroying our remembrance of the 'primal past' of primitive communism.[112] As Wolin observes, Benjamin

is disturbed that the abyss separating the modern world from past
historical life has expanded to the point where an entire array of
tradition-bound meanings have become unrecognizable, if not patently
unserviceable, to us in the present. Not only does he fear the loss of
past experience, but also the serious impairment of the present-day
capacity to assimilate experience in general.[113]

If Benjamin is right, then it seems as if the development of
capitalism progressively denies us our memories of the classless past.
But if this is so, how can these memories serve to stimulate
revolutionary action? Conceiving revolution as the restoration of
primal harmony merely reiterates the antinomy we noted in section
5.1, between the mystified everyday world of commodity fetishism, of
Sartrean seriality and the *Jetztzeit* of revolution.

The threat which bourgeois society represents to our memories of
the past is indeed one of the main themes of Benjamin's 'Theses':

> Every image of the past that is not recognized by the present as one of
> its own concerns threatened to disappear irretrievably. . . . In every era
> the attempt must be made anew to wrest tradition away from a
> conformism that is about to overpower it. . . . Only that historian will
> have the gift of fanning the spark of hope in the past who is firmly
> convinced that *even the dead* will not be safe from the enemy if he
> wins. And this enemy has not ceased to be victorious.[114]

A similar thought has recently been made fashionable, albeit in a
far more abstract and indeed dehistoricized form by the Czech
novelist Milan Kundera: 'man's struggle against power is the struggle
of memory against forgetting.'[115] In Benjamin's case, however, his
concern is with the 'tradition of the oppressed', which constitutes
the second main aspect of his reflections on revolution's relation to
the past.

> The class struggle, which is always present to a historian influenced by
> Marx, is a fight for the crude and material things without which no
> refined and spiritual things could exist. Nevertheless, it is not in the
> form of the spoils which fall to the victor that the latter make their
> presence felt in the class struggle. They manifest themselves in this
> struggle as courage, humour, cunning, and fortitude. They have
> retroactive force and will constantly call into question every victory,
> past and present, of the rulers. As flowers turn toward the sun, by dint
> of a secret heliotropism the past strives toward that sun which is rising
> in the sky of history. A historical materialist must be aware of this most
> inconspicuous of all transformations.[116]

It is the memory of past exploitation and struggle which sustains the proletariat in its battles with capital:

> Not man or men but the struggling oppressed class itself is the depository of historical knowledge. In Marx it appears as the last enslaved class, as the avenger that completes the task of liberation in the name of generations of the downtrodden. . . . Social democracy thought fit to assign to the working class the role of redeemer of future generations, in this way cutting the sinews of its greatest strength. This training made the working class forget both its hatred and its spirit of sacrifice, for both are nourished by the image of enslaved ancestors rather than that of liberated grandchildren.[117]

Historical materialism, like the angel of history, faces backwards, seeking to reconstruct and keep alive the 'tradition of the oppressed', as Edward Thompson puts it, to rescue past struggles from the 'vast condescension of posterity'.[118] One of the most powerful affirmations of this attitude is to be found in G. E. M. de Ste Croix's *The Class Struggle in the Ancient Greek World*, whose frontispiece is Van Gogh's *The Potato Eaters*. Ste Croix calls the picture 'the most profound and moving representation in art of "the peasant". . . . These are the voiceless toilers, the great majority – let us not forget it – of the population of the Greek and Roman world, upon whom was built a great civilization which despised them and did all it could to forget them'.[119]

The preservation of the memory of past struggles is not, however, an end in itself. 'Historical materialism conceives historical understanding as an afterlife of that which is understood', Benjamin writes, 'whose pulse can still be felt in the present.'[120] The 'tradition of the oppressed' provides the impetus for revolutionary action. Here indeed Benjamin offers a concept of tradition which is neither the memory of an imaginary past binding together exploiter and exploited nor the remembrance of a mythical primitive communism but rather the sedimented experience of class struggle. But while the concept of the 'tradition of the oppressed' is not open to the kinds of objections raised against these other notions of tradition, the consciousness which it designates is subject to the constant danger of erosion. Memories of past struggle are vulnerable to the tendency Benjamin identifies towards 'the serious impairment of the present-day capacity to assimilate experience'. That this threat does not merely exist in Benjamin's imagination is indicated by the wholesale disintegration over the past generation of the all-embracing nexus of cultural, political and social institutions which grew up around the

European workers' parties, both social democratic and Communist, in the first half of this century.

Merely to focus on this kind of fragmenting of collective experience would nevertheless be misleading. Benjamin writes:

> In the long run, without self-confidence, no class can engage in political action with any success. But it makes a difference whether this optimism is felt for the active strength of the class, or for the circumstances in which it operates. Social democracy inclined towards the second, more questionable kind of optimism.[121]

Benjamin is right to say that one cannot merely rely on the historical process itself to bring about revolution, but to counterpose, as he does, objective 'circumstances' and the 'active strength' of the proletariat is equally fallacious. It contrasts sharply with Marx's insistence that 'in revolutionary activity the changing of oneself coincides with the changing of circumstances.'[122] Capitalism's contradictory development stimulates class battles which both increase workers' 'active strength' and revitalize the 'tradition of the oppressed.'

The central weakness of Benjamin's theory of revolution thus lies in the absence from it of Marx's analysis of the proletariat, the 'special class' formed within bourgeois relations of production but 'trained, united and organized by the very mechanism of the capitalist process of production' (see section 5.2 above). It is workers' collective experience of exploitation which leads them to organize against it, and to develop a consciousness of the antagonism between labour and capital and an awareness of their 'active strength'. To put it in terms of Gramsci's concept of 'contradictory consciousness' (see section 4.3 above), participation in class struggle alters the balance between the two 'conceptions of the world' present in that consciousness, increasing the weight of the elements of revolutionary class-consciousness *vis-à-vis* those beliefs which bind workers to the status quo. It intensifies the struggle between different identifications, encouraging workers to imagine themselves as part of the international community of class rather than of the narrow fraternities of race, nation, tribe.

While the experience of class struggle heightens the contradictions within workers' existing consciousness, there is, however, no guarantee that the outcome will be the development of revolutionary class-consciousness. Marx seems to have thought that the proletariat's mental horizons would continually expand until they possessed the confidence, consciousness and organization necessary to expropriate capital. He left out of account the fact that experience is never self-interpreting. Workers will interpret their experience of struggle in the light of their existing beliefs. *Solidarność* is a good example. The enormous organized strength of the Polish working class after the August 1980 strikes found expression through a particular appropriation of traditional nationalist ideology, which in turn sanctioned the strategy of 'self-limiting revolution'. Other great proletarian movements have displayed a similar pattern: the German Revolution of November 1918 had the immediate effect of reinvigorating the political forces of traditional social democracy, rather than that of greatly strengthening the revolutionary left around Rosa Luxemburg and Karl Liebknecht.[123]

Workers therefore do not simply slough off the 'tradition of all the dead generations' when they move into struggle on a large scale. The reason has to do with more than the fact that experience always admits of more than one interpretation. Organizations and the particular interests which may grow up around them help to sustain workers' prevailing beliefs. The idea that *Solidarność* and the Polish regime could somehow peacefully coexist with one another drew support from two forces with great influence over the workers' movement – the church, with long experience of using its ability to restrain political opposition in order to secure concessions from the state, and the union's own bureaucractic apparatus, 40,000-strong by the time of *Solidarność*'s national congress in September 1981.[124] More generally, an essential condition of the incorporation of the working class in the advanced capitalist countries has been the emergence of the trade-union bureaucracy, that is, of a layer of full-time officials based on workers' collective organization but acting as intermediaries between labour and capital. Their existence has made possible the institutionalized separation of economics and politics characteristic of Western capitalism, since they have tended to encourage workers to limit their struggles to securing improvements in wages, conditions and the like, rather than to launch any frontal assault against the bourgeois state. Examples of such conduct range from the behaviour of the general council of the Trades Union Congress during the British General Strike of May 1926 to the way in which the leaders of the main French union federation, themselves all members of the Communist Party, sought to bring the insurrectionary strikes and factory occupations of May–June 1968 to a speedy negotiated conclusion.[125]

The 'dual consciousness' characteristic of the Western working class, which combines both a sense of class antagonism and the pragmatic acceptance of capitalist society, is therefore not simply a reflection of workers' situation. It is sustained by the active intervention within the workers' movement of a social layer whose interests spring from their role in negotiating the terms on which labour is exploited by capital. The trade-union bureaucracy finds its political expression in the various social democratic parties (to which the Communist Parties have increasingly assimilated themselves in the past generation). The pursuit of reform within the structures of bourgeois democracy is the mirror image of the negotiated improvement of workers' material conditions by the trade unions; both are aspects of the separation of economy and polity.[126]

To identify the material interests which help to blot out of workers' consciousness any realistic perspective for achieving a society in which they are not longer exploited is not to treat this consciousness as a mental prison from which they have no way of escaping. For great class battles do highlight inconsistencies in prevailing beliefs, even if they do not automatically provide the means of resolving them. They are learning processes which offer at least the opportunity for experience to be clarified. Barker puts it very well:

> Workers' movements are involved in a collective problem-solving activity, through which they make history. In this, the various leaderships and members shape and reshape their forms of organization, their own capacities, the tasks they set themselves. All the while they are practically testing various theories concerning the nature and possibilities of their own movement, and the character, the interests and the capabilities of their antagonists.[127]

All the great revolutionary experiences of the modern working class – Russia 1905 and 1917, Germany from 1918 to 1923, Spain from 1936 to 1937, Hungary 1956, France 1968, Portugal 1974 to 1975, Poland 1980 to 1981 – have displayed this pattern. They have been relatively protracted processes, involving retreats and advances, skirmishes and confrontations, through which the two sides test each other's and their own strengths, pending a final, inevitable settling of accounts. Usually within each great struggle a minority of workers has begun to challenge the ideology prevailing within their movement, and to grope towards an alternative theory and the different strategy it would imply. Thus, to take the most recent example again, there emerged within *Solidarność* during the six months before the coup a minority of 'radicals' who were increasingly critical of the strategy of 'self-limitation'.[128]

The Russian Revolution of October 1917, the only case where the proletariat did seize power (albeit only to succumb subsequently to the effects of the Revolution's isolation and encirclement),[129] suggests that the missing ingredient in the other instances was the minority's lack of access to an alternative tradition as a framework for developing a strategy for defeating capital. That tradition could only be provided by classical Marxism. Gramsci writes of revolutionary theory not as imposed on the working class from without, but as 'a theory which, by coinciding and identifying itself with the decisive elements of the practice itself, can accelerate the historical process that is going on, rendering practice more homogeneous, more coherent, more efficient in all its elements, and thus, in other words, developing its potential to the maximum.'[130] The role of Marxist theory is, then, to resolve the conflict which exists within workers' consciousness, to elicit from within it those elements which represent revolutionary consciousness in embryonic form and give them a coherent, articulated expression.

Gramsci's formulation identifies the continuity between working-class struggle and revolutionary socialist theory at the price – no doubt because of his anti-realist reduction of theories to the conscious expression of practical needs – of understating the break which also exists between the two. The point may be clarified by returning to Benjamin's notion of the 'tradition of the oppressed'. Now there is a real sense in which historical materialism *is* this tradition, that it reflects the concentrated experience of 150 years of working-class struggle, beginning with the Chartists and the Lyons weavers, through the great revolutionary movements of the twentieth century, to such present-day phenomena as the British miners' strike and the rise of powerful industrial proletariats in countries such as South Africa and Brazil. Such a view of Marxism is expressed in Trotsky's description of the revolutionary party as the 'memory of the class'. However, historical materialism does not simply transcribe the pattern of past struggles passively. It seeks to assimilate these experiences of these struggles critically and reflectively. Only such an appropriation of the past can produce historical knowledge 'whose pulse', in Benjamin's words, 'can still be felt in the present'. For the point of remembering past victories and defeats is to learn from them and to put their lessons to work in the future. That is why revolutionary Marxism is not a tradition in Scruton's sense (see section 5.4). The fact that workers have struggled in the past and the manner in which they have done so are not reasons for following in their path now. The memory of past struggles does not 'still the desire for a justifying aim', as Scruton puts it. Calling them to mind may provide inspiration for political action in the present but it is, from the perspective of historical materialism, an occasion for critical reflection, not for the sleep of reason. Classical Marxism is the theoretically clarified experience of the international working-class movement. What allows it to play this role is the fact that it is more than a phenomenology of the class struggle, that it is historical materialism, an empirical theory which roots the mechanisms of social change in the structural properties of successive modes of production. Without this structural dimension Marxism would lack the means of identify both the possibilities and the limits of change in particular circumstances, the powers which individual and collective actors can invoke.

Classical Marxism is a tradition rather in the etymological sense of the word – it is a body of theory and historical knowledge that has been handed down and developed by generations of revolutionary socialists: Marx and Engels, Plekhanov and Kautsky, Lenin and the Bolsheviks, the Communist International in its early years, Trotsky and the Left Opposition. To be a living tradition requires its constant renewal, which involves both theoretical reflection and empirical study. It also requires organizational embodiment. For classical Marxism the revolutionary party is the indispensable intermediary between historical materialism and the class struggle. This is for two reasons. First, Marxist social theory can only be tested through attempts to apply it. Only through an interaction between socialist theory and practice, in which each is subjected to critical scrutiny by the other, can Marxism continue to be a living tradition. Secondly, to counteract the pressures encouraging workers to accept the status quo, however reluctantly, which hold them back even in periods of great social conflict, requires the minority of revolutionary socialists, however small it may initially be, to organize independently in order to influence the majority of the proletariat. The classic example of this relationship is that between the Bolsheviks and the Russian working class in 1917. Far from conforming to the Stalinist myth of a monolithic party imposing its will on and substituting itself for the masses, the Bolsheviks related to the Russian proletariat in a manner very similar to that described above by Gramsci, helping to draw out the logic of workers' struggles, to render them fully conscious and to direct them towards the seizure of state power. Trotsky described the relationship of revolutionary party and working class well: 'Without the guiding organization the energy of the masses would dissipate like steam not enclosed in a piston box. But nevertheless, what moves things is not the piston or the box, but the steam.'[131]

Trotsky's *History of the Russian Revolution*, from which this passage is drawn, brings out a central feature of proletarian revolutions, that they consist in 'the forcible entry of the masses in the

realm of rulership over their own destiny'.[132] Perry Anderson called
the Russian Revolution 'the inaugural incarnation of a new kind of
history, founded on an unprecedented form of agency' – 'self-
determination' (see section 1.1) – i.e. 'those collective projects which
have sought to render their initiators authors of their collective mode
of existence as a whole, in a conscious programme aimed at creating
or remodelling whole social structures'.[133] The importance of
theoretical clarity and the centrality of conscious political leadership
to socialist revolutions are consequences of the role played by self-
determination within these upheavals. The overthrow of capitalism is
a self-conscious project in a sense that no previous social revolution
was.

Consideration of the organic crises of previous modes of production
confirms this claim. Ste Croix's analysis of the decline of classical
antiquity focuses on a series of structural changes: the shift from
supplying slaves by conquest to breeding them which followed the
end of Roman expansionism under the Principate; the consequent
decline in the rate of exploitation of slave-labour, since breeding was
far more costly; the propertied classes' response, to increase the rate
of exploitation of the hitherto free peasant majority by progressively
reducing them to the status of *coloni*, serfs tied to the land; this in
turn undermined the military strength of the Roman Empire, which
had relied on armies recruited from free-holding peasants and made it
therefore more vulnerable to barbarian incursions.[134] Anderson
observes that class struggles 'bear little or no explanatory weight' in
this account:

> The real mechanisms, indicated by Ste Croix, rather form an instance
> of that *other* fundamental theme of historical materialism: namely,
> that modes of production change when the *forces and relations of
> production* enter into decisive contradiction with each other. The
> maturation of such a contradiction need involve no conscious class
> agency on either side, by exploiters and exploited – no set battle for the
> future of economy and society; although its subsequent unfolding, on
> the other hand, is unlikely to unleash relentless social struggles between
> those opposing forces.[135]

Anderson's point is presented as a general historical thesis, and as
such it is correct: organic crises arise from the fettering of the forces
by the relations of production, not from action consciously directed
at producing such crises (see section 5.3 above). But a more specific
point should be added, namely that the conscious agency of the
masses played a comparatively minor part in resolving the crisis of
classical antiquity.The decisive part seems to have been played by

Roman landowners in the Western Empire who, faced in the fifth century with a choice between the bureaucratic imperial state constantly exacting more taxes from them to finance its armies, and the embryonic barbarian successor-states, opted for the latter. The *coloni* and slaves who made up the overwhelming majority of the population did not themselves consciously reshape their social world, even if they probably benefitted from the less efficient mechanisms of surplus-extraction which replaced the Roman state.[136]

The balance between the role played by structural contradictions and conscious human agency in resolving organic crises has shifted from the former to the latter in the course of the past, 1,500 years. The transition from feudalism to capitalism occupies an intermediate position in this respect between the fall of the Roman Empire and the Russian Revolution. Marxist historians have in recent years challenged the idea that bourgeois revolutions are necessarily (or even usually) the work of the bourgeoisie itself. Thus Gareth Stedman Jones wrote (prior to his conversion to post-structuralism):

> The triumph of the bourgeoisie should be seen as the global victory of a particular form of property relations and a particular form of control over the means of production, rather than as the conscious triumph of a class subject which possessed a distinct and coherent view of the world. . . . If the definition of a bourgeois revolution is restricted to the successful installation of a legal and political framework in which the free development of capitalist property relations is assured, there is then no necessary reason why a 'bourgeois revolution' need be the direct work of the bourgeoisie.[137]

One motivation for so conceiving bourgeois revolutions is the need to deal with cases such as that of nineteenth-century Germany, which went through a series of political transformations creating the conditions for the prevalence of industrial capitalism, under the aegis of the Prussian monarchy and its quasi-feudal *Junker* supporters, rather than through their overthrow.[138] But the thesis that bourgeois revolutions do not arise from the conscious action of the bourgeoisie can be applied to other cases, as it has been by Christopher Hill to the English Revolution of 1640 to 1660:

> The English Revolution, like all revolutions, was caused by the breakdown of the old society; it was brought about neither by the wishes of the bourgeoisie, nor by the leaders of the Long Parliament. But its *outcome* was the establishment of conditions far more favourable to the development of capitalism than those which prevailed before 1640. The hypothesis is that this outcome, and the

Revolution itself, were made possible by the fact that there had already been a considerable development of capitalist relations in England, but it was the structures, fractures, and pressures of the society, rather than the wishes of leaders, which dictated the outbreak of revolution, and shaped the state which emerged from it.[139]

It is, nevertheless, in the epoch of the classical bourgeois revolutions, those of 1640, 1776 and 1789, that the concept of self-determination, of the mass of the people collectively shaping their destiny, first came to be formulated, for example, during the celebrated Putney debates within the Parliamentary army in October 1647. Various factors were no doubt involved, but two are worth mentioning in this context. First, the development of capitalism involved the emergence of production relations in which exploiter and exploited are, for the first time, legal equals, even if the underlying economic relationships continue to involve structural inequalities. Formal political equality and class exploitation became, in principle at least, mutually compatible, although the protracted emergence of bourgeois democracy, with three centuries separating the English Revolution from the general acceptance of universal adult suffrage, shows that they can actually coexist only in specific historical conditions.[140]

Secondly, the question of political power assumes a particular importance in the case of bourgeois revolutions. In arguing that the English Revolution falls under the latter category, Hill focuses on the transformation of the state which it accomplished (see section 4.4 above). This analysis can be generalized. Capitalist production relations, since they are associated with (though not reducible to) the growing circulation of commodities, develop in a decentralized and molecular fashion. A point is reached, however, where the further expansion of capitalism depends on the restructuring of the state. A bourgeois revolution is therefore required – in Stedman Jones's words, the 'installation of a legal and political framework in which the free development of capitalist property relations is assured'. But this change need not involve the forcible overthrow of the existing state. As Lenin put it:

> The survivals of serfdom may be abolished either as a result of the transformation of landlord economy or as a result of the abolition of the landlord latifundia, i.e. either by reform or by revolution. Bourgeois development may proceed by having big landlord economies at the head, which will gradually become more and more bourgeois and gradually substitute bourgeois for feudal methods of exploitation. It may also proceed by having small peasant economies at the head,

which in a revolutionary way, will remove the 'excrescence' of the feudal latifundia from the social organism and then freely develop without them along the path of capitalist economy.[141]

Bismarckian Germany is the classic instance of bourgeois revolution from above (indeed Lenin called this path to capitalism the 'Prussian road'), France under the Jacobin dictatorship the chief example of bourgeois revolution from below. The era after 1848 can be seen that of what Gramsci called 'passive revolutions', the symbiosis of industrial bourgeoisie and landed aristocracy, not just in Germany, but also in the Italy of the *Risorgimento* and Japan of the Meiji restoration. Geoff Eley observes:

> To make sense, 'revolution from above' requires the overall European context, both in its spatial and its temporal dimensions. In other words, we need something like the classical Marxist concept of 'uneven and combined development'. On the one hand, German and Italian unifications occupied a distinct temporality when compared with the earlier sequence of the Dutch, British, American and French Revolutions. Where the latter occurred before the global victory of capitalist relations on a European, let alone a world, scale – the former actively presupposed the triumph of capitalism; where the earlier revolutions were driven forward by broad coalitions of large and small property owners, the later ones lost their popular impetus to an intervening process of social differentiation which . . . set the bourgeoisie proper against the mass of pauperized small producers and the infant working class.[142]

The revolutionary inventions of tradition we discussed in section 5.4 were appropriate to the conditions of the classic bourgeois revolutions, helping to cement together the 'broad coalitions of large and small property owners', as they have been to the class alliances involved in the main kind of twentieth-century bourgeois revolutions, the national liberation struggles in the Third World. But such coalitions are only possible where the working class had not emerged as an independent force. The Revolutions of 1848 and above all the bloody June struggles between Parisian workers and the bourgeois National Guard, marked the death-knell of the plebeian mass mobilizations which had swept away French Absolutism, pushing capitalists and landowners together throughout Europe in an uneasy partnership which nevertheless, under the leadership of ambiguous figures such as Bismarck and Cavour, transformed the Continent.[143]

Socialist revolution differs fundamentally from all bourgeois revolutions, whatever their variations. Anderson has, however, on occasions assimilated the structure of socialist to that of bourgeois revolution: 'Capitalism does not automatically or everywhere require a victorious industrial bourgeoisie to launch it – any more than socialism requires a victorious industrial proletariat to impose it.'[144] The analogy suggested here does not hold. The bourgeoisie develops its control over the means of production prior to its acquisition of political power, through the development of trade, the separation of the direct producers from the land and the concentration of wealth in capitalist hands. Since capitalism typically involves a separation of economy and polity, there is no need for the bourgeoisie itself to staff the state apparatus, provided that the state operates in a manner that maintains capitalist relations of production. Bourgeois revolutions bring it about that the state does so function. The working class, by contrast, is defined by its structural separation from the means of production. It can only overcome this separation by establishing collective control over the economy: any piecemeal conquest, say in the form of workers' co-operatives, will be undermined by the competitive logic of capital accumulation. But to acquire overall economic control the proletariat must first attain political power. The conquest of state power is a prerequisite of the proletariat becoming the economically dominant class.[145]

Treating bourgeois and socialist revolutions as identical in structure also obscures the radically democratic character of the latter. Every major proletarian upheaval since the Paris Commune has involved the emergence of organs of working-class power which, like the *soviets* during the Russian Revolutions of 1905 and 1917, have been based on the active participation and control of the masses and the direct election and recall of representatives. *Solidarność* is merely the latest instance, with its democratic and participatory structures and its programmatic aspirations to a 'Self-Managing Republic'.[146] Such political forms are not contingent features of the struggle for socialism. To suppose, as Anderson does, that some force other than the proletariat (for example, Stalinist movements in the Third World), can seize power on its behalf and abolish capitalism by nationalizing the means of production, is to confuse the juridical form of workers' power with its reality.[147] Socialist revolution, as the establishment by the direct producers of collective control over the means of production, can only take the form of the mass of workers dismantling the existing state apparatus and replacing it with their own organs of democratic self-govement.

So claims classical Marxism. But the degeneration of the Russian Revolution and other more recent disappointments have led many socialists to challenge the conception of proletarian revolution expounded and defended in this chapter. Does not the very dynamic of revolutionary processes lead to the replacement of workers' democracy by the kind of bureaucratic and authoritarian structures characteristic of Stalinism? Are not socialist societies likely to suffer from much more pervasive conflicts than Marx had envisaged, whose regulation would require some kind of state? Is not one of these conflicts that arising from the oppression of women by men, a form of domination irreducible to class antagonisms and, unless addressed separately, likely to survive their abolition? Will not a socialist economy of necessity rely on decentralized market mechanisms, contrary to Marx's predictions and Stalinist practice? Urgent and important though these questions are, it is not the place of this book to answer them.

CONCLUSION

One of Bruegel's most extraordinary paintings is called *Dulle Griet*. It shows a group of housewives storming Hell. Some attack and plunder devils, while their leader, clad in armour, her basket fully of booty, advances on the gates of Hell itself. 'Griet' was a proverbial Netherlandish name for a shrewish wife, and the picture is thought to have been an attack on domineering women who fail to respect their husbands' authority: 'Dulle Griet and her ravaging army may be understood as archetypes of all women who usurp masculine perogatives or otherwise defy standards of behaviour considered proper for them.'[1]

Sexist though Bruegel's imagery may have been intended to be, the painting can provoke other reactions from the viewer. This not because, as the post-structuralists and even neo-conservative critics like Roger Scruton would claim, the consumer determines the meaning of a work of art. Rather, what *Dulle Griet* depicts – poor women in arms before the gates of Hell – can be taken in more than one way. Caryl Churchill exploited this fact in the wonderful opening scene of her play *Top Girls*, where Griet appears alongside Pope Joan and other famous women of the past.

Walter Benjamin argued that the perspective from which we view the past will be shaped by the struggles in which we engage in the present. *Dulle Griet* is one of the most powerful images I know of the central theme of this book, the efforts made by human beings to resist and, where possible, to transform, a harsh and often unendurable social reality. The existence of this kind of human agency, at its high point in revolution attaining to what Perry Anderson calls 'self-determination', is clearly incompatible with any view of persons as the 'bearers' of social structures. There are, however, two other theoretical pitfalls in seeking to understand historical agency, perhaps less obvious because they are made by opponents of structuralism. One is, quite simply, to sentimentalize human beings, to drown the fact of collective action in expressions of admiration for the actors' courage and endurance, treating any attempt to examine the objective conditions in which historical struggles unfold as almost obscene, the dissection of a living body. Edward Thompson has sometimes been guilty of such an attitude, less in his historical writings proper than in polemics such as *The Poverty of Theory*. The other mistaken stance represents in one respect the opposite extreme. The formal analyses of rational-choice theory decompose the structures of individual and collective action with painstaking care. They too, however, bracket the objective context of action, so that often the causes and course of social struggles become incomprehensible.

Perhaps it may be of some use if, in conclusion, I were to set out how the argument of this book avoids these various traps, and how far it gets us:

(1) An adequate theory of agency must be a theory of the causal *powers* persons have. Intentional explanations of human action, invoking beliefs and desires as reasons for acting, are necessary because of the peculiar kind of living organisms human beings are – in particular, because of the especial capacities they possess for consciously reflecting on and altering not merely their actions, but also their thoughts. Action-explanations contain a hidden premiss referring to the agent's power to perform the action in question. In normal circumstances this premiss may be ignored, since the capacities assumed are those possessed by any healthy adult person, but this is by no means always the case when the explanation of social events is in question.

(2) Structures play an ineliminable role in social theory because they determine an important subset of human powers. These are what I have called, following Erik Olin Wright, *structural capacities*, the powers an agent has in virtue of his or her position within the relations of production. Viewing structures from this perspective involves breaking with the idea of them as *limits* on individual or collective action, providing a framework within which human agency can then have free play. In so far as their position in structures delimits the possibilities open to agents, they are also presented with the opportunity to pursue their goals in particular directions. Anthony Giddens among contemporary social theorists has most forcefully expressed this basic insight – structures enable as well as constrain. But he then undermines his argument by identifying structure with the resources available to agents. The effect is to keep structure within the framework of the utilitarian theory of action, for resources are, as Giddens puts it, the media of power, means used by

agents to further their ends, not in any sense determinants of action.[2] Resources of different kinds – material, culture, organizational – are, however, available to agents because of their position within production relations. It is as the determinant of the access people have to resources, and not as the resources themselves, that structure figures in social theory.

(3) Historical materialism is itself a theory of structural capacities. Marx indeed quite explicitly identifies the development of the productive forces in bourgeois society with 'the absolute working-out [humanity's] creative potentialities, with no presupposition other than the previous historic development, which makes this totality of development, i.e. the development of all human powers as such the end in itself.'[3] The productive forces are thus best understood as the productive *powers* of humanity, reflecting a particular, technically determined form of labour-process. But the relations of production also involve particular kinds of powers. This is clearest in G. A. Cohen's analysis of production relations as the powers agents have over labour-power and the means of production, but this is one version of a theme going back to Marx, according to which property-relations are to be understood as relations of effective control. Agents' structural capacities are thus determined by their relative access to productive resources, to labour-power and means of production.

(4) This analysis of structures in terms of their role in determining agents' causal powers allows us to avoid the dead-end of structuralism in both its Althusserian and Parsonian forms. These theories seek to reconcile the fact of agency with the causal role of structures by treating persons as social constructs, their motivation and understanding formed through processes which lead them to internalize the prevailing ideology. Rational-choice theorists such as Jon Elster rightly wish to give proper scope to agents' rationality. The concept of structural capacities allows us to do so without, as Elster does, reducing structures to the unintended consequences of individual action. It leaves open the question of how agents' thoughts have been formed: structures nevertheless figure ineliminably in the explanation of social events, since they help determine the powers that persons draw on when acting in the light of their beliefs and desires (however formed).

(5) Indeed, the present treatment of structure is consistent with a much stronger theory of agency than that to which rational-choice theorists subscribe. As chapter 3 should make clear, there is much to be said for the view of persons put forwards by hermeneutically inclined philosophers such as Charles Taylor. Taylor argues that

agents are capable of transcending the instrumental, means–end rationality ascribed to them by the utilitarian theory of action, and making 'strong evaluations' concerning the kinds of desires they ought to have, and the kind of persons they should be. This approach, however, seems to pull away from the focus on crisis, conflict, and struggle made by Marxism, towards a more consensual and evolutionary conception of society. This is so, I suggest, only so long as we ignore agents' structural capacities. These give them different interests, in as much as to realize their ends people must engage in particular kinds of collective action, reflecting their specific position in production relations and bringing them often into conflict with those in other positions. This argument by no means nullifies the considerations advanced by Taylor: indeed, strong evaluations and the commitments they entail are essential to explaining why agents engage in collective action when, in narrowly instrumental terms, it is irrational for them to do so. Taylor's broader conception of agency is indispensable if we are to understand why, despite the Prisoner's Dilemma and the free-rider problem, resistance, rebellion, and even revolution occur.

(6) The existence of structural capacities is not equivalent to that of collectivities exercising them. The construction of collectivities, of groups of agents coordinating their actions in the light of a common identity which they believe themselves to share, formed the central theme of chapters 4 and 5. Only certain issues were pursued – the nature of the beliefs involved in social action (ideologies); the historical conditions in which two kinds of collectivity are formed (class and nation); and the relationship between certain kinds of belief (those held to be 'traditional') and the rarest, if – literally – most epoch-making type of collective action (revolutions). There is, however, enormous scope for empirical inquiry into the specific conditions favouring or impeding the formation of collectivities of one sort or another.[4] If the arguments put forward in this book are correct, they may be of some help in formulating better questions for such investigations to seek to answer.

(7) My underlying preoccupation in developing these arguments, however, has been less with better social theory than with a better social world. Chapter 5 in particular was concerned with clarifying the nature of socialist revolution. I sought to do so partly by criticizing what seemed to me mistaken arguments for its impossibility, namely that the working class is disappearing and that revolution is irrational even for the dwindling band of proletarians, and partly by trying to identify the subjective conditions for its realization, the kind of beliefs and organization which must be

present for it to succeed. There are many, many outstanding objections to revolutionary socialism, some of which were noted at the end of chapter 5. My intention, however, has not been to offer a comprehensive theory capable of dealing with all such objections, but rather to show how socialist revolution fits into the general account of agency defended in this book. The most important instance of structural capacity is that possessed by the world working class to replace capitalism with communism. Whether or not workers ever exercise this capacity cannot be settled by this, or any other book.

Theodor Adorno wrote in 1951 that 'the only philosophy which can responsibly be practised in the face of despair is the attempt to contemplate things from the standpoint of redemption.'[5] Adorno owed this orientation to Walter Benjamin. We have seen that Benjamin came increasingly to identify redemption with socialist revolution. Unlike Adorno he did not despair of such a deliverance. I hope I have given some reasons for practising social theory from the perspective of socialist revolution.

NOTES

ABBREVIATIONS

CW   K. Marx and F. Engels. *Collected Works* (50 vols published or in preparation, London 1975–)
IS   *International Socialism*
JP   *Journal of Philosophy*
KMTH   G. A. Cohen, *Karl Marx's Theory of History – A Defence* (Oxford, 1978)
NLR   *New Left Review*
P & P   *Past and Present*

INTRODUCTION

1 P. Abrams, *Historical Sociology* (West Compton House, 1982), pp. 6–7, x.
2 A. Giddens, *Central Problems in Social Theory* (London, 1979), p. 230.
3 The precise significance of these studies is controversial: see L. Stone, 'The Revival of Narrative', *P & P*, 85 (1979); and E. J. Hobsbawm, 'The Revival of Narrative: Some Comments', *P & P*, 86 (1980).
4 P. Anderson, *In the Tracks of Historical Materialism* (London, 1983), p. 24. See also my review of this book, 'Perry Anderson and "Western Marxism" ', *IS*, 2, 23 (1984).
5 See, for example, E. J. Hobsbawm, 'The Historians' Group of the Communist Party', in M. Cornforth, ed., *Rebels and their Causes* (London, 1978); and B. Schwarz, ' "The People" in History: the Communist Party Historians' Group', in Centre for Contemporary Cultural Studies, *Making Histories* (London, 1982).
6 To some degree one can say that these younger historians have also followed a model of historiography provided by Maurice Dobb's *Studies in the Development of Capitalism* (1946), a seminal influence on the CP historians but one whose example they have not tended to pursue: see R. Johnson, 'Edward Thompson, Eugene Genovese and Socialist–Humanist History', *History Workshop*, 6 (1978). Robert Brenner has highlighted the importance of 'the Marxist idea of the mode of production' for the *Studies*: 'It is perhaps [Dobb's] . . . central contribution that through developing the mode of

production conception in relation to the long-run trends of the European feudal economy he is able to begin to lay bare its inherent developmental tendencies or "laws of motion" '; 'Dobb on the Transition from Feudalism to Capitalism', *Cambridge Journal of Economics*, 2 (1978). p. 121. Such a preoccupation with modes of production and their laws of motion is a common feature of Brenner and other younger Marxist historians, though it is much more rare among the previous generation, with the very important exception of G. E. M. de Ste Croix, whose *Class Struggle in the Ancient Greek World* (1981) was described by Perry Anderson as 'one of the most strenuously theoretical works of history ever to be produced in this country'; 'Class Struggle in the Ancient World', *History Workshop*, 16 (1983), p. 58.

7 P. Anderson, *Arguments within English Marxism* (London, 1980), p. 65.

8 Anderson, *In the Tracks*, p. 26.

9 Ibid., p. 34.

10 See T. Benton, *The Rise and Fall of Structural Marxism* (London, 1984).

11 For a representative selection, see J. Roemer, ed., *Analytical Marxism* (Cambridge, 1986).

12 *KMTH*, pp. ix, x.

13 G. A. Cohen, 'Reply to Elster on "Marxism, Functionalism, and Game Theory" ', *Theory and Society*, 11, 4 (1982), p. 489.

14 J. Elster, *Making Sense of Marx* (Cambridge, 1985), p. 531.

15 See J. Molyneux, *What is the Real Marxist Tradition?* (London, 1985).

16 I am, of course, far from alone in this attitude. Compare, for example, the notorious declaration that 'the study of history is not only scientifically but also politically valueless', by Barry Hindess and Paul Hirst in *Pre-Capitalist Modes of Production* (London, 1975), p. 312, with Hirst's much more positive appraisal of historiography in *Marxism and Historical Writing* (London, 1985), ch. 1.

CHAPTER 1   SUBJECTS AND AGENTS

1 CW, XI, pp. 103–4.

2 P. Anderson, *Arguments within English Marxism* (London, 1980), pp. 19–20.

3 Ibid., pp. 21. Incidentally the adjective 'natural–human' is Anderson's addition to Althusser's formula 'history is a process without a subject or goals' and seems to involve a misunderstanding on the former's part.

4 A. Giddens, *A Contemporary Critique of Historical Materialism* (London, 1981), p. 172.

5 S. A. Marglin, 'What Do the Bosses Do?', in A. Gorz, ed., *The Division of Labour* (Hassocks, 1976).

6 Anderson, *Arguments*, p. 19.

7 See M. Weber, *Economy and Society* (Berkeley, 1978), Part One, ch. I.

8 J. Elster, *Explaining Technical Change* (Cambridge, 1983), p. 69.

9 Ibid., p. 71. The reference is to F. Jacob, *The Logic of Living Systems* (London, 1974).

10 D. Dennett, *Brainstorms* (Brighton, 1981), pp. 269–71, 281–5.

11 Ibid., p. 3.

12 P. Pettit, 'A *Priori* Principles and Action-Explanation', *Analysis*, 46, 1 (1986), p. 39.

13 See D. Davidson, *Essays on Actions and Events* (Oxford, 1980); and *Inquiries in Truth and Interpretation* (Oxford, 1984).

14 Dennett, *Brainstorms*, p. 19.

15 G. Macdonald and P. Pettit, *Semantics and Social Science* (London, 1981), pp. 60, 12.

16 See Pettit, 'A *Priori* Principles', p. 39.

17 Elster, *Explaining*, p. 72. See also Weber, *Economy*, pp. 24ff.

18 See K. R. Popper, 'The Rationality Principle', in D. Miller, ed., *A Pocket Popper* (London, 1983).

19 As Elster concedes: *Explaining*, p. 74.

20 Macdonald and Pettit, *Semantics*, pp. 125, 122.

21 Ibid., 126.

22 Ibid., 99, 103. Pettit's more recent article, 'A *Priori* Principles', simply restates the distinction between nomothetic and action-explanation in terms of a higher distinction between 'regularizing' and 'normalizing' explanations, where the latter seems to be simply another name for intentional explanation.

23 G. Deleuze and F. Guattari, *Mille plateaux* (Paris, 1980), p. 9, following the translation of the introduction (from which this passage is drawn) by P. Foss and P. Patton in *Ideology & Consciousness*, 8 (1981), p. 49.

24 Ibid., pp. 14–15 (tr. pp. 53–4).

25 A.W.H. Adkins, *From the Many to the One* (London, 1970), pp. 15–16.

26 Ibid., p. 267.

27 Ibid., p. 44.

28 Macdonald and Pettit, *Semantics*, p. 100.

29 Weber, *Economy*, p. 4.

30 J. Habermas, *The Theory of Communicative Action*, I (London, 1984), pp. 47–8.

31 C. Levi, *Christ Stopped at Eboli* (Harmondsworth, 1982), pp. 75, 115.

32 B. A. O. Williams, *Descartes* (Harmondsworth, 1978), pp. 65–7, 237–49.

33 See A. J. P. Kenny, 'Cartesian Privacy', in G. Pitcher, ed., *Wittgenstein* (London, 1970). The crucial distinction between primary and secondary qualities is also drawn by Galileo: see S. Drake, ed., *Discoveries and Opinions of Galileo* (Garden City, 1957), pp. 273ff.

34 Habermas, *Theory*, p. 51.

35 M. Foucault, *L'Usage des plaisirs* (Paris, 1984), p. 13, note 1.

36 C. Taylor, 'Rationality', in M. Hollis and S. Lukes, eds, *Rationality and Relativism* (Oxford, 1982), p. 89. See also, on *theōria*, H-G. Gadamer, *Truth and Method* (London, 1975), pp. 110–11.

37 See especially, A. Koyré, *Etudes Galiléenes* (Paris, 1966).

38 For a stimulating discussion of the problems which arise here, see R. Rorty et al., eds, *Philosophy in History* (Cambridge, 1984).

39 See C. Taylor, 'The Validity of Transcendental Arguments', *Proceedings of the Aristotelian Society*, n.s. LXXXIX (1978).

40 W. E. Connolly, *The Terms of Political Discourse*, 2nd edn (Oxford, 1983), p. 239; and see generally pp. 231–43, added in the 2nd edn.

41 M. Foucault and R. Sennett, 'Sexuality and Solitude', in *London Review of Books: Anthology One* (London, 1981), pp. 170–1.

42 See L. Althusser, 'Ideology and the Ideological State Apparatuses', in L. Althusser, *Lenin and Philosophy and Other Essays* (London, 1971).

43 M. Foucault, 'The Subject and Power', Afterword to H. L. Dreyfus and P. Rabinow, *Michel Foucault* (Brighton, 1982), p. 208.

44 See M. Foucault, *Power/Knowledge* (Brighton, 1980), pp. 194–5. The concept of *dispositif* bears at least a family resemblance to Deleuze and Guattari's notion of *agencement* (assemblage).

45 Ibid., p. 98.

46 Ibid., p. 90.

47 M. Foucault, *La Volonté de savoir*, (Paris, 1976), pp. 125–6.

48 Foucault, *Power/Knowledge*, p. 141. On the problem of resistance, see N. Poulantzas, *State, Power, Socialism* (London, 1978), pp. 146–53; and P. Dews, 'The *Nouvelle Philosophie* and Foucault', *Economy and Society*, 8, 2 (1979).

49 R. A. Dahl, 'The Concept of Power', in R. Bell *et al.* eds, *Political Power* (New York, 1969), p. 80.

50 Foucault, *Volonté*, p. 208.

51 Foucault, 'The Subject and Power', p. 221.

52 Foucault and Sennett, 'Sexuality', pp. 171–2.

53 Foucault, *Usage*, pp. 16–17.

54 Foucault, 'The Subject and Power', p. 221.

55 G. E. R. Lloyd, 'The Mind on Sex', *New York Review of Books*, (13 March 1986).

56 See M. Foucault, 'Questions of Method', *Ideology and Consciousness*, 8 (1981); and, among commentaries, P. Veyne, 'Foucault révolutionne l'histoire', appendix to P. Veyne, *Comment on écrit l'histoire* (Paris, 1979); and Dreyfus and Rabinow, *Foucault*.

57 I. Hacking, review of Dreyfus and Rabinow, *Foucault*, (2nd ed.), *JP*, LXXXII, 5 (1985), p. 277.

58 S. J. Gould, *Ever Since Darwin* (Harmondsworth, 1980), pp. 252–3.

59 N. Geras, *Marx and Human Nature* (London, 1983), p. 97.

60 D. Wiggins, *Sameness and Substance* (Oxford, 1980), p. 188.

61 M. Midgeley, *Beast and Man* (London, 1978), pp. 58, 331.

62 Geras, *Marx*, p. 24.

63 A. Heller, 'Habermas and Marxism', in J. B. Thompson and D. Held, eds, *Habermas: Critical Debates* (London, 1982), pp. 21, 22.

64 But see, for example, M. Merleau-Ponty, *Phenomenology of Perception* (London, 1962); A. Heller, *The Theory of Need in Marx* (London, 1976); B. S. Turner, *The Body and Society* (Oxford, 1984); and R. Scruton, *Sexual Desire* (London, 1986).

65 J. Elster, *Making Sense of Marx* (Cambridge, 1985), p. 62.

66 *CW*, III, p. 276.

67 Ibid., V, p. 31.

68 See, for example, S. Hook, *From Hegel to Marx* (London, 1936), pp. 272–307; and A. W. Wood, *Karl Marx* (London, 1981), p. 32.

69 *CW*, V, pp. 446, 44.

70 K. Marx, *Grundrisse* (Harmondsworth, 1973), p. 84. See also V. N. Voloshinov, *Marxism and the Philosophy of Language* (New York, 1973).

71 S. Rose, *The Conscious Brain* (Harmondsworth, 1976), p. 173–4.

72 Geras, *Marx*, pp. 106, 107.

73 Ibid., pp. 78–9. See A. Callinicos, *Marxism and Philosophy* (Oxford, 1983), pp. 40–7, on the shift in Marx's thought in the mid-1840s.

74 G. A. Cohen, 'Reconsidering Historical Materialism', in J. R. Pennock and J. W. Chapman, eds, *Marxism: Nomos XXVI* (New York, 1983), pp. 243, 242.

75 K. Marx and F. Engels, *Selected Works* (3 vols, Moscow, 1973), III, p. 19; K. Marx, *Capital*, III (Moscow, 1971), p. 820. The contrast here is between what Alan Ryan calls the 'self-developmental' and 'instrumental' attitudes to work and property: see his *Property and Political Theory* (Oxford, 1984), pp. 1–13.

76 Cohen, 'Reconsidering', p. 233.

77 Ibid., 242.

78 Elster, *Making Sense*, p. 83.

79 For examples of such condemnations, see S. Lukes, *Marxism and Morality* (Oxford, 1985), ch. 2.

80 N. Geras, 'The Controversy about Marx and Justice', *NLR*, 150 (1985), p. 70.

81 Elster, *Making Sense*, p. 216. See also G. A. Cohen, review of A. W. Wood, *Karl Marx*, *Mind*, XCII (1983).

82 Marx and Engels, *Selected Works*, III, pp. 18, 19.

83 J. Elster, 'Exploitation, Freedom, and Justice', in Pennock and Chapman, eds, *Marxism*, p. 296. See, in addition to this article, Elsen, *Making Sense*, pp. 216–33. Geras, 'Marx and Justice', pp. 79–84, deals with arguments against treating the needs principle as a principle of justice.

84 See, for example, R. W. Miller, 'Marx and Morality', in Pennock and Chapman, eds, *Marxism*.

85 See Lukes, *Marxism*, ch. 3, and for versions of moralities of *Recht*, H. L. A. Hart, 'Are There Any Natural Rights?'; and J. L. Mackie, 'Can There be a Right-Based Moral Theory?'; both in J. Waldron, ed., *Theories of Rights* (Oxford, 1984).

86 R. W. Miller, 'Marx and Aristotle: A Kind of Consequentialism', in K. Nielsen and S. C. Patten, eds, *Marx and Morality, Canadian Journal of Philosophy*, supp. vol. VII, (1981), p. 323. See also H. Marcuse, *Reason and Revolution* (London, 1968); and G. Lukács, *Toward the Ontology of Social Being* (London, 1978, 1980).

87 Miller, 'Marx and Aristotle', pp. 324–5, 333, 347–8, 349. In the light of the interpretation given in this article, Miller's denial that Marx had at least an implicit moral theory seems just perverse. See also A. Gilbert, 'Marx's

Moral Realism', in T. Bell and J. Farr, *After Marx* (Cambridge, 1984).

88 A. MacIntyre, *After Virtue* (London, 1981), pp. 139, 140, 141.

89 Ibid., pp. 152–3, 245.

90 F. G. Whelan, 'Marx and Republican Virtue', in Pennock and Chapman, eds, *Marxism*, p. 67. On classical republicanism, see especially Q. Skinner, *The Foundations of Modern Political Thought*, (2 vols, Cambridge 1978); and 'The Idea of Negative Liberty', in Rorty *et al.*, *Philosophy in History*.

91 A. Gilbert, 'Historical Theory and the Structure of Moral Argument in Marx', *Political Theory*, 9, 2 (1981), pp. 192, 185. See also A. Gilbert, *Marx's Politics: Communists and Citizens* (Oxford, 1981).

92 Anderson, *Arguments*, p. 86.

93 Geras, 'Marx and Justice', p. 85.

94 See, for example, Cohen, 'Reconsidering'; and Elster, *Making Sense*, pp. 82–92.

95 Lukes, *Marxism, passim*. Note, however, that Lukes does not wholly reject appraising actions in terms of their consequences. Indeed, he is prepared in certain circumstances to justify the use of torture, even though he concedes that the Bolsheviks rejected such a proposal with contempt in the summer of 1918: see ibid., pp. 67, 109–10, and R. Medvedev, *Let History Judge* (Nottingham, 1976), p. 261–2. Nor does he establish any inconsistency between Marx's consequentialism and the kind of account of rights offered by Joseph Raz in 'On the Nature of Rights', *Mind*, XCIII (1984), and 'Rights-Based Moralities', in Waldron, ed., *Theories of Rights*.

96 Wiggins, *Sameness*, p. 185.

97 See, for example, in addition to MacIntyre's writings, I. Murdoch, *The Sovereignty of Good* (London, 1970); D. Wiggins, *Truth, Invention and the Meaning of Life* (Oxford, 1976); S. Lovibond, *Realism and Imagination in Ethics* (Oxford, 1983); and B. A. O. Williams, *Ethics and the Limits of Philosophy* (London, 1985).

98 See J. Raz, ed., *Practical Reasoning* (Oxford, 1978).

99 Aristotle, *Nicomachean Ethics*, vii. 1–10.

100 G. H. von Wright, 'On So-Called Practical Inference', in Raz, ed., *Practical Reasoning*, p. 56.

101 See G. E. M. de Ste Croix, *The Class Struggle in the Ancient Greek World* (London, 1981). The main source for the Spartacus revolt is Appian, *Civil Wars*, I.xiv.

CHAPTER 2   STRUCTURE AND ACTION

1 A. Giddens, *Central Problems in Social Theory* (London, 1979), p. 76.

2 I owe this formulation to E. O. Wright: see *Class Structure and Income Determination* (New York, 1979).

3 D. Lockwood, 'Social Integration and System Integration', in G. K. Zollschan and W. Hirsch, eds, *Explorations in Social Change* (Boston, 1964), pp. 245, 249.

4 Ibid., pp. 245, 249–50.

5 Giddens, *Central Problems*, pp. 64, 65–6.

6 Ibid., p. 64.
7 L. Althusser and E. Balibar, *Reading Capital* (London, 1970), p. 207, note 5.
8 N. Poulantzas, *Political Power and Social Classes* (London, 1973), p. 13.
9 Ibid., p. 15.
10 See P. Anderson, *Arguments within English Marxism* (London, 1980), p. 39. This is not to say that the notion of the social formation as an 'articulation' of modes of production cannot, and has not been abused. Althusserians have tended to neglect a peculiar property of the capitalist mode of production, its tendency to establish a world system of which individual social formations are component parts, and which is subject to processes of uneven and combined development: see especially L. Trotsky, *The Third International after Lenin* (New York 1970). Failure to recognize adequately this dimension of the capitalist mode has led often to an underestimation of its dominance within particular national economies. See A. Foster-Carter, 'The Modes of Production Controversy', *NLR*, 107 (1978).
11 K. Marx, *Capital*, III (Moscow, 1971), p. 791. Hal Draper comments: 'If one had to select from Marx's writing a single statement which contains the main body of his theoretical work *in ovo*, this would be it', *Karl Marx's Theory of Revolution*, I (New York, 1977), p. 571. The chief merit of the 1859 Preface, by contrast, is that it focuses on the dynamic aspect of Marx's theory, arising from the fettering of forces by relations of production. See section 2.3 below.
12 See, for example, *KMTH*, pp. 28–9.
13 Ibid., pp. 32, 61.
14 G. Therborn, *Science, Class and Society* (London, 1976), pp. 355–6, 362–3. Therborn's entire discussion of 'the social and theoretical formation of historical materialism', ibid., pp. 317–413, is very helpful.
15 K. Marx, *Capital*, I (Harmondsworth, 1976), p. 290.
16 *KMTH*, p. 32.
17 Althusser and Balibar, *Reading*, p. 235.
18 Marx, *Capital*, I, p. 452, note 20.
19 KMTH, pp. 92–3, 94, 113–14, 98. See also ibid., p. 107.
20 *CW*, V, p. 43.
21 Marx, *Capital*, I, p. 286.
22 Althusser and Balibar, *Reading*, p. 173.
23 *KMTH*, pp. 45–7. Compare K. Marx, *Grundrisse* (Harmondsworth, 1973), pp. 699ff.
24 K. Marx, *Capital*, II (Moscow, 1967), pp. 33, 36–7.
25 Marx, *Grundrisse*, p. 96.
26 *KMTH*, pp. 34–5.
27 B. Hindess and P. Q. Hirst, *Pre-Capitalist Modes of Production* (London, 1975), especially ch. 5.
28 CW, XXXVIII, p. 99. See S. Lukes, *Marxism and Morality* (Oxford, 1985), pp. 28ff., on *Recht*.

29 R. Brenner, 'The Social Basis of Economic Development', in J. Roemer, ed., *Analytical Marxism* (Cambridge, 1986), pp. 26, 46, 43, 40–8.

30 A. Callinicos, *Marxism and Philosophy* (Oxford, 1983), pp. 48–9.

31 Therborn, *Science*, pp. 368, 371, and see generally 365–75.

32 C. Harman, 'Base and Superstructure', *IS*, 2, 32 (1986), p. 21. See my comments on this article in *IS*, 2, 34 (1987).

33 Harman, 'Base and Superstructure', p. 22.

34 See, for example, P. Anderson, *Lineages of the Absolutist State* (London, 1974), pp. 462–549.

35 J. Elster, *Making Sense of Marx* (Cambridge, 1985), pp. 257–8. Elster's other main criticism of Cohen's ownership table, that it omits the guild system (pp. 256–7), seems much less interesting.

36 C. Wickham, 'The Other Transition', *P & P*, 103 (1984), p. 6; C. Wickham, 'The Uniqueness of the East', *Journal of Peasant Studies*, 12, 2 & 3(1985), p. 170.

37 Wickham, 'Uniqueness', pp. 183, 184, and *passim*; on the rise of Western feudalism, see 'Other Transition', *passim*. Draper argues that Marx's analysis of 'Oriental Depotism' is one of a tributary mode of production: *Theory*, I, ch. 22. I am grateful to Chris Harman for reminding me of this argument.

38 Elster, *Making Sense*, p. 258. He adds a third condition, 'the rules governing acquisition and transfer of property', reflecting his Quixotic desire to elevate the guild system into a mode of production.

39 Marx, *Grundrisse*, pp. 414, 651, 657. For commentaries which stress the importance of such passages see R. Rosdolsky, *The Making of Marx's 'Capital'* (London, 1977); and A. Callinicos, *The Revolutionary Ideas of Karl Marx* (London, 1983).

40 Marx, *Capital*, I, pp. 344, 325.

41 G. E. M. de Ste Croix, *The Class Struggle in the Ancient Greek World* (London, 1981), p. 51.

42 Althusser and Balibar, *Reading*, p. 193.

43 Ste Croix, *Class Struggle*, pp. 43–4. See also *KMTH*, pp. 73–7; and Wright, *Class Structure*, ch. 1. Ste Croix's claim, in *Class Struggle*, pp. 98ff., that women in classical antiquity were a class is rightly challenged by Perry Anderson: see 'Class Struggle in the Ancient World', *History Workshop*, 16 (1983), p. 65.

44 Wright, *Class Structure*, p. 22.

45 Ste Croix, *Class Struggle*, pp. 44, 57–69.

46 Ibid., pp. 90–1.

47 A. Levine and E. Sober, 'What's Historical about Historical Materialism', *JP*, LXXXII, 6 (1985), p. 322.

48 See A. Callinicos, *Is There a Future for Marxism?* (London, 1982), ch. 5; and *Marxism and Philosophy*, chs 2 and 3. Michael Rosen's discussion of the intrinsic relationship between Hegel's 'method' and 'system' is definitive: *The Hegelian Dialectic and its Criticism* (Cambridge, 1982).

49 Therborn, *Science*, p. 396. Compare Ste Croix, *Class Struggle*, p. 50.

50 Elster, *Making Sense*, p. 48.

51 *CW*, VI, pp. 168, 174.
52 Compare Giddens, *Central Problems*, p. 141.
53 K. Marx, *A Contribution to the Critique of Political Economy* (London, 1971), p. 21.
54 Levine and Sober, 'What's Historical', pp. 313–14.
55 *KMTH*, p. 134.
56 Ibid., p. 160.
57 Ibid., pp. 259–60, 278, 261, 263.
58 See Marx, *Capital*, I, part 4, and 'Results of the Immediate Process of Production', appendix to ibid.
59 *KMTH*, p. 162; see also p. 180.
60 See J. Elster, *Ulysses and the Sirens* (Cambridge, 1979), pp. 1ff.; and *Explaining Technical Change* (Cambridge, 1983), pp. 49–55. On natural selection, see especially F. Jacob, *The Logic of Living Systems* (London, 1974); and E. Sober, *The Nature of Selection* (Cambridge, MA, 1984).
61 Elster, *Explaining*, p. 57. (See also Elster, *Ulysses*, p. 28.)
62 Ibid., pp. 59–60. See also Elster, *Making Sense, passim*.
63 *KMTH*, p. 266 (see also pp. 271, 285–6); and G. A. Cohen, 'Functional Explanation: Reply to Elster', *Political Studies*, XXXVIII, 1 (1980), p. 131.
64 Elster, *Explaining*, p. 64.
65 Ibid., p. 66.
66 *KMTH*, p. 282.
67 See R. Harré and E. Madden, *Causal Powers* (Oxford, 1975); and R. Bhaskar, *A Realist Theory of Science* (Hassocks, 1975). Elster has recently retreated from the criticisms of functional explanation cited in the text. He now says of Cohen's analysis of functional explanations that 'it is vulnerable to strong pragmatic objections, but on the level of principle, it is hard to fault it', 'Further Thoughts on Marxism, Functionalism and Game Theory', in Roemer, ed., *Analytical Marxism*, p. 204. This retreat seems quite unnecessary. As Harré and Madden argue, 'the only sure way of distinguishing lawful and accidental universal statements is to point out that in the former cases we see why the regularity must hold, while in the latter we do not'. Harré and Madden, *Causal Powers*, p. 37. But this condition can be met only by identifying the mechanism responsible for this regularity: see Bhasker, *Realist Theory, passim*. If this is so, then Cohen's weaker condition, that a consequence-explanation is valid so long as some mechanism exists even if we do not know what it is, is inherently unsatisfactory, not merely objectionable on 'pragmatic' grounds. For more on Elster's retreat, see 'Further Thoughts', pp. 202–7, and his exchange with Allen Wood in *Inquiry*, 29; 1 (1986).
68 P. van Parijs, *Evolutionary Explanation in the Social Sciences* (London, 1981); and 'Marx's Central Puzzle', in T. Ball and J. Farr, eds, *After Marx* (Cambridge, 1984).
69 A. Levine, *Arguing for Socialism* (London, 1984), pp. 164–74. An earlier version of this critique of *KMTH* is to be found in A. Levine and E. O. Wright, 'Rationality and Class Struggle', *NLR*, 123 (1980).
70 *KMTH*, pp. 152–3.

71 Ibid., p. 156.
72 G. A. Cohen, 'Reconsidering Historical Materialism', in J. R. Pennock and J. W. Chapman, *Marxism: Nomos XXVI* (New York, 1983), p. 228.
73 See M. Elvin, *The Pattern of the Chinese Past* (London, 1973).
74 J. Cohen, review of *KMTH*, *JP*, LXXIX, 5 (1982), pp. 271, 268.
75 Brenner, 'Social Basis', p. 27. He argues that there is no pertinent difference in this respect between the slave and feudal modes: ibid., pp. 32–3, note 6.
76 Ibid., pp. 28–9, 32.
77 Ibid., pp. 33, 34.
78 *CW*, VI, p. 487. See also Elster, *Making Sense*, p. 273: 'Marx explained the dynamic of pre-capitalist societies in terms of the extensive development of the productive forces, as opposed to the intensive development implied by the general theory'. i.e. the 1859 Preface.
79 G. Bois, *Crise du féodalisme* (Paris, 1976). See also section 4.4 below.
80 *KMTH*, p. 151.
81 Althusser and Balibar, *Reading*, p. 235. Balibar only explicitly writes of *capitalist* relations dictating the '*type of development*' of the productive forces, but it is clear that the point is intended more generally.
82 G. A. Cohen, 'Forces and Relations of Production', in B. Matthews, ed., *Marx: A Hundred Years On* (London, 1983), pp. 123, 121.
83 G. A. Cohen, 'Historical Inevitability and Human Agency in Marxism', (unpublished MS), pp. 5, 22. See also ch. 5, note 61 below.
84 Levine, *Arguing*, pp. 174, 176. On slave revolts, see M. I. Finley, *Ancient Slavery and Modern Ideology* (Harmondsworth, 1983), pp. 114ff.
85 G. A. Cohen, 'Reply to Elster on "Marxism, Functionalism and Game Theory" ', *Theory and Society*, 11, 4 (1982), p. 488.
86 Elster, *Making Sense*, pp. 6–7.
87 J-P. Sartre, *Critique of Dialectical Reason* (London, 1976), pp. 36–7.
88 Ibid., pp. 80, 122, 123, 123, 161ff., 164. Elster also uses the example of peanuts causing soil erosion by clearing trees as a case of collective irrationality: *Sour Grapes* (Cambridge, 1983), pp. 27–9.
89 J. Elster, *Logic and Society* (London, 1978), pp. 99, 106. See also Elster, *Making Sense*, pp. 37ff.
90 Sartre, *Critique*, p. 69.
91 Anderson, *Arguments* p. 53. See generally ibid., pp. 51–3; and R. Aronson, *Jean-Paul Sartre – Philosophy in the World* (London, 1980), pp. 275–86.
92 Sartre, *Critique*, p. 817.
93 Ibid., pp. 151, 162–3.
94 Ibid., pp. 165, 183, 250, 251, 132, 149.
95 Aronson, *Sartre*, p. 257. See generally ibid., pp. 243–86.
96 See ibid., 324–52 for a discussion of *The Family Idiot* and, on Wilhelm II, J-P. Sartre, *War Diaries* (London, 1985), pp. 300–1, 302–9, 311–13, 316–19. The latter is a remarkable document, which 'contains anticipations of almost every major theme of [Sartre's] . . . post-war output', P. Anderson, *In the Tracks of Historical Materialism* (London, 1983), p. 70, note 19.
97 See J. Elster, 'Marxism, Functionalism, and Game Theory', *Theory and Society*, 11, 4 (1982).

98 J. Roemer, *A General Theory of Exploitation and Class* (Cambridge, MA, 1982), pp. 19–20. See also G. A. Cohen, 'The Labour Theory of Value and the Concept of Exploitation', in M. Cohen *et al.*, eds, *Marx, Justice and History* (Princeton, 1980).

99 E. O. Wright, 'The Value Controversy and Social Research', in I. Steedman *et al.*, *The Value Controversy* (London, 1981), pp. 51, 63 and *passim*.

100 E. O. Wright, 'Reconsiderations', ibid., pp. 138, 159.

101 E. O. Wright, 'The Status of the Political in the Concept of the Class Structure', *Politics and Society*, 11, 3 (1982), p. 338 and *passim*.

102 E. O. Wright, *Classes* (London, 1985), pp. 56–7, 71–2, 79, 87.

103 See E. O. Wright, *Class, Crisis and the State* (London, 1978), pp. 134–7.

104 Wright, 'Reconsiderations', p. 150.

105 See, for example, F. Parkin, *Marxism and Class Theory* (London, 1979).

106 See especially Roemer, 'Reply', *Politics and Society* 11, 3 (1982).

107 See especially B. Fine and L. Harris, *Rereading 'Capital'* (London, 1979); J. Weeks, *Capital and Exploitation* (London, 1981); C. Harman, *Explaining the Crisis* (London 1984); and E. Mandel and A. Freeman, eds, *Ricardo, Marx, Sraffa* (London, 1984).

108 Elster, *Making Sense*, pp. 52, 142, 390, 513–14. The contributions by Scott Meikle and Cliff Slaughter to the symposium on his book published in *Inquiry*, 29, 1 (1986) do not really engage with Elster's arguments, but it is easy to sympathize with their outrage at his casual and dismissive attitude to Marx's *Capital*.

109 See, for example, L. von Bortkiewicz, 'Value and Price in the Marxian System', *International Economic Papers*, 2 (1952); S. Himmelweit, 'The Continuing Saga of the Rate of Profit', *CSE Bulletin*, 9 (1974); and, for a generalization of these results, I. Steedman, *Marx after Sraffa* (London, 1977).

110 J. Weeks, 'Equilibrium, Uneven Development and the Tendency of the Rate of Profit to Fall', *Capital and Class*, 16 (1982), p. 66.

111 See I. Prirogine and I. Stenghers, *Order out of Chaos* (London, 1984).

112 A. Freeman, 'The Logic of the Transformation Problem', in Mandel and Freeman, eds, *Ricardo*, p. 238.

113 See A. Shaikh, 'Marx's Theory of Value and the "Transformation Problem" ', in J. Schwartz, ed., *The Subtle Anatomy of Capitalism* (Santa Monica, 1977); A. Shaikh, 'The Transformation from Marx to Sraffa', in Mandel and Freeman, eds, *Ricardo*; and Harman, *Explaining*, pp. 38–43.

114 Freeman, 'Logic', p. 239. Michel De Vroey stresses the importance of the interaction between the 'instantaneous' nature of the value-relationship and the 'intertemporal' logic of the irreversible processes of change characteristic of the capitalist mode: see 'Value, Production, and Change', in Steedman *et al.*, *Value Controversy*. Failure to appreciate the second aspect undermines the argument of Cohen, 'Labour Theory'.

115 See Fine and Harris, *Rereading*; Weeks, *Capital*; Weeks 'Equilibrium'; and P. Green, 'Once More on the Rate of Profit'. *IS*, 2, 32 (1986).

116 See, as an example of this kind of analysis, Harman, *Explaining*; and N. Harris, *Of Bread and Guns* (Harmondsworth, 1983). In a different

theoretical mode there is the stimulating work of the 'regulation' school. See especially M. Aglietta. *A Theory of Capitalist Regulation* (London, 1979); and M. Davis, *Prisoners of the American Dream* (London, 1986).

117 H. G. Romero, 'Marx, Sraffa and the Neo-Classicals in Context', in Mandel and Freeman, eds, *Ricardo*, p. 113.

118 I have discussed Roemer's book at some length elsewhere: see 'Exploitation, Justice, and Socialism', University of York, *Morell Studies in Toleration*, Discussion Paper 16 (1985). See also J. Elster, 'Roemer vs. Roemer', *Politics and Society*, 11, 3 (1982). J. Roemer, 'Should Marxists be Interested in Exploitation?', in Roemer, ed., *Analytical Marxism*, explains why he isn't, not why Marxists are.

119 For an important recent contribution to this discussion, see D. Blackbourn and G. Eley, *The Peculiarities of German History* (Oxford, 1984). See also section 5.5 below.

120 Elster, *Explaining*, pp. 217, 226. See generally ibid. pp. 209–36; and Elster, *Making Sense*, pp. 259ff. Cohen defends 'Use Fettering' in 'Forces and Relations', pp. 125–31.

121 Elster, *Making Sense*, pp. 155–61, 165.

122 A good example was 'The Trump of Capitalism', a talk given by Cohen on Channel Four Television on 3 September 1986. Similarly, when reviewing what's left of Marx, Elster concludes that 'the critique of exploitation and alienation remains central'; *Making Sense*, p. 531. See E. Wood, *The Retreat from Class* (London, 1986) for a critical survey of the contemporary intellectual revival of Utopian socialism, which, however, omits analytical Marxism.

123 Elster, 'Marxism, Functionalism', pp. 453, 454, 463. Note that this is a stronger version of MI than Popper's. The latter concedes that 'our actions cannot be explained without reference to our social environment, to social institutions and to their manner of functioning'; *The Open Society and its Enemies* (2 vols, London, 1966) II, p. 90.

124 Elster, *Ulysses*, p. 18.

125 See R. D. Luce and H. Raiffa, *Games and Decisions* (New York, 1957).

126 Elster, 'Marxism, Functionalism', p. 453.

127 Roemer, *General Theory*, p. 15.

128 Elster, 'Marxism, Functionalism', p. 464.

129 *CW*, VI, p. 485.

130 See Callinicos, *Future*, chs 5 and 8.

131 A. Przeworski, *Capitalism and Social Democracy* (Cambridge, 1985), p. 93.

132 G. V. Plekhanov, *Fundamental Problems of Marxism* (London, 1969), pp. 164, 171.

133 E. Mandel, 'The Role of the Individual in History: the Case of World War Two', *NLR*, 157 (1986), pp. 70, 73.

134 Ibid., p. 72. Indeed, in *The Meaning of the Second World War* (London, 1986), Mandel gives many examples of strategic and tactical mistakes committed by actors.

135 L. Trotsky, *The History of the Russian Revolution* (3 vols, London, 1967), I, p. 310.

136 A. MacIntyre, *Against the Self-Images of the Age* (London, 1971), p. 59, commenting on I. Deutscher, *The Prophet Outcast* (London, 1967), pp. 242–7. Ironically, Deutscher himself has recently been criticized for exaggerating the role of one individual – namely Stalin: see J. A. Getty, *Origins of the Great Purges* (Cambridge, 1985).

137 See E. O. Wright, 'Giddens's Critique of Marx', *NLR*, 138 (1983), pp. 14–17.

138 Elster, *Making Sense*, p. 6.

139 Roemer, *General Theory*, p. 113.

140 Giddens, *Central Problems*, pp. 69–70. See also Giddens, *The New Rules of Sociological Method* (London, 1976).

141 Giddens, *Central Problems*, p. 91. For the discussions Giddens has in mind, see S. Lukes, *Power* (London, 1974).

142 See A. Callinicos, 'Anthony Giddens: A Contemporary Critique'; and A. Giddens, 'Marx's Correct Views on Everything', *Theory and Society*, 14 (1985).

143 Wright, *Class, Crisis*, pp. 99, 101.

144 Przeworski, *Capitalism*, pp. 94–5.

145 Ibid., p. 95.

146 G. A. Cohen, 'The Structure of Proletarian Unfreedom', in Roemer, ed., *Analytical Marxism*, pp. 239, 238. See also Elster, *Making Sense*, pp. 211–16.

147 Cohen, 'Proletarian Unfreedom', pp. 240, 243.

148 Ibid., 244, 248, 245.

149 Marx, *Capital*, I, p. 899.

150 Elster, *Making Sense*, p. 6.

151 Elster, 'Reply to Comments', *Inquiry*, 29, 1 (1986), p. 67.

152 R. Bhaskar, *The Possibility of Naturalism* (Brighton, 1979), p. 43.

153 Ibid., pp. 49, 43. There is clearly some similarity between my critique of Elster and Scott Lash's and John Urry's argument in an interesting article I only read after completing this book, 'The New Marxism of Collective Action: A Criticial Analysis', *Sociology*, 18, 1 (1984). How much similarity there is, however, is unclear, since their account of 'class capacity' as 'the strength of the organizational and cultural resources which the grouping may mobilize' (ibid., p. 46) is highly compressed; if developed it might turn out to suffer from the same defects as Gidden's conception of structure.

154 W. V. O. Quine, 'On What There Is', in *From a Logical Point of View* (New York, 1963).

155 G. Bachelard, *Le Rationalisme appliqué* (Paris, 1970), p. 113.

156 Levine and Sober, 'What's Historical', p. 323.

157 Levine, *Arguing*, pp. 194–5.

158 Wright, 'Giddens's Critique', pp. 27–9. See also Harman, 'Base and Superstructure', pp. 16–18.

159 Wickham, 'Uniqueness', pp. 185, 187.

160 Lockwood, 'Social Integration', p. 252.

161 A. Gramsci, *Selections from the Prison Notebooks* (London, 1971), p. 178.

162 Analyses of the organic crises of the slave and feudal modes are to be found

in, respectively, Ste Croix, *Class Struggle*, pp. 226–59; and Bois, *Crise*, *passim*. See also section 5.5 below.

CHAPTER 3   REASONS AND INTERESTS

1 H.-G. Gadamer, *Truth and Method* (London, 1975), pp. 212, 213.
2 See C. J. Hempel, *Aspects of Scientific Explanation* (New York, 1965).
3 M. Weber, *Roscher and Knies* (New York, 1975), pp. 173, 241, note 24.
4 See J. Habermas, *Knowledge and Human Interest* (London, 1972), p. 180. See also ibid., pp. 177–86; and Gadamer, *Truth*, pp. 193ff.
5 Weber, *Roscher*, p. 166.
6 Gadamer, *Truth*, pp. 230, 258, 273, 431.
7 C. Taylor, *Philosophical Papers* (2 vols, Cambridge, 1985), I, pp. 255–6, 256–7, 259, 260, 269.
8 Ibid., pp. 280, 232.
9 Gadamer, *Truth*, p. 432.
10 H. Dreyfus, 'Holism and Hermeneutics', *Review of Metaphysics*, LXXXIV, 1, 33 (1980), pp. 7, 8, 17.
11 A. Giddens, *The New Rules of Sociological Method* (London, 1976), p. 19; A. Giddens, *Profiles and Critiques in Social Theory* (London, 1982), pp. 5, 31.
12 W. G. Runciman, *A Treatise on Social Theory*, I (Cambridge, 1983), p. 144.
13 Ibid., pp. 1, 15, 20, 294, 226–7, 236, 295.
14 Ibid., pp. 267–8.
15 Ibid., p. 55.
16 A. MacIntyre, *After Virtue* (London, 1981), pp. 84, 86–7, 89–95.
17 R. Bhaskar, *A Realist Theory of Science* (Hassocks, 1975), *passim*.
18 R. Bhaskar, *The Possibility of Naturalism* (Brighton, 1979), pp. 57, 58.
19 Runciman, *Treatise*, p. 168.
20 See R. Brenner, 'Agrarian Class Structure and Economic Development in Pre-Industrial Europe', *P & P*, 70 (1976). See also section 4.4 below.
21 W. G. Runciman, 'Comparative Sociology or Narrative History', *Archives européenes de sociologie*, XXI (1980), pp. 172, 163, 163–71. Anderson himself has criticized the 'theoretical fallacy . . . that there cannot be a sociology at once historical and comparative', and defended 'real comparisons' as 'indispensable empirical controls': 'Those in Authority', *Times Literary Supplement*, 12 December 1986.
22 Runciman, *Treatise*, pp. 32, 150.
23 Ibid., pp. 27, 22, 95.
24 Ibid., p. 85.
25 D. Davidson, *Inquiries into Truth and Interpretation* (Oxford, 1984), p. 142.
26 See W. V. O. Quine, *Word and Object* (Cambridge, MA, 1970), ch. 1; and 'On the Reasons for Indeterminacy of Translation', *JP*, LXIII (1970). On the underdetermination of all sentences by observation see, for example, K. R. Popper, *The Logic of Scientific Discovery* (London, 1968), ch. 1.

27 Davidson, *Inquiries*, pp. 148, 152. Note that Davidson agrees with Quine's arguments about indeterminacy: see, for example, 'The Inscrutability of Reference', ibid.

28 Ibid., p. 137.

29 W. V. O. Quine, 'Comment on Donald Davidson', *Synthese*, 27 (1974), p. 328.

30 Davidson, *Inquiries*, p. 137.

31 Ibid., p. 125; and *passim*. See A. Tarski, 'The Concept of Truth in Formalized Languages', in A. Tarski, *Logic, Semantics, Metamathematics* (Oxford, 1969).

32 Davidson, *Inquiries*, pp. 48, 136, note 16.

33 Taylor, *Papers*, II, pp. 281, 275.

34 M. A. E. Dummett, *Truth and Other Enigmas* (London, 1978), p. 403. See also H. Putnam, 'The Meaning of "Meaning" ', in H. Putnam, *Mind, Language and Reality* (Cambridge, 1975); and S. Kripke, *Wittgenstein on Rules and Private Language* (Oxford, 1982).

35 See J. McDowell, 'Anti-Realism and the Epistemology of Understanding', in H. Parret and J. Bouveresse, eds, *Meaning and Understanding* (Berlin, 1981), pp. 239–40. See also J. Bouveresse, 'Herméneutique et linguistique', ibid., pp. 128–33.

36 C. McGinn, 'Charity, Interpretation and Belief', *JP*, LXXIV, 9 (1977), pp. 522–3.

37 G. Macdonald and P. Pettit, *Semantics and Social Science* (London, 1981), pp. 29–30. See also R. Grandy, 'Reference, Meaning and Belief', *JP*, LXX, 14 (1973).

38 D. Wiggins, *Sameness and Substance* (Oxford, 1980), p. 222.

39 Ibid., pp. 222–3.

40 L. Wittgenstein, *Remarks on the Foundations of Mathematics* (Oxford, 1978), pt. VI. 39.

41 Id., *Philosophical Investigations* (Oxford, 1968), pt. I. 206; pt. II. xi.

42 See R. Bernstein, ed., *Habermas and Modernity* (Cambridge, 1985); and J. Habermas, *Autonomy and Solidarity* (London, 1986).

43 J. Habermas, *A Theory of Communicative Action*, I (London, 1984), pp. 287, 305, 302.

44 Ibid., pp. 302, 307–8.

45 Habermas, *Knowledge*, p. 314. See also J. Habermas, *Communication and the Evolution of Society* (London, 1979).

46 J. Habermas, *Legitimation Crisis* (London, 1976), p. 105.

47 *The Collected Papers of Charles Sanders Peirce* (Cambridge, MA, 1960), 5. 311.

48 See K. R. Popper, *Realism and the Aim of Science* (London, 1982).

49 M. Rosen, 'Critical Theory: the Persistence of Philosophy', in S. Mitchell and M. Rosen, eds, *The Need for Interpretation* (London, 1982).

50 C. McGinn, *Wittgenstein on Meaning* (Oxford, 1984), pp. 42 (italics removed from first quotation), 42 note 42.

51 Davidson, *Inquiries*, p. 280.

52 Macdonald and Pettit, *Semantics*, p. 12.

53 T. Parsons, *The Structure of Social Action* (2 vols, New York, 1968), I, pp. 60, 58, 59, 60.

54 J. Roemer, ' "Rational-Choice" Marxism', in J. Roemer, ed., *Analytical Marxism* (Cambridge, 1986).

55 See Habermas, *Theory, passim.*

56 Parson, *Structure*, I, p. 110. See also M. Olson, *The Logic of Collective Action* (Cambridge, MA, 1971), pp. 102–10.

57 D. Lockwood, 'The Weakest Link in the Chain? Some Comments on the Marxist Theory of Action', in R. L. and I. H. Simpson, eds, *Research in the Sociology of Work*, I (1981) (Greenwich, CT, 1981), p. 437.

58 Ibid., pp. 441, 442, 453, 476. See also Parsons, *Structure*, I, part II.

59 *CW*, VI, p. 409.

60 Ibid., p. 410.

61 K. Marx, *Capital*, I (Harmondsworth, 1976), pp. 758, 758–9, note 51.

62 C. Taylor, 'What is Human Agency?', in T. Mischel, ed., *The Self: Psychological and Philosophical Issues* (Oxford, 1977), pp. 103–4.

63 Ibid., pp. 104, 107, 112, 114.

64 Taylor, 'Understanding and Explanation in the *Geisteswissenschaften*', in S. H. Holtzmann and C. M. Leich, *Wittgenstein: To Follow a Rule* (London, 1981), p. 200. See also P. Pettit, 'Reply: Evaluative "Realism" and Interpretation', ibid.

65 A. K. Sen, 'Rational Fools', in A. K. Sen, *Choice, Welfare and Measurement* (Oxford, 1982), pp. 89, 92, 103, 99, 100–101. See also A. K. Sen, 'Behaviour and the Concept of Preference', ibid.

66 J. Elster, *Ulysses and the Sirens* (Cambridge, 1979), pp. 154–5.

67 See D. Davidson, 'Hempel on Explaining Action', in D. Davidson, *Essays on Actions and Events* (Oxford, 1980).

68 J. Elster, *Explaining Technical Change* (Cambridge, 1983), pp. 74, 87–8. See also J. Elster, *Sour Grapes* (Cambridge, 1983), ch. I.

69 Pettit, 'Reply', pp. 242, 239.

70 M. J. Sandel, *Liberalism and the Limits of Justice* (Cambridge, 1982), p. 53.

71 J. Rawls, *A Theory of Justice* (Oxford, 1971), pp. 126ff.

72 Sandel, *Liberalism*, pp. 54, 64, 150, 183.

73 Rawls, *Theory*, p. 129.

74 W. E. Connolly, *The Terms of Political Discourse* (Oxford, 1983), p. 46.

75 Ibid., p. 46.

76 A. Giddens, *Central Problems in Social Theory* (London, 1979), p. 189.

77 R. A. Dahl, 'A Critique of the Ruling Elite Model', in R. Bell *et al.*, eds, *Political Power* (New York, 1969), p. 39.

78 P. Bachrach and M. S. Baratz, 'Two Faces of Power', in Bell *et al.*, *Power*; and on the whole 'power debate', S. Lukes, *Power* (London 1974).

79 N. Polsby, 'How to Study Community Power', in Bell *et al.*, eds, *Power*, p. 33.

80 Connolly, *Terms*, pp. 64, 68.

81 J. Elster, *Making Sense of Marx* (Cambridge, 1985). p. 349. See also A. E. Levine, *Arguing for Socialism* (London, 1984), p. 110.

82 E. O. Wright, *Class, Crisis and the State* (London, 1978), p. 89.

83 E. O. Wright, *Classes* (London, 1985), p. 249.
84 G. Therborn, *The Ideology of Power and the Power of Ideology* (London, 1980), pp. 5, 10.
85 G. Stedman Jones, *Languages of Class* (Cambridge, 1983), p. 21.
86 Ibid., pp. 20, 21–2.
87 Ibid., p. 8.
88 See A. Callinicos, 'Post-Modernism, Post-Structuralism, Post-Marxism?', *Theory, Culture & Society*, 2, 3 (1985). For a critical discussion of *Languages of Class*, see E. M. Wood, *The Retreat from Class* (London, 1986), ch. 7.
89 Therborn, *Ideology*, p. 17.
90 T. Parsons, *The Social System* (London, 1951), pp. 205–6, 208, 211.
91 See Therborn, *Ideology*, pp. 20–2.
92 Wright, *Class, Crisis*, p. 98.
93 Giddens, *Central Problems*, p. 189.
94 Ibid., p. 189.
95 Levine, *Arguing*, p. 110.
96 Elster, *Sour Grapes*, p. 25.
97 Marx, *Capital*, I, p. 275.
98 Quoted in J. Brecher, *Strike!* (Boston, 1977), p. xiv.
99 Wright, *Class, Crisis*, p. 99.

CHAPTER 4 IDEOLOGY AND POWER

1 T. Burns, 'On the Rationale of the Corporate System', in R. Marris, ed., *The Corporate Society* (London, 1974), p. 152.
2 A. Giddens, *The Class Structure of the Advanced Societies* (London, 1981), pp. 111–13.
3 M. Mann, *The Sources of Social Power*, I (Cambridge, 1986), p. 219.
4 B. Anderson, *Imagined Communities* (London, 1983), p. 15.
5 See, for example, Robert Michels's classic *Political Parties* (New York, 1962).
6 E. O. Wright, *Classes* (London, 1985), p. 242.
7 See G. Stedman Jones, 'The Marxism of the Early Lukács', *NLR*, 70 (1971).
8 Wright, *Classes*, p. 244.
9 J. Elster, *Making Sense of Marx* (Cambridge, 1985), p. 464. Asserting, as is stated in (2), that the acceptance of ideologies is socially caused, side-steps the issue of the *formation* of beliefs and thus avoids the common objection to the Marxist theory of ideology, that it is self-refuting. See ibid., pp. 473–6.
10 J. Larrain, *The Concept of Ideology* (London, 1979), pp. 58, 61. See also H. Barth, *Truth and Ideology* (Berkeley and Los Angeles, 1976).
11 See generally J. Elster, *Sour Grapes* (Cambridge, 1985), ch. IV.
12 CW, V, p. 59.
13 Ibid., p. 4. See also Larrain, *Concept*, p. 26.
14 K. Marx, *Capital*, I (Harmondsworth, 1976), 165.

15 See A. Callinicos, *Marxism and Philosophy* (Oxford, 1983), pp. 129–34.
16 N. Abercrombie *et al.*, *The Dominant Ideology Thesis* (London, 1980), pp. 1–2.
17 Elster, *Sour Grapes*, p. 164.
18 I. Wallerstein, *The Modern World System*, I (New York, 1974), pp. 143–4.
19 K. Thomas, *Religion and the Decline of Magic* (Harmondsworth, 1973), pp. 206, 189, and see generally pp. 189–206 on religious indifference, ignorance and scepticism.
20 C. Ginzburg, *The Cheese and the Worms* (London, 1980), p. 112.
21 Abercrombie *et al.*, *Dominant Ideology*, pp. 75–6. See generally P. Burke, *Popular Culture in Early Modern Europe* (London, 1978).
22 E. P. Thompson, 'Anthropology and the Discipline of Historical Context', *Midland History* (1972), pp. 51–2.
23 Burke, *Popular Culture*, p. 207, and see generally ibid., ch. 8.
24 Ginzburg, *Cheese*, p. 126.
25 M. Foucault, *Discipline and Punish* (London, 1977), pp. 57, 80–1.
26 A. Giddens, *A Contemporary Critique of Historical Materialism* (London, 1981), pp. 169, 170, 103, 165.
27 Mann, *Sources*, pp. 170, 174–5. See ibid., pp. 137–46 on the logistics of imperial power.
28 Ibid., p. 7.
29 E. P. Thompson, 'Time, Work-Discipline and Industrial Capitalism', *P & P*, 38 (1967). See more generally Burke, *Popular Culture*, ch. 9.
30 M. Mann, 'The Social Cohesion of Liberal Democracy', *American Sociological Review*, 35, 3 (1970), pp. 432, 435.
31 M. Mann, *Consciousness and Action among the Western Working Class* (London, 1973), pp. 33, 21, 68.
32 H. Beynon, *Working for Ford* (Harmondsworth, 1973), pp. 98–9.
33 Ibid., p. 121.
34 T. Nichols and P. Armstrong, *Workers Divided* (London, 1976). pp. 47, 58, 59.
35 G. Therborn, *The Ideology of Power and the Power of Ideology* (London, 1980), pp. 108–9. See generally the discussion of 'forms of ideological domination' in ibid., ch. 5.
36 See especially Abercrombie *et al.*, ch. 6 and appendix; and the critical discussion of their book in G. Therborn, 'New Questions of Subjectivity', *NLR*, 143 (1984).
37 K. Marx, *A Contribution to the Critique of Political Economy* (London, 1971), p. 21.
38 Therborn, *Ideology*, pp. 1–2.
39 See Callinicos, *Marxism*, ch. 6.
40 See for example A. Giddens, *The Constitution of Society* (Cambridge, 1984), ch. 1.
41 G. Macdonald and P. Pettit, *Semantics and Social Science* (London, 1981), p. 27.
42 M. Foucault, *La Volonté de savoir* (Paris, 1976), p. 125.
43 H. Pim, 'Some Aspects of the South African Native Problem', *South African*

Journal of Science, 4 (1905), quoted in M. Legassick and D. Innes, 'Capital Restructuring and Apartheid', *African Affairs*, 76 (1977).

44 Foucault, *Volonté*, p. 125. See C. Taylor, 'Foucault on Freedom and Truth', in D. C. Hoy, ed., *Foucault* (Oxford, 1986).

45 See M. Williams, 'An Analysis of South African Capitalism', *CSE Bulletin*, IV, 1 (1975).

46 Elster, *Making Sense*, p. 474.

47 Ibid., p. 465.

48 See especially Elster, *Sour Grapes*, chs I and IV.

49 W. H. Shaw, 'Marxism and Moral Objectivity', in K. Neilsen and S. C. Patten, eds, *Marx and Morality, Canadian Journal of Philosophy*, supp. vol. VII (1981), p. 28.

50 See B. A. O. Williams, *Ethics and the Limits of Philosophy*, (London, 1985) ch. 8; and John McDowell's review of this book in *Mind*, XVC (1986).

51 A. Giddens, *Central Problems in Social Theory* (London, 1979), p. 196.

52 Therborn, *Ideology*, p. 77.

53 A. Gramsci, *Selections from the Prison Notebooks* (London, 1971), pp. 368, 328.

54 Ibid., p. 327.

55 Ibid., p. 333.

56 C. Harman, personal communication.

57 See C. Hill, 'The Norman Yoke', in C. Hill, *Puritanism and Revolution* (London, 1968).

58 L. Althusser, *Lenin and Philosophy and Other Essays* (London, 1971), pp. 162–3.

59 Therborn, *Ideology*, p. 2.

60 Althusser, *Lenin*, p. 169. I would hazard that it is because he rejects such an oversocialized view of human beings that Wright insists, against Therborn, that 'ideology concerns the process of formation of human *consciousness* not the totality of human subjectivity', *Classes*, p. 245.

61 Therborn, *Ideology*, p. 78.

62 *CW*, VI, p. 503.

63 G. A. Cohen, 'Reconsidering Historical Materialism', in J. R. Pennock and J. W. Chapman, eds, *Marxism: Nomos XXVI* (New York, 1983), p. 233.

64 Ibid., p. 235.

65 Anderson, *Imagined Communities*, ch. 1.

66 E. Gellner, *Nations and Nationalism* (Oxford, 1983), pp. 49, 57.

67 Ibid., p. 38; and see generally ch. 3.

68 E. Gellner, *Thought and Change* (London, 1964), p. 118. See K. Kumar, *Prophecy and Progress* (Harmondsworth, 1978) for a useful discussion of the problematic of industrial society.

69 See also E. P. Thompson, 'Notes on Exterminism, the Last Stage of Civilization', *NLR*, 121 (1980).

70 T. Skocpol, *States and Social Revolutions* (Cambridge, 1979), pp. 32, 22.

71 Giddens, *Contemporary Critique*, pp. 250, 25.

72 Mann, *Sources*, ch. 1.

73 Ibid., pp. 222–3. See also chs 5, 7, and 9.

74 M. Weber, 'The Nation-State and Economic Policy', *Economy and Society*, 9, 4 (1980), p. 438.

75 M. Weber, *Economy and Society* (Berkeley, 1978), p. 941.

76 See, for example, F. Parkin, *Marxism and Class Theory* (London, 1979).

77 See especially L. Trotsky, *1905* (Harmondsworth, 1973), part I, ch. 1.

78 See N. Bukharin, 'Towards a Theory of the Imperialist State', in N. Bukharin, *Selected Writings on the State and the Transition to Socialism* (Nottingham, 1982).

79 T. Cliff, *State Capitalism in Russia* (London, 1975); T. Cliff, *Neither Washington nor Moscow* (London, 1982); M. Kidron, *Western Capitalism Since the War* (Harmondsworth, 1970); M. Kidron, *Capitalism and Theory* (London, 1974); and C. Harman, *Explaining the Crisis* (London, 1984).

80 C. Barker, 'The State as Capital', *IS*, 2, 1 (1978); and A. Callinicos, *Is There a Future for Marxism?* (London, 1982), ch. 8.

81 Mann, *Sources*, p. 11.

82 H. H. Gerth and C. W. Mills, *From Max Weber* (London, 1970), p. 78. For an argument from the libertarian right for the interdependence of territorial regulation and military power, see R. Nozick, *Anarchy, State, and Utopia* (Oxford, 1974), pp. 16–17. See also J. Hall, *Powers and Liberties* (Harmondsworth, 1985), p. 19, note 13.

83 R. Brenner, 'The Social Basis of Economic Development', in J. Roemer, ed., *Analytical Marxism* (Cambridge 1986), pp. 31–2. Perry Anderson gives a more tentative version of this argument with respect to feudalism: see *Lineages of the Absolutist State* (London, 1974), pp. 31–2.

84 Marianne Weber, *Max Weber* (New York, 1975), p. 222. For a discussion of the way such an assumption is central to the work even of a theorist who seeks to distance himself from Weber, see A. Callinicos, 'Anthony Giddens: A Contemporary Critique', *Theory and Society*, 14 (1985).

85 R. Brenner, 'The Agrarian Roots of European Capitalism', *P & P*, 97 (1982), p. 38.

86 M. Elvin, *The Pattern of the Chinese Past* (London, 1973), p. 97.

87 Mann, *Sources*, pp. 534, 511; see also ibid., chs 3, 4, 7, 12–15.

88 Hall, *Powers*, p. 136; see generally ch. 5.

89 Brenner, 'Social Basis', p. 36. See also R. Brenner, 'The Origins of Capitalist Development: A Critique of Neo-Smithian Marxism', *NLR*, 104 (1977).

90 Mann, *Sources*, p. 393; see especially ibid., ch. 12. Mann and Hall lay great stress on the 'normative regulation' of mediaeval Europe provided by the Catholic church. Thus: 'its normative pacification enabled more produce to be traded over longer distances than could usually occur between the domains of such a large number of small, often highly predatory, states and rulers', ibid., p. 383. Hence their admiration for Trevor-Roper's unashamedly 'Europa-centric' *The Rise of Christian Europe* (London, 1965), which dismisses the pre-colonial history of Africa as 'the unrewarding gyrations of barbarous tribes in picturesque but irrelevant parts of the globe', pp. 11, 9. Treating Christendom as the *sine qua non* for the mediaeval expansion of trade does not account for the central role played in commerce and banking by the Jews, on which see Abram Leon's classic

study, *The Jewish Question: A Marxist Interpretation* (New York, 1970), especially chs II and III.

91 G. Bois, *Crise du féodalisme* (Paris, 1976), pp. 54, 62–3, 299–308.

92 M. M. Postan, *The Mediaeval Economy* (Harmondsworth, 1975), pp. 39–44, 73, 49. See generally ch. 4 and, on technological stagnation in late mediaeval and early modern Normandy, Bois, *Crise*, pp. 185–90.

93 Hall, *Powers*, pp. 122–3.

94 See the essays in T. Ashton, ed., *Crisis in Europe 1560–1660* (London, 1965), especially E. J. Hobsbawm, 'The Crisis of the Seventeenth Century'; and G. Parker, *Europe in Crisis 1598–1648* (London, 1979), though the latter puts down the crisis to climactic changes.

95 M. M. Postan and J. Hatcher, 'Population and Class Relations in Feudal Europe', *P & P*, 78 (1978), p. 28. See also ibid., pp. 28–30; and Postan, *Mediaeval Economy, passim*.

96 R. Brenner, 'Agrarian Class Structure and Economic Development in Pre-Industrial Europe', *P & P*, 70 (1976), pp. 48, 50.

97 Brenner, 'Agrarian Roots', pp. 37–8.

98 Bois, *Crise*, pp. 203ff.

99 Brenner, 'Agrarian Roots', pp. 78, 81. See also his critical discussion of Bois, ibid., pp. 41ff. Bois himself stresses the growing importance of royal exactions and the pressure they placed on the peasantry: see *Crise*, pp. 254–5, 272–4.

100 Brenner, 'Agrarian Roots', pp. 54, 45–51, 65; Brenner 'Agrarian Class Structure', pp. 63, 65–6.

101 Anderson, *Lineages*, pp. 18–19, 32. See generally ibid., ch. 1.

102 C. Tilly, 'Reflections on the History of European State-Making', in C. Tilly, ed., *The Formation of Nation-States in Western Europe* (Princeton, 1975), pp. 15, 74.

103 C. Hill, 'A Bourgeois Revolution?', in J. G. A. Pocock, ed., *Three British Revolutions: 1641, 1688, 1776* (Princeton, 1980), pp. 134–5. 'The post-Restoration state, and especially the post-1688 state, was strong in external relations, weak at home', ibid., p. 120. See also C. Hill, 'Braudel and the State', in *The Collected Essays of Christopher Hill*, III (Brighton, 1986).

104 P. Anderson, *Arguments within English Marxism* (London, 1980), p. 91.

105 Mann, *Sources*, pp. 483–5.

106 G. Ardant, 'Financial Policy and Economic Infrastructure of Modern States and Nations', in Tilly, ed., *Formation*, p. 202, and *passim*. See also Brenner, 'Agrarian Roots', p. 89, on how absolutism undermined economic development. By contrast, the capitalist landed aristocracy of England was prepared to finance overseas military expansion. 'By the early eighteenth century its members were fully convinced that England's strength lay in its overall commercial prosperity, and they were ready and willing to finance and build an invincible navy to open up the markets of the world to English enterprise', L. Stone and J. F. C. Stone, *An Open Elite? England 1540–1880* (Oxford, 1984), p. 420. 'Although in the eighteenth century they transferred the greatest burden of taxation to the poor through the excise, they also voted to impose an equally severe land tax upon themselves, which in times

of war amounted to four shillings in the pound, or 20 per cent of nominal gross income. This self-imposed tax amounted to at least 25 per cent of the total net income of the state.' (Ibid., p. 413; see also pp. 282–6, 420–1).

107 The best discussion of the economic trends involved here is Harman, *Explaining*. For a brilliant survey of their social and political impact, see N. Stone, *Europe Transformed 1879–1919* (London, 1983).

108 Gellner, *Nations*, p. 6.

109 E. J. Hobsbawm, 'Introduction: Inventing Traditions', in Hobsbawm and T. Ranger, eds, *The Invention of Tradition* (Cambridge, 1983), pp. 1, 14.

110 E. J. Hobsbawm, 'Mass-Producing Traditions: Europe, 1870–1914', in ibid., pp. 264–5.

111 See T. Zeldin, *France 1848–1945* (2 vols, Oxford, 1975; 1977), II, p. 3. Zeldin comments: 'The French nation had to be created', ibid., p. 3. See also E. Weber, *Peasants into Frenchmen* (London, 1977).

112 Hobsbawm, 'Mass-Producing', pp. 269–73.

113 D. Cannadine, 'The Context, Performance and Meaning of Ritual: the British Monarchy and the "Invention of Tradition", *c.* 1820–1977', in Hobsbawm and Ranger, eds, *Invention*.

114 Elster, *Making Sense*, pp. 391ff.

115 Giddens, *Contemporary Critique*, pp. 4, 104.

116 M. I. Finley, *The Ancient Economy* (London, 1973), pp. 51, 50; see generally ibid., chs I and II.

117 Marx, *Capital*, I, pp. 175–6, note 35.

118 See Callinicos, *Future*, pp. 163–7.

119 *KMTH*, p. 216.

120 Elster, *Making Sense*, pp. 33–4. Italics added.

121 C. Harman, 'Base and Superstructure', *IS*, 2, 32 (1986), p. 14. See my comments on the article in *IS*, 2, 34 (1987).

122 Marx, *Contribution*, p. 21. See *KMTH*, pp. 28–31 for Cohen's argument for a restrictive usage of 'economic structure'.

123 K. Marx, *Capital*, III (Moscow, 1971), p. 817. The distinction between explanatory and descriptive concepts is relative, given what is sometimes called the theory-ladenness of observation. See D. Papineau, *Theory and Meaning* (Oxford, 1979).

124 G. E. M. de Ste Croix, *The Class Struggle in the Ancient Greek World* (London, 1981), pp. 57–96.

125 Harman, 'Base and Superstructure', p. 21.

126 Brenner, 'Agrarian Roots', p. 128.

127 Marx, *Capital*, III, pp. 790–1. But see B. Hindess and P. Hirst, *Pre-Capitalist Modes of Production* (London, 1975), ch. 5.

128 G. Bois, 'Against the Neo-Malthusian Orthodoxy', *P & P*, 79, (1978), pp. 67, 63.

129 Brenner, 'Agrarian Roots', p. 32.

130 M. Dobb, *Studies in the Development of Capitalism* (London, 1946), pp. 199–200.

131 Some important recent Marxist contributions on the subject of gender are L. German, 'Theories of Patriarchy', *IS*, 2, 12 (1981); T. Cliff, *The Class*

Struggle and Women's Liberation (London, 1984); C. Harman, 'Women's Liberation and Revolutionary Socialism', *IS*, 2, 23 (1984); and J. Brenner and M. Ramas, 'Rethinking Women's Oppression', *NLR*, 145 (1984). I write 'supposed race' in the text since 'any use of racial categories must take its justifications from some other source than biology. The remarkable feature of human evolution and history has been the very small degree of divergence between geographical populations as compared with the genetic variation among individuals', S. Rose *et al.*, *Not in Our Genes* (Harmondsworth, 1984), p. 127; see also ibid., pp. 119–27. Racial differences are historically constructed within oppressive social relationships, not biologically given.

CHAPTER 5   TRADITION AND REVOLUTION

1 See E. Bloch *et al.*, *Aesthetics and Politics* (London, 1977), pp. 100–141, with a Presentation by Perry Anderson.
2 Ibid., p. 125. On the background to the debate, see M. Jay, *The Dialectical Imagination* (London, 1973), pp. 197–212.
3 See, for example, J. Roberts, *Walter Benjamin* (London, 1982). 'Bolshevism', which Roberts defines as 'revolutionary Leninism', is far too crude a category with which to analyse the political commitments of any Marxist in this period, since it does not distinguish between the various currents claiming to be Bolshevik – not just Stalinism and Trotskyism, but also, for example, Gramsci, Bukharin, Brandler.
4 M. Löwy, 'Revolution against "Progress": Walter Benjamin's Romantic Anarchism', *NLR*, 152 (1985), p. 59.
5 R. Wolin, *Walter Benjamin: An Aesthetic of Redemption* (New York, 1982), pp. 260–1.
6 W. Benjamin, *Illuminations* (London, 1970), pp. 259–60, 263. See also W. Benjamin, 'Eduard Fuchs, Collector and Historian', in W. Benjamin, *One-Way Street and Other Writings* (London, 1979).
7 Quoted in Wolin, *Benjamin*, p. 261.
8 Benjamin, *Illuminations*, pp. 262–3.
9 Ibid., pp. 262–3, 264.
10 Wolin, *Benjamin*, p. 38. Benjamin's 'Janus-faced' orientation towards both revolutionary Marxism and Jewish mysticism is explored in Gershom Scholem's memoir, *Walter Benjamin: The Story of a Friendship* (London, 1982), pp. 157–234.
11 Wolin, *Benjamin*, pp. 48, 57–8.
12 Löwy, 'Revolution', p. 58. See Wolin, *Benjamin*, chs 2 and 3, on Benjamin's early, quasi-Kabbalistic epistemology and philosophy of language.
13 Benjamin, *Illuminations*, p. 259. For similar criticisms to those stated in the text, see T. Eagleton, *Walter Benjamin or Towards a Revolutionary Criticism* (London, 1981).
14 T. W. Adorno, *Minima Moralia* (London, 1974), p. 247.
15 J-P. Sartre, *Critique of Dialectical Reason* (London, 1976), pp. 269, 266, 277, 351–2.

16 Ibid., pp. 357, 386, 401.

17 Ibid., pp. 412, 418.

18 Ibid., p. 322.

19 A. Gorz, *Farewell to the Working Class* (London, 1982), p. 20; see generally ibid., ch. 1.

20 The best account of the development of Marx's views on the working class is M. Löwy, *La Théorie de la révolution chez le jeune Marx* (Paris, 1970). See Wolin, *Benjamin*, pp. 112–14, on the impact *History and Class Consciousness* made on Benjamin; and A. Callinicos, *Marxism and Philosophy* (Oxford, 1983), pp. 70–80, on the book itself.

21 *CW*, III, p. 186.

22 Ibid., VI, p. 496.

23 F. Mulhern, '*Towards 2000*, or News from You-Know-Where', *NLR*, 148 (1984), p. 22. See also H. Draper, *Karl Marx's Theory of Revolution*, II (New York, 1978), ch. 2.

24 See especially K. Marx, 'Results of the Immediate Process of Production', appendix to K. Marx *Capital*, I (Harmondsworth, 1976).

25 Sartre, however, argues that 'it would be completely mistaken to reduce these [i.e. serial] structures and their mode of expression to capitalist society, and to regard them as a historic product of capital: others can be found, different in content but similar in essence, in socialist societies too'; *Critique*, p. 305, note 88. One might prefer to treat this fact as grounds for refusing to regard such societies as socialist.

26 Draper, *Theory*, p. 73.

27 Marx, *Capital*, I, pp. 412–13, 929.

28 *CW*, X, p. 626. 'Civil war' is to be understood here, as in the foregoing quotation from *Capital*, as class struggle rather than (necessarily) armed conflict. See generally Draper, *Theory*, ch. 5; and A. Callinicos, *The Revolutionary Ideas of Karl Marx* (London, 1983), ch. 7.

29 *Statistical Abstract of the United States, 1984* (Washington, 1983), table 705.

30 *Department of Employment Gazette*, (January 1986).

31 Marx, *Capital*, I, pp. 574–5.

32 See H. Braverman, *Labour and Monopoly Capital* (New York, 1974); E. O. Wright, *Class, Crisis and the State* (London, 1978); E. O. Wright, *Class Structure and Income Determination* (New York, 1979); N. Harris, *The End of the Third World* (London, 1986); A. Callinicos, 'The "New Middle Class" and Socialist Politics', *IS*, 2, 20 (1983); and C. Harman, 'The Working Class after the Recession', *IS*, 2, 33 (1986). It is characteristic of Gorz's method that he should approvingly quote a Brazilian theorist of urban guerilla warfare from the late 1960s on the revolutionary role of the lumpenproletariat, ignoring the very considerable growth of the industrial working class in Brazil during the 1970s, which culminated in the emergence of a powerful and increasingly politicized workers' movement at the end of that decade: see *Farewell*, pp. 68–9, note 1.

33 See texts by Wright cited in the last note above.

34 E. O. Wright, *Classes* (London, 1985). Cohen describes this book as

'masterful', in 'Peter Mew on Justice and Capitalism', *Inquiry*, 29, 3 (1986), p. 323, note 16.

35 Wright, *Classes*, pp. 87, 89.

36 Ibid., pp. 85–6, 184–5.

37 B. Hindess and P. Q. Hirst, *Pre-Capitalist Modes of Production* (London, 1975), ch. 5.

38 Wright, *Classes*, p. 79.

39 R. E. Pahl and J. T. Winkler, 'The Economic Elite: Theory and Practice', in P. Stanworth and A. Giddens, eds, *Elites and Power in British Society* (Cambridge, 1974), pp. 114–15. See also J. Scott, *Corporations, Classes and Capitalism* (London, 1979).

40 Wright, *Classes*, p. 56.

41 E. O. Wright, 'The Value-Controversy and Social Research', in I. Steedman *et al.*, *The Value Controversy* (London, 1981), p. 71.

42 Wright, *Class Structure*, p. 138.

43 Wright, *Classes*, pp. 93–4. For an illuminating analysis of 'strategic jobs', see J. Goldthorpe, 'On the Service Class, its Formation and Future', in A. Giddens and G. Mackenzie, eds, *Social Class and the Division of Labour* (Cambridge, 1982).

44 Wright, *Classes*, pp. 55–6.

45 Wright, 'Capitalism's Futures', *Socialist Review*, 68 (1983).

46 See T. Cliff, *State Capitalism in Russia* (London, 1975); T. Cliff, *Neither Washington nor Moscow* (London, 1982); and C. Harman, *Class Struggles in Eastern Europe, 1945–81* (London, 1984).

47 E. O. Wright, 'What is Middle about the Middle Class', in J. Roemer, ed., *Analytical Marxism* (Cambridge, 1986), p. 117.

48 M. Olson, *The Logic of Collective Action* (Cambridge, MA, 1971), pp. 14, 15–16.

49 Ibid, pp. 71, 76, 105, 106. See also A. Buchanan, 'Revolutionary Motivation and Rationality', in M. Cohen *et al.*, eds, *Marx, Justice, and History* (Princeton, 1980).

50 W. H. Shaw, 'Marxism, Revolution, and Rationality', in T. Ball and J. Farr, *After Marx* (Cambridge, 1984), p. 21.

51 Buchanan, 'Revolutionary Motivation', p. 286.

52 CW, VI, p. 495.

53 R. D. Luce and H. Raiffa, *Games and Decisions* (New York, 1957), p. 101.

54 Shaw, 'Marxism', pp. 27–8.

55 G. A. Cohen, 'Historical Inevitability and Human Agency in Marxism', pp. 8–9. I am grateful to Jerry Cohen for providing me with this unpublished MS. He has asked me to make it clear that his discussion of the collective-action problem 'is a draft which will undergo further revision . . . before final publication.'

56 Ibid., pp. 5, 8.

57 Buchanan, 'Revolutionary Motivation', p. 279.

58 A. K. Sen, *Choice, Welfare and Measurement* (Oxford, 1982), pp. 96, 93.

59 Ibid., p. 106. See also B. A. O. Williams, *Ethics and the Limits of Philosophy* (London, 1985).

60 C. Taylor, 'What is Human Agency?', in T. Mischel, ed., *The Self: Psychological and Philosophical Issues* (Oxford, 1977), p. 114.

61 Shaw, 'Marxism', pp. 30–1.

62 Sen, *Choice*, p. 70. According to Cohen, 'Marx thought that . . . class interest would not motivate in the absence of a normative representation of it', 'Peter Mew', p. 319.

63 A. Przeworski, *Capitalism and Social Democracy* (Cambridge, 1985), p. 174.

64 Ibid., p. 176, and ch. 5 *passim*.

65 Ibid., ch. 1.

66 N. I. Bukharin, *The Economics of the Transformation Period* (New York, 1971), pp. 105–6. Lenin's marginal comment on this passage was 'True!' ibid., p. 216. Engels to Kautsky, 12 September 1882: 'all sorts of destruction . . . [are] inseparable from all revolutions'; K. Marx and F. Engels, *Selected Correspondence* (Moscow, 1965), p. 351.

67 Przeworksi, *Capitalism*, p. 198.

68 See, for example, J. Harrison, *Marxist Economics for Socialists* (London, 1978).

69 Przeworski, *Capitalism*, p. 180.

70 Ibid., p. 217.

71 See R. Rosdolsky, *The Making of Marx's 'Capital'* (London, 1977), pp. 282–313.

72 See C. Harman, *Explaining the Crisis* (London, 1984).

73 Quoted in T. Cliff, *The Crisis: Social Contract or Socialism* (London, 1975), p. 126.

74 See C. Barker, *Festival of the Oppressed* (London, 1986).

75 R. Scruton, *The Meaning of Conservatism* (Harmondsworth, 1980), pp. 42–3.

76 See D. O'Meara, *Volkskapitalisme* (Johannesburg, 1983); and also T. D. Moodie, *The Rise of Afrikanerdom* (Berkeley, 1980); and H. Adam and H. Gilliomee, *Ethnic Power Mobilized* (New Haven, 1979).

77 T. Ranger, *The Invention of Tribalism in Zimbabwe* (Gweru, 1985), pp. 3, 17, 6, and *passim*.

78 T. Ranger, *Peasant Consciousness and Guerilla War in Zimbabwe* (London, 1985), appendix I.

79 See N. Alexander, *Sow the Wind* (Johanesburg, 1985); and 'An Approach to the National Question in South Africa', *Azania Worker*, 2, 2 (1985).

80 CW, XI, pp. 103–4.

81 See C. Hill, 'The Norman Yoke', in C. Hill, *Puritanism and Revolution* (London, 1968).

82 G. Deleuze, *Différence et répétition* (Paris, 1969), p. 121.

83 CW, XI, pp. 104–5.

84 Ibid., p. 106.

85 G. Therborn, *The Ideology of Power and the Power of Ideology* (London, 1980), pp. 121–2.

86 See D. Martin and P. Johnson, *The Struggle for Zimbabwe* (London, 1981), pp. 74–8; Ranger, *Peasant Consciousness*, ch. 6; and D. Lan, *Guns and*

Rain: Guerillas and Spirit Mediums in Zimbabwe (London, 1985).

87 Lan, *Guns and Rain*, pp. 218–19.

88 Ibid., p. 222.

89 See B. Anderson, *Imagined Communities* (London, 1983), especially ch. 7.

90 See T. Cliff, *Deflected Permanent Revolution*, new edn. (London, 1986).

91 F. Halliday, *The Making of the Second Cold War* (London, 1983), pp. 94–5. See generally ibid., ch. 4, on the 'third wave' of Third World revolutions in the 1970s.

92 N. Davies, *God's Playground* (2 vols, Oxford, 1981), I, p. 162; II, pp. 11, 13.

93 Barker, *Festival*, pp. 60, 64. See generally ibid., ch. 4.

94 Ibid., pp. 65–6.

95 Ibid., pp. 134–5.

96 Anderson, *Imagined Communities*, pp. 15–16.

97 E. J. Hobsbawm, 'Falklands Fallout', in S. Hall and M. Jacques, eds, *The Politics of Thatcherism* (London, 1983), p. 268.

98 E. Laclau, *Politics and Ideology in Marxist Theory* (London, 1977), pp, 99, 117, 128–9.

99 S. Hall, 'The Problem of Ideology', in B. Matthews, ed., *Marx: A Hundred Years On* (London, 1983), pp. 77–8.

100 See E. Laclau and C. Mouffe, *Hegemony and Socialist Strategy* (London, 1985). For a critique of such a philosophy of language, see A. Callinicos, 'Post-Modernism, Post-Structuralism, Post-Marxism?', *Theory, Culture & Society*, 2, 3 (1985).

101 E. J. Hobsbawm, 'Some Reflections on "The Break-up of Britain" ', *NLR*, 105 (1977), p. 23.

102 W. Benjamin, *Charles Baudelaire* (London, 1973), p. 159.

103 Ibid., pp. 139, 141.

104 Löwy, 'Revolution', pp. 55–6.

105 Wolin, *Benjamin*, p. 175.

106 Block *et al.*, *Aesthetics*, pp. 112–113.

107 M. M. Bakhtin, *The Dialogic Imagination* (Austin, 1981), pp. 206–10.

108 See J. Berger, *Pig Earth* (London, 1979), appendix.

109 Benjamin, *Illuminations*, pp. 263–4.

110 For stimulating reflections on this subject, see M. Berman, *All that is Solid Melts into Air* (London, 1983); P. Anderson, 'Modernity and Revolution', *NLR*, 144 (1984); and M. Berman, 'The Signs in the Street', *NLR*, 144 (1984).

111 See W. Benjamin, 'The Work of Art in the Age of Mechanical Reproduction', in Benjamin, *Illuminations*; but compare Benjamin *One-Way Street*, pp. 357–8.

112 See, for example, W. Benjamin, 'Some Motifs in Baudelaire', in both Benjamin, *Baudelaire* and *Illuminations*.

113 Wolin, *Benjamin*, p. 217.

114 Benjamin, *Illuminations*, p. 257.

115 M. Kundera, *The Book of Laughter and Forgetting* (Harmondsworth, 1983), p. 3.

116 Benjamin, *Illuminations*, pp. 256–7.

117 Ibid., p. 262.

118 E. P. Thompson, *The Making of the English Working Class* (Harmondsworth, 1980), p. 12.

119 G. E. M. de Ste Croix, *The Class Struggle in the Ancient Greek World* (London, 1981), pp. 209–10.

120 Benjamin, *One-Way Street*, pp. 351–2.

121 Ibid., p. 370.

122 CW, V, p. 214.

123 See C. Harman, *The Lost Revolution* (London, 1982).

124 Barker, *Festival*, p. 184.

125 For a review of Marxist approaches to the trade-union bureaucracy, see T. Cliff and D. Gluckstein, *Marxism and Trade Union Struggle* (London, 1986), part 1.

126 See I. Birchall, *Bailing Out the System* (London, 1986).

127 Barker, *Festival*, p. 86.

128 See, for example, ibid., pp. 92–3.

129 See P. Binns, T. Cliff, C. Harman, *Russia: From Workers' State to State Capitalism* (London, 1987).

130 A. Gramsci, *Selections from the Prison Notebooks* (London, 1971), p. 365.

131 L. Trotsky, *The History of the Russian Revolution* (3 vols, London, 1967), I, p. 19. On the theory and practice of the Bolsheviks, see C. Harman, *Party and Class*, new edn., (Chicago, 1986); T. Cliff, *Lenin* (4 vols, London, 1975–9); J. Molyneux, *Marxism and the Party* (London, 1978); A. Rabinowich, *The Bolsheviks Come to Power* (London, 1979); S. Smith, *Red Petrograd* (Cambridge, 1983); and A. Callinicos, 'Party and Class before 1917', *IS*, 2, 24 (1984).

132 Trotsky, *History*, I, p. 15.

133 P. Anderson, *Arguments within English Marxism* (London, 1980), p. 20.

134 Ste Croix, *Class Struggle*, pp. 226–59.

135 P. Anderson, 'Class Struggle in the Ancient World', *History Workshop*, 16 (1983), p. 68.

136 C. Wickham, 'The Other Transition: From the Ancient World to Feudalism', *P & P*, 103 (1984).

137 G. Stedman Jones, 'Society and Politics at the Beginning of the World Economy'. *Cambridge Journal of Economics*, 1 (1977), p. 86. See also G. Lukács, *History and Class Consciousness* (London 1971), p. 282; and C. Hill, 'Conclusion', in C. Hill, *Change and Continuity in Seventeenth-Century England* (London, 1974).

138 See especially D. Blackbourn and G. Eley, *The Peculiarities of German History* (Oxford, 1984).

139 C. Hill, 'A Bourgeois Revolution?', in J. G. A. Pockock, ed., *Three British Revolutions: 1641, 1688, 1776* (Princeton, 1980), p. 111. Lawrence Stone broadly agrees with this assessment, though he jibs at calling the result of the revolution 'a bourgeois society, because of the continued dominance of an admittedly entrepreneurial landed elite'; 'The Bourgeois Revolution of Seventeenth-Century England Revisited', *P & P*, 109 (1984), p. 54. But his study of the English landed class, L. Stone and J. F. C. Stone, *An Open*

Elite? England 1540–1880 (Oxford, 1984), fully confirms Robert Brenner's claim that the distinctiveness of English development lay in 'the rise of a *capitalist aristocracy* which was presiding over an *agricultural revolution*'; 'The Agrarian Roots of European Capitalism', *P & P*, 97 (1982), p. 89.

140 See G. Therborn, 'The Rule of Capital and the Rise of Democracy', *NLR*, 103 (1977).
141 V. I. Lenin, *Collected Works* (Moscow, 1964), XIII, p. 239.
142 G. Eley, 'The British Model and the German Road', in Blackbourn and Eley, *Peculiarities*, p. 85. See also Stedman Jones, 'Society and Politics'; and, on uneven and combined development, Trotsky, *History*, I, ch. I; and *The Third International after Lenin* (New York, 1970), pp. 18–24.
143 The American Civil War is arguably another case of bourgeois revolution from above: see G. Novack, ed., *America's Revolutionary Heritage* (New York, 1976).
144 P. Anderson, 'Socialism and Pseudo-Empiricism', *NLR*, 35 (1966), p. 9.
145 See Lukács, *History*, pp. 280–4.
146 See Barker, *Festival*, ch. 9; and T. G. Ash, *The Polish Revolution* (London, 1985), pp. 222–31.
147 P. Anderson, 'Trotsky's Interpretation of Stalinism', in T. Ali, ed., *The Stalinist Legacy* (Harmondsworth, 1984).

CONCLUSION

1 W. S. Gibson, *Bruegel* (New York, 1977), p. 107.
2 See A. Callinicos 'Anthony Giddens – a Contemporary Critique', *Theory and Society*, 14 (1985).
3 K. Marx, *Grundrisse* (Harmondsworth, 1973), p. 488.
4 An illuminating discussion of various conditions of collective action is provided in S. Lash and J. Urry, 'The New Marxism of Collective Action: A Critical Analysis', *Sociology*, 18, 1 (1984). I strongly disagree, however, with the authors when they claim, in *The End of Organized Capitalism* (forthcoming), that the conditions of working-class collectivity have been eroded to the point where other forms of collectivity are replacing them.
5 T. W. Adorno, *Minima Moralia* (London, 1974), p. 247.

INDEX